The BIG BOOK of BACON

Savory Flirtations, Dalliances, and Indulgences
with the Underbelly of the Pig

JENNIFER L.S. PEARSALL

Skyhorse Publishing

Skyhorse Publishing books may be purchased in bulk at special discounts for sales promotion, corporate gifts, fund-raising, or educational purposes. Special editions can also be created to specifications. For details, contact the Special Sales Department, Skyhorse Publishing, 307 West 36th Street, 11th Floor, New York, NY 10018 or info@skyhorsepublishing.com.

Skyhorse® and Skyhorse Publishing® are registered trademarks of Skyhorse Publishing, Inc.®, a Delaware corporation.

Visit our website at www.skyhorsepublishing.com.

10 9 8 7 6 5 4 3 2 1

Library of Congress Cataloging-in-Publication Data is available on file.

Cover design by Rain Saukas
Cover photo credit Thinkstock

Print ISBN: 978-1-62914-555-6
Ebook ISBN: 978-1-62914-871-7

Printed in China

Dedication

To my Grandmother Smith for her turkey tetrazzini, Grandfather Smith for always having bread with dinner, Grandmother Evans for the only Thanksgiving turkey I can ever remember really liking, and Grandfather Evans for his baby carrots with real butter. This is also for my father, for egg in the hole and geometric school lunch sandwiches. But above all, this is for my mother, for her spaghetti sauce, her way with leftovers, and the hundreds of things she taught me over the stove.

Contents

ACKNOWLEDGMENTS

There are many people to thank on many levels for the privilege of writing this book. Indeed, it's a little tough to know where to start, to sift through the names running through my head, the dishes and bottles we've shared together. For all those moments and people have contributed something to this book getting done.

The first people to come to mind are my grandparents, both Evans and Smith, all gone now, but their impressions and memories still strong within me. Snapshots of Thanksgiving dinner at the farm in Pennsylvania, home of my grandparents Evans, the smell of the tin-lined breadbox drawer and bacon frying early in the morning, a plug-in coffee percolator with its bubbling knob, are forever with me. So, too, are the vanilla milkshakes and open-faced tomato cheese sandwiches scalding hot from under the broiler, my grandmother's apron, and Pepperidge Farm white sandwich bread that always tasted better than the bread we had at home, and the salt steak dipped in melted butter are what call the hardest to me from my grandparents Smith. I am forever thankful that those memories are so strong with me, that they produced a love for cooking and eating. I wish I'd known this when they were alive, for I'd surely have thanked them then.

My mom and dad without a doubt get thanks, more than I could ever say, more than I could ever write. I was lucky to have them and a family dinner every night, where we all sat down; I don't think a lot of families do that anymore. That my mother is a genius with leftovers and at making something out of nothing I could never say enough about. She taught me all the basics, held my hand through bread and canning competitions in 4-H, and, now, in my adult years, allows me to take over her kitchen during the couple times of year we all see each other. How do you ever thank parents like that?

My brother, C.T., gets a thank-you, too. He knew I was on to something with the bacon even before I signed the contract to write this book. That year, I got salted bacon chocolate and a bacon refrigerator magnet in my Christmas stocking from him. This year, he sent me Perfect Bacon Bowls.

I very much want to thank my long-time friend Lisa Lambiasi Albert. It was her idea to have a "cookbook night" two or three times a month, back when I was still living in Virginia. We'd pick a theme, then create three, four, eight courses from cookbooks and recipes we'd never cooked from before. It got us out of the comfort food rut. If anything spurred my willingness, my excitement to experiment with food and drink, to go beyond what was safe and didn't need a book or directions, it was those evenings we shared almost more than anything else.

Finally, many thanks go to my editor, Jay Cassell. I know I did a double-take when we ran into each other at a trade show and you said, "I've seen the blog. Can we have the book?" You had faith in this project before I even knew it was one.

INTRODUCTION

I't's funny how things turn out.

My professional background has long been in the outdoor and shooting sports industry, most of it spent as a writer and editor. I've gone from staff jobs to freelance and back to staff jobs, and somewhere along the line I started a blog. That was about the time social media was fast becoming the juggernaut it is today, and I worked it, gathering up a pretty good following along the way.

Now, most of the folks who pay attention to my Facebook and Twitter feeds are hunters and outdoorsmen. Just in case you're not, you should know that most of us take huge pride in eating what we successfully hunt. For us, it's the ultimate farm to table.

For those who haven't eaten game meat before, you should know that it needs time and attention that other, farm-raised meats don't require. They're very lean for the most part, and, yes, some things do taste gamey. My fellow Facebook friends often post recipes they've come up with, a way of sharing the hunt and ideas for using the animals we've taken. Especially for the guys, many of whom love good food but don't cook much, the exchange of recipes and techniques is a great way to eat their deer or pheasant without passing off the chore of cooking to their wives.

One day, in November 2012, someone showed up on my Facebook feed looking for help with some sort of game meat or another, I can't remember what. Several friends posted tips on marinades and cooking temps, and I ended up weighing in with "Wrap it in bacon." Bacon is a natural choice with lean game meats; the added fat from the smoked pork belly is a moisturizer of sorts and a flavor booster, too. The next day, someone messaged me looking for help with another piece of game meat. I offered up a recipe, then ended the post with "Wrap it in bacon."

Now, my friends, especially my editorial colleagues, are a pretty sharp bunch. Soon, "Wrap it in bacon" was added to damn near every post on the site. Boyfriend broke up with you? Wrap it in bacon. Went to leave for work and found a flat tire? Wrap it in bacon. Katie got an "A" on her homework? Wrap it in bacon. And on and on and on. It was the running joke that just would not stop—and that's when I decided to have some fun with it.

I started cooking and created my website, www.TheBaconAffairs.com. I didn't expect anything to come out of it (though I secretly hoped someone at the Food Network would discover me and make me their next star). Then I ran into a colleague and friend of mine at our annual trade show. Turns out he'd seen the blog, thought it was right on trend, and asked for the book. And, so, here we are.

A couple things to know and consider as you thumb through these pages and, I hope, find some inspiration.

First, I'm not a professional cook. I have never attended the Culinary Institute of America or *Le Cordon Bleu,* nor even a cooking class at a community college. That doesn't mean I don't know what I'm doing in the kitchen any more than it means you're not a good cook because you don't have a day job as a sous chef.

I'm also not a dietician or nutritionist. Everyone thinks they know bacon is "bad" for you, but I've seen several news item over the last year while I've developed this book that say it's often good for you. How much or how often? Who knows. One day lettuce, coffee, and wine are bad for you, and the next they seem to be superfoods. Could be the same with bacon. Should you eat it every day? Probably not. If you're really worried about your bacon consumption, see your doctor. Some would say the sheer number of recipes in this book would make me an advocate of eating bacon as often as possible. I'm not, not really. I had a book to fill. That means I cooked, on average, about three pounds of bacon a week, and I ate a lot of it. That's a ton of bacon by anyone's standard. But you're not writing a book about bacon. So, while I'm not advocating you eat bacon every day, just as I'm not telling you to put bacon in everything you cook, there is something I hope you take away from this book, something I discovered in creating these recipes.

Bacon, it turns out, is nearly *umami* in nature. *Umami* is a Japanese word, and without getting into the science of it all (Wikipedia has a sound enough explanation if you'd like to read it), suffice it to say that it's the fifth taste, after sweet, sour, salty, and bitter. *Umami* is less tangible, less directly identifiable than the other four tastes. It does have its own taste, but really it tends to amplify flavors. The best example of *umami* is MSG, that often (and, it turns out, probably wrongly) maligned ingredient in Asian dishes. Compare a dish of your favorite General Tso's chicken or beef and broccoli side by side with the same dish minus the MSG, and you'll quickly see the difference.

I discovered bacon can serve in much the same capacity. Yes, I deliberately cooked with it so that bacon was highlighted as a definitive ingredient, one you'd bite into and know immediately you were biting into bacon; you don't want to wonder if your bacon cheeseburger has bacon on it. Other times I worked it into a dish in a much more subtle capacity. It was those dishes that I made the discovery on. Dishes I'd cooked before and again because I liked them—cornbread, stews, etc.—were elevated to an entirely new level. I can't tell you how many times I tasted something and went "Wow!" just because I'd added bacon to it.

I never would have realized—and this is going to sound corny—the "power of bacon," had it not been for the writing of this book. And that, more than anything, is what I want you to take away from this book. Whether you eat it once a year, once a month, or every day, work bacon into a dish you hadn't thought to try it in before. I'd bet my next slice of succulent, salty, savory bacon that you won't be sorry.

BACON BASICS

BAKING BACON

A while ago, I bemoaned to my bacony friends on Facebook that, while I loved all things bacon, I had issues with the aftermath. Well, more than "issues." When you get right down to it, I *loathe* the grease spatter on my glass cooktop—I don't care what grease-cutting cleaning agent you use, it still takes three passes to get back to the glass proper. Then there's the ugly, congealed nastiness in the pan, not to mention the kitchen sponge that will never ever return to its full usefulness once you've cleaned said pan with it. Love/hate, hate/love. I was torn. I had the inklings of this book bouncing around my head, but I wasn't sure I wanted to clean up all the mess on a regular enough basis to make a go of it. And then someone suggested baking bacon in the oven.

Now, I've been around the butcher block a time or two, and one look at my burgeoning kitchen cabinets will tell you there's nothing I truly need from Williams-Sonoma anymore, but I had never heard of baking bacon. I doubted my friends' advice.

"Gawd, it's bad enough cleaning the stovetop, the oven's got to be worse," I commented on a Facebook post.

"There's actually no spatter at all this way!" came the reply.

"Okay, but I don't want to miss the aroma of it cooking," I whined.

"You won't! You can still smell it, there's just no mess!"

And, so, I tried it. What follows is how the first two trials went and, I have to admit, this is the way to go.

Farmland Reduced Sodium—This is a national brand that quickly became my favorite (other than a little detour, when it was announced that Smithfield, which owns the Farmland brand, had been bought by a Chinese conglomerate, but more on that later). It comes in regular thin slices, a medium cut, and a super thick butcher's cut. All the cuts have good consistent flavor—even the reduced sodium slices—and you'll have more bacon than grease when you're done cooking; this is not always the case with some lesser-known and off-brand bacons, so, if Farmland isn't available where you live, just do some experimenting until you find your preference.

After Googling a bunch of oven-baked bacon processes—foil or parchment, 375°F or 425°F, bacon touching or space between—here's how it went down for the Farmland medium thick cut in my oven.

1. I used a preheated 375°F oven. Now, unless I'm baking bread, cakes, or pies, I rarely preheat, but it seemed prudent to at least try this the recommended way, and I figured it would yield more consistent results and help get the timing down.

2. All but one slice of the one pound of bacon was placed, edges touching, on a large, foil-covered jellyroll pan. At the last minute, I went wild hare and sprinkled three of the slices with fresh ground pepper, and three with cracked red chili pepper (these intended for use in the first bacon recipe to be tried). In the oven the pan went, atop the forgotten but now-hot pizza stone. I set the timer for 15 minutes.

3. I took a look when the stove buzzer went off. Coming along nicely, but not near enough done. Six minutes more on the timer.

4. Good, more progression, still not enough. Another 7 minutes on the timer.

5. Better, almost there. Strips at the edge of the pan were attractive and nearly done, those in the middle still not quite. I poured off the pooling fat, then took my favorite tongs and turned all the slices over before setting the timer for another 7 minutes.

6. Done and out. Total time 35 minutes, with one grease pour and one slice turnover in a pre-heated 375°F oven. Bacon is perfectly cooked and not curled at all, grease is golden coming off the pan, rather pure-looking, actually. (As a side note, the spiced slices were delicious!)

Nueske's Applewood Smoked Bacon—A friend at work told me about Nueske's when I was telling him about the running bacon joke my friends and I had going on. "If you want to get serious about it, get to Nueske's," he said. I didn't get there, at least not yet (the main company store is in a small town called Wittenberg, about forty miles north of my small town here in central Wisconsin—not far, but when I found the brand in one of my area's grocery stores, I snagged just one pound. At roughly $10 and change, it was twice the price of the big-brand packages. Still, I'd seen some "gourmet" bacon online that was pushing $20 a pound, so I figured, well, better go big or go home.

Nueske's website tells its story better than I can, but the short version is that it's a Wisconsin company, bravely begun in 1933 when most other companies were disappearing in the Great Depression. I guess the attitude was something like "Smoke the meat and they will come." Not a

Nuekse's bacon is a Wisconsin favorite, but it can be ordered off the web and shipped to you. Sweet and smoky, the slices are thick and meaty, but a little on the pricey side.

bad philosophy, especially if you've ever happened past a barbeque joint in Memphis or South Carolina and had that whip-your-head-around aroma from the smoker out back hit your nostrils. Yup, you've been there, and you've followed that smell of smoky goodness to its origins like a stud dog following a bitch in heat. You are not in control. The smoke beckons. Apparently that's worked for Nueske's for the last eighty years. Can't argue with that.

The Nueske's bacon slices were thicker than the Farmland brand, though the package hadn't been labeled thick-cut. Nor were they ham-steak thick. The slices also looked carved, like they'd come straight from the underbelly of the pig. And I imagine they did.

1. I upped the oven, already hot from cooking the Farmland bacon, to 385°F and set the timer for 20 minutes. I doctored none of the slices as I had the Farmland strips.
2. A look at the bacon when the timer went off revealed really nice progression, so I flipped the slices and set the timer for 7 more minutes.
3. That was all she wrote. Perfect bacon, and just a little more grease for the bacon fat container.

BACON BRANDS

This might be a good time to talk about bacon brands. I've experimented with probably nearly a dozen different brands overall in putting together this book. Among these, I sampled Patrick

Cudahy (which had a distinct, artificial—almost chemical—smoke taste to it that I did not care for); Wright Brand (my absolute top pick, but, sadly, mostly an East Coast brand and not available much where I live); the offerings from two different local butchers (if you have a private butcher convenient enough to you, by all means, give their bacons a try—they tend to be better priced per pound than the store brands, they tend to be thicker cut, and they tend to be more deeply smoke-flavored if that appeals to you); Gwaltney and Smithfield (again, mostly available on the East Coast by my experience, but certainly worth buying if they're available to you); some off-brand one of my grocers carries called CornKing (good flavor, but wildly inconsistent meat-to-fat ratios, so, if you get a really fatty package, the shrinkage is stupendous); Oscar Meyer (just fine, not a thing wrong with it); and my grocers' own store brand (better than the CornKing, but the same criticism still applies, and I'd anticipate your store brand would be the same—you'll have to debate the price savings against the quality, but my biggest criticism of these low-rent types is that they're just inconsistent).

After all that baconating, I tend to use Farmland most, as I find it to be the most consistent bacon in the $5 per pound range, with Oscar Meyer running a close second. If one's not on sale, I buy the other. My one criticism of Oscar Meyer is that one end of the slices in a package almost always seems to be all fat. Sometimes it's heavy enough that I simply cut off the solid fat end, so my bacon's not just swimming in rendered fat as it cooks.

I occasionally take a pound of my butchers' bacons, but they are heavily smoked, and while I like that for eating the bacon all by itself, that smokiness tends to become the pervasive flavor profile when worked into a dish, and that's not generally what I'm looking for. The biggest benefit to a private butcher's bacon cut is usually found in the thickness of the slices and the meatiness of the bacon. Sometimes it's nearly ham-like, which I don't find at all unpleasant.

That brings me back to the low-rent off-brands. In general, unless you just gotta have bacon and really need to save that extra dollar a pound, I'd skip them. Not only do the slices tend to be super thin—sometimes you can see light through them!—they also shrink so much that, if you need a couple cups of cooked bacon for one of these recipes in this book or your own concoctions, you're going to end up cooking three packs instead of two of one of the better brands, and then your savings have just plum gone out the window.

On the other end of the spectrum are those so-called "gourmet" bacons. Okay, so they're flavored with this or smoked with that. That justifies $10 or more a pound? Oh, and that pound you see may not actually be a pound. I've seen some purveyors selling 12- or 13-ounce packages with the weight listed only in the small print, at exorbitant prices well past that $10 mark. Save yourself the trouble. Either make your own (there are plenty of charcuterie books out there to tell you how to do this, but really it's not much more difficult than taking a slab of pork, curing it in curing salts for a week, then smoking it for a few hours), or simply spice or sweeten up your bacon before baking (I'll show you how to do that in a bit).

The lesson here, really, is that if this book inspires you to work bacon into more of your dishes, then experiment a little. The worst you'll end up doing is cooking a second batch, and what's so bad about that?

ADDITIONAL COOKING TIPS

As I was getting settled into this cookbook, I discovered a few things about cooking bacon. I think you'll find these tips helpful.

- When possible, try to cook a full pound of bacon at one time, laying the slices on the foil so that they're touching. If you must cook just a few slices, reduce your cooking time and keep an eye on the oven. Just a few slices spaced apart cook much faster than a full pan.
- I finally settled on 380°F preheated. When I set mine at 375°F the bacon, no matter what type, seemed to just kind of boil along in its own rendered fat, never really quite getting the

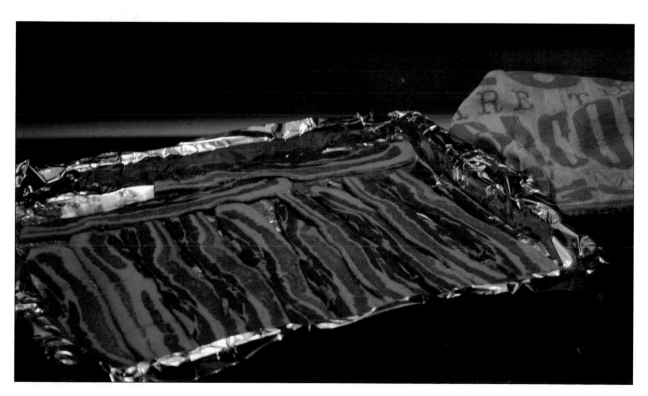

Fill your pan from edge to edge and as much as possible from top to bottom. A few gaps are okay, but the bacon will cook more evenly if the pan is full and the slices are touching.

A finished pan. If you're feeding a crowd, simply pour off the grease, gently lift the cooked strips with a fork, and put them on a plate lined with a paper towel to drain, then start the next batch.

edges crisp and browning. At 375°F, and even when I poured off the grease, the bacon really took too long to cook, up to 35 minutes for regular slices. That might not be an issue for you if you're not feeding a crowd and need to make several batches, but it might be important if you're timing your bacon to be done at the same time other dishes you're cooking are finished.

Raising the temperature up developed another set of problems. Not only did I get a lot of oven spatter, which caused my oven and, eventually, the entire house to be filled with bacon smoke, when I boosted the temp to something like 400°F or 425°F, cooking time became very unpredictable. If you're not keeping an eagle eye on your pan, you can go from almost there to burnt in a flash.

All this said, every oven is different. You're going to have to play with yours to find out what works best for you. Regardless what temp and how long you settle on, preheating is a must. You will never get predictable results if you start with a cold oven.

🐖 I start all but the thinnest bacon at the 20-minute mark to end up with bacon that has started to crisp but is still soft to the tooth. I'm not a fan of dark, super-crispy bacon, preferring mine more on the flexible side. Obviously, if you like yours crispier, you're going to extend your cooking time.

You will need to adjust your starting time based on the thickness and meatiness of your bacon. Really thick, meaty slices will, of course, take longer—I've had some go as long as 35 minutes—than their thinner counterparts. With thicker bacon, especially that which has a heavy fat content, you may also need to either pour off the fat or turn the slices over near the end of the cooking time (or both).

- When cooking for a large crowd and working up several pounds of bacon, there's no need to switch the foil out in between batches. I routinely cooked three to four pounds of bacon every weekend in the course of developing this book, and so long as you pour the fat off in between batches, you're good to go. The foil does get pretty dark towards the end of the third pound, due to all those little bits and pieces continuing to bake, so, if your crowd is army-sized and you need to cook much more than that, then, yes, I would swap out the foil to keep new batches from taking on that burnt flavoring.

- If you're making your bacon ahead of time for something like burgers or sandwiches and intend the bacon to be hot when you do use it in the dish or as a side, undercook it a little bit. When you're close to serving, spread the mostly cooked bacon across a foiled cookie sheet and reheat for a few minutes at 350°F (or lower). It takes almost no time at all for bacon to reheat, and it continues to cook as it does, thus my advice to undercook a bit when you're first whipping up a pound. Do not reheat in the microwave. Microwaving reheats far too quickly, and the spatter on the inside of the appliance will drive you to madness—I don't care how well you think you've covered it.

- When you're ready to remove the finished bacon to drain (like you would any other time you cook bacon, on a plate lined with a paper towel), gently lift them off the foil with a fork. I say gently, because if you don't poke the foil, the grease won't leak through, and all you'll have as cleanup duty is to fold up the foil, toss, and put the still-clean tray back in the cabinet.

- You might be tempted to go with organic bacon. I've also seen something called an "uncured, nitrate-free" bacon, but that's like saying "non-dairy ice cream" or "meatless hamburger." There is no such thing. If it's not cured with that pink, nitrate-containing curing salt, then it's not bacon. Yes, some bacon can be had that's been cured with things like celery salt and such, but I tried a couple of these and was very disappointed. One disaster I remember in particular was a pound of Oscar Mayer's new Smoked Uncured Bacon. It developed *terrible* shrinkage—think a manly man gone all polar bear plunge—and it was *not* due to the overcooking. In fact, even at the still-flexible stage I like my bacon, I was left with miniature bacon strips. They weren't good for anything but a couple finger sandwiches with the Queen.

I tried a couple other organic and uncured bacons, but the results were the same for all. I was left with mini-me strips no matter what I tried. Not only that, they were all excessively salty and yet managed to lack the deep bacony taste we cook the darn stuff for to begin with. If that weren't enough to dissuade you, consider this: the organic and uncured bacons I found were all sold in those deceptive 12-ounce packages and at prices approaching $10 or more a pound. Ridiculous.

SPICED AND CANDIED BACONS

Peppered bacon and maple-flavored bacon are routinely found in every grocery store I've ever been in. Too, following hot on the heels of the salted caramel trend comes candied bacon, as well as bacon dipped in chocolate. I'll cover that last in the chapter Baconated Desserts, but making your own flavored bacon is so simple you'll wonder why you haven't tried it before—and, in the case of peppered bacon, you don't get stuck with all that heavy cracked pepper on just the edge of your bacon, as happens with store-bought peppered bacon.

All you need is a pound of bacon, a gallon ziplock bag, and whatever flavoring ingredient you like. For cracked pepper, I'd go with about two tablespoons of medium-fine grind. For hot-sauce flavor, a quarter-cup or up to a half ought to do it. For candied bacon, you'll need about a half-cup of light brown sugar. Whichever route you're going, separate your strips of bacon and put them one at a time into the ziplock bag. Add in your flavoring, zip the bag shut, and shake and massage until the strips are evenly coated. From there, simply bake as usual on your foil-wrapped jellyroll pan.

A couple notes on candied bacon. First, keep a really close eye on the bacon, but don't let the color fool you. Because the brown sugar caramelizes and combines with the rendered fat, it gets dark before it's actually done. You may want to lower the oven temp just a tad, and you'll certainly want to pour off excessive renderings so it doesn't start to burn. Second, this stuff is ridiculously sticky when it's done. Better to place it on wax paper to cool than your standard paper towel. Finally, when it does cool, the bacon will be very stiff, thanks to the cooled, caramelized sugar coating. Thick bacon can resemble jerky in texture—but it won't matter, because this stuff is beyond addictive.

DECORATIVE BACON

This is another thing that's easier than it looks. If you want to garnish a dish with a bacon rose, simply take a strip of bacon and roll it around your finger, starting with the smallest end of the strip, so that the widest end becomes the opening "petal." Once rolled, set them on their bottoms in a small gratin dish or in the corner of the jellyroll pan with your other bacon and

Decorative roses are as simple as wrapping bacon around your little finger—literally. Bake like you normally would and garnish a dish with them for some bacony fun!

cook until done. You can toothpick them if you want to make sure they hold together, but I haven't found it to be necessary.

BACON BOWLS

By now you've probably seen those ads on TV for this little upside-down funnel that you simply wrap bacon around and bake to make bacon bowls. They have a moat around their base to collect the grease as the bacon cooks. Given that these ads contain the usual overzealous host screaming that they're "only $19.95 and, if you act now, you'll get a second set FREE!" along with the weird disclaimer of no C.O.D.s allowed for New Jersey orders (seriously, who sends anything C.O.D. anymore?), I dismissed them as being as hokey as every other made-for-TV gadget. Then my brother, as a joke, sent them to me for Christmas.

Ha! Joke was on me. These things work *brilliantly*! The plastic is really solid, they drain just like the ad said they would, and you do indeed end up with this perfect bacon bowl that you can stuff with anything your heart desires. Cleanup's a snap; just put them in the top rack of your dishwasher. The only drawback I found was that you really can't reheat your bacon bowls, as they

As seen on TV indeed! The author's brother sent her the Perfect Bacon Bowls as a joke, but it turns out they work just as advertised. So much for gimmicks.

shrink up into something more resembling a slightly curved bacon plate than their neato-keeno original bowl.

It looks like the official name of this product is the Perfect Bacon Bowl. You can find them at www.buyperfectbacon.com, as well on Amazon. They're cheaper on the company website, four for $10 plus shipping and handling, but you get the ubiquitous second set of four for free for a total of eight. Amazon was selling them as a set of two for $15.

BACON GREASE—IT'S A GOOD THING

When cooking multiple batches of bacon, you'll need to pour off the rendered, liquid fat in between. Find a heat-proof glass container, cup the foil at one edge of your jellyroll pan to form a kind of spout, and merely tip the pan up to pour. (Do I have to tell you to do this with potholders on your hands? Well, there you go.)

Pour off your grease into a heat-safe glass container and save if it comes out really clear. It's a great addition to sautéed vegetables, steaming rice, and even for basting things like biscuits, pie crusts, and breads.

I use a spare two-cup Pyrex measuring cup or one of my many ceramic mixing bowls and save my grease unless my pour-off has a lot of blackened pieces in it. You can stick it in the fridge if you like, but in a cool kitchen, it really doesn't go bad. If you think you've had yours too long, merely discard the solidified fat in the garbage pail (not down your kitchen drain) and start fresh with the next batch of bacon you make. I use bacon fat all the time for things like sautéing veggies and sometimes chicken, just for that little extra boost of flavor. I'll also baste biscuits or bread in it now and again, as well as add some to refried beans made from scratch instead of lard, and I'll stir a dab into my rice when I'm cooking. I don't know, it just adds something you can't get with anything else.

BACON—THE END IS NEAR

No, no, no. Hang on a minute, take a deep breath. There's absolutely no reason to go about reliving the momentary—and, as it turns out, untrue—Bacon Panic of 2012. It's not happening—or not not happening—again. But the end of bacon *is* near. Well, it's as near as a good butcher who handles pork and makes his own bacon. I'm talking about bacon ends.

What are bacon ends? They are everything from the cured and smoked pork belly that doesn't make it into nice, neat rows of display case-perfect slices or that fit conveniently and uniformly into pre-sized vacuum-packed bags. They do not fit tidily onto a BLT.

You are likely going to have to find a butcher for bacon ends, as its uncoordinated, "leftovers" state just doesn't meet the definition of most grocery store fare. There are some packaged brands, but the problem with these is that they tend to be uncured. My butcher smokes his own

Bacon ends are all the pretty stuff that doesn't make the cut for those display-case packages. You'll likely not find these at your local grocer, but rather will need to locate a butcher. It's worth hunting one down, as bacon ends provide depth, texture, and different flavor profiles than its neatly sliced cousin.

sausages, bratwursts, and bacon. His is a pretty decent-sized shop, and while he's not terribly accommodating when it comes to cuts beyond the basics, he always has a steady supply of bacon, pork belly, and bacon ends, the latter of which are cured and smoked. The ends come vacuum packed in quantities of roughly 3¼ pounds, and the price per pack runs $3.69 to $3.89 a pound, significantly less than the uniform slices he also sells, and often more than $2 a pound less than the packaged bacon in the grocery store. Based on that alone, it's worth seeking out, but I've discovered there are some other benefits to it as well.

When I cut open my first pack, I thought I was going to find lots of bits and pieces. I did not. I found big, meaty, fatty chunks, thick-cut strips that were clearly from the last of a pork belly end run through the slicer, and then these decadently thick, almost steak-like hunks with a thick ridge of ham-like meat that tapered to beautiful white fat at the ends. I pondered the pile before me— talk about non-uniform—then whipped out one of my bigger Wusthoff knives and chunked it up in more or less like-size pieces. I figured that was probably the best way to get it cooked evenly, especially given the array of content from nearly all meat to nearly all fat.

Chunked up and spread out on my foil-lined jellyroll tray, I set it for my usual: 385°F, twenty-five minutes. I checked it at twenty-ish, poured off the fat—there's quite a bit, though it's deliciously clear and well worth saving—and then set it back in the oven to run out the last five minutes on the timer. Some batches have taken a little longer, but this is the time and temp I get most of it done.

It was love at first bite. Here I had bacon, ham, and pork belly, all in one, with the spectrum of flavor and richness I'd been searching for in the dozens of brands of uniform slices I've bought in the name of this book, but had not quite found. Textures ran from chewier on the ham side, to fatty delight on the pieces that were half-and-half meat and fat, to the insane decadence of perfectly roasted pork belly. Left cold, buttered (yes, *buttered!*) in their own softened fat, they were the ultimate definition of "meat candy" everyone jokes about bacon being—with a cooked tray sitting on the counter and cooling, I could *not* keep my hands off it. Best of all, when cooked and then further chopped up to make easier to incorporate, the bacon ends imparted a depth to other dishes that I don't believe regular strips of bacon are capable of.

Don't get me wrong. Bacon strips will always have a place in my cooking. Truly, I couldn't live without strips, especially when I *do* want a very uniform product that crumbles or purées to great consistency. But sometimes it's hit or miss when it comes to the actual amount of bacon *flavor* they impart, especially when you're trying to balance the texture of a dish against what can be chewy and crunchy bacon bits; the more you reduce bacon in its size, the more the flavor it exports to the dish can dissipate. And let's be real—while I don't think most people put enough bacon in a dish that calls for it as an ingredient—seriously, two or three strips on a BLT, what the heck's up with *that?*—when you put too much in, you end up with a greasy, soggy mess that slicks on the tongue and lets no other flavor through.

Bacon ends seem to solve a great deal of that power struggle between texture and flavor. I get the deepness, richness, and distribution of flavor I'm looking for in something like bacon cornbread or the baconated smoked pork and *poblano* appetizer wraps you'll find among these pages, but without the hard crunchy bits from crumbled bacon that rather "interrupt" the bite of such dishes. Both a compromise and a bonus I hadn't expected in the world of cured pork and pork belly delights, bacon ends are something I'm very glad I discovered. My advice to you? Find a good butcher and experiment with bacon ends, should you find them. Well worth your time in the pursuit of bacon love.

BACONATED BREAKFAST AND BRUNCH

- Apple Bacon Cinnamon Rollups
- Bacon Berry Buttermilk Pancakes
- Bacon Choco Pumpkin Pancakes
- Baconated Breakfast Caper
- Baconated Parmesan Grits and Eggs
- Baconated Breakfast on the Grill
- Berry Bacon Cheddar Breakfast Bread Pudding
- Chorizo Breakfast Pizza
- Double Pork Breakfast Hash and Gravy
- French-Kissed Elvis
- Porcine Polenta Breakfast in Bed
- Sausage and Bacon Pancake Pie
- Swiss Scramble with Grilled Steak Toppings
- Three-Pig Breakfast Pie

APPLE BACON CINNAMON ROLLUPS

Some aromas sing to your heart (and stomach) more than others. Bacon frying. Fresh-made bread. Bacon Frying. Onions sautéing. Bacon frying. Hot-out-of-the-oven apple pie. Bacon frying. Fresh-brewed coffee. Bacon frying. Did I mention bacon frying? For me, I also add to the list—and curse every airport I go through with fifteen minutes in between connections and therefore not enough time to breathe, let alone time to stop for a cup of coffee—that heavenly aroma known as Cinnabon.

I like Cinnabons well enough, but mostly just the portion of these behemoth cinnamon rolls that's saturated with icing and dripping liquefied cinnamon; I could leave behind the dry insides without ever thinking I've missed something in life. Still, after a couple bites, and despite how terrific they smell, I've had enough. It's like I can't get that super-sweetness off my tongue, and it seems to coat my mouth in a way that only a strong cup of coffee and a toothbrush follow-up can handle.

The other morning, I had a yearning for a cinnamon roll. I refuse to use the stuff in a can, and the closest Cinnabon is probably Chicago O'Hare, which would make it a $400 cinnamon roll with the airfare from central Wisconsin. I rummaged through my bookcase of cookbooks and came up with a base dough out of Alisa Huntsman's *Desserts from the Famous Loveless Café*, then ratified it to suit my ever-lovin' bacon desires. Here's what you'll need:

For the Dough
2 cups of all-purpose flour
¼ cup of sugar
2 teaspoons of baking soda
¼ teaspoon of salt
1 stick of butter, cold from the fridge
½ cup of buttermilk

For the Filling
8 to 10 strips of cooked bacon
1½ to 2 regular sized apples (I used Pink Ladies)
¾ cup of dark brown sugar
3 tablespoons of cinnamon
1½ teaspoons cloves
1 teaspoon of nutmeg
1 teaspoon of ground ginger
2 tablespoons of butter

1. Peel and core the apples and chop them small. Melt the butter in a sauté pan and, when the butter's bubbly, add in the apples and half measures of the listed spices. Sautée until the apples are fork-tender, then set them aside to cool.

2 The pastry is up next, and this one is stupid easy. Again, I give all the proper shout-outs to The Loveless Café in Nashville, Tennessee, and this wonderful book it sent me, along with all the appropriate credit for the dough base components. To make the dough, combine the dry ingredients, then slice the butter in half-tablespoon chunks and cut them into the dry ingredients with a pastry cutter until incorporated and the base resembles tiny pebbles in texture. Pour in the buttermilk a little at a time, working it through the dry ingredients with a fork. Once all is well moistened—not wet, not sloppy, not gooey—flour your hands and form the dough into a loose ball. Dough should be sticky, but not so much that you think you'll have to reconsider a career choice as Spiderman/woman because you're never gonna get it from between your fingers.

3 Take your ball of dough and put it on a large floured cutting board or other suitable surface. Now, the Loveless Café book advised to just press the dough out by hand into a suitable rectangle. I chose to flour a rolling pin and roll to produce a more uniform rectangle. Go *gently* with the pin, as this dough can tear if you're not careful, and, and also because it's just sticky enough that, if you press too hard, and even on a floured surface, you run the risk of sticking the dough to the board.

④ Once you've got a good, evenly distributed rectangle about thirteen inches long by six or seven inches wide, turn the board so that one of the rectangle ends is facing toward you. Sprinkle the other half of the spices and all the brown sugar onto the surface of the dough. Lay out the bacon strips, an end of the strips of half of them touching the dough edge nearest you, the one you're going to roll forward from, the other end free of anything but spices and sugar for its last 1½ inches. Finally, on top of the bacon, ladle on the cooled apples, again stopping just short of the dough edge farthest away from you.

⑤ Carefully lift the end of the rectangle where the bacon ends touch it and start to roll forward. Yes, some of the bacon will start to poke through. Pay these tiny tears no attention, just keep slowly rolling forward; there's enough dough to cover them as you continue rolling. Before you get to the last, un-baconed 1½ inches of dough, moisten that naked end. Finish the roll, pressing lightly down on the wetted end to seal the roll.

⑥ I flipped over the roll to have the seam on the bottom, then trimmed the bit of loose dough flapping on either end so that the roll had its stuffing evenly distributed end to end (more or less). Now, take a very sharp knife (one with a non-serrated edge) and make eight even

slices out of the roll, pressing down decisively to cut through the bacon and dough in one motion—don't saw through the roll, or you'll both drag out the insides and tear the pastry. Take each round slice and lay it on one of its sides on a cookie sheet lined with parchment paper. Into the oven at 375°F for about twenty minutes, maybe a little longer to toast up the outer ring of pastry. I brushed the tops with warm bacon fat during my last five minutes in the oven.

7 These are delicious! You get all the aroma of a Cinnabon shop, but in a much lighter and less saturated sweet treat. I took a condiment bottle and filled it with melted butter, turbinado sugar, and cinnamon that I'd warmed a bit on the stove, then drizzled the mix over the top of these biscuity rollups, but even that wasn't necessary—truly, all these tasty breakfast bites needed were a peaceful morning and a hot cup of coffee.

Note: You could certainly use Pepperidge Farm's puff pastry for this, but the scratch dough comes together so quickly that, by the time you remember you have a roll of puff pastry in your freezer, take the time to let it come to room temperature, and then roll it out, you'll already be biting into the rollups with the dough made with your own hands.

BACON BERRY BUTTERMILK PANCAKES

I confess, I have a weak spot for greasy diner breakfasts. Establishments on my faves list sporting such nap-inducing morning fare include a few of the big chains: *IHOP, Denny's,* and that never-miss-one-while-you're-road-tripping *Waffle House* and *Huddle House.* (Can you say, "Grits smothered and covered?" Of course you can!) Anyway, while I tend to always order a protein-laden plate—eggs, sausage, bacon, stuffed omelets, etc.—sometimes I give in to those pretty pictures of fruit-topped pancakes dripping with bright red strawberry sauce or oozing deep purple blueberry juice from between their golden, buttery layers. Still, no matter how many times I do this, I always regret it. They're always too cloyingly, almost always sickening sweet (plus they preclude the use of syrup and butter, and I can't do without the butter). Yuck, I can never get that canned-peach syrup flavor off my tongue. You'd think I'd learn.

Well, I might not have learned, but I did fix it. Here's what you'll need.

2 eggs	1 teaspoon of vanilla extract
1 cup of buttermilk	3 tablespoons of melted butter
1 heaping cup of all-purpose flour	1½ cups of red raspberries
1½ teaspoons of baking powder	1½ cups of blueberries
½ teaspoon of baking soda	1 cup of chopped pre-cooked bacon
1 teaspoon of salt	1 jar of Smucker's blueberry dessert topping
2 tablespoons of sugar	

❶ For the pancake batter, mix together the dry ingredients to combine, then fork-whisk in the eggs, buttermilk, melted butter, and vanilla extract. Add a little more buttermilk if you think you need it, but, because of the added ingredients going in once the griddle is hot, you don't want a thin, super-spreading flapjack batter. Keep the "cake" in pancake, that's all I'm saying.

❷ Heat up your griddle close to medium-high, or just about 375°F if you're using an electric pan. Spread some of the chopped bacon, about two tablespoons for each pancake, in a close-knit, but single-layer round pattern and let it heat up a little. You don't want to really cook the bacon more than it already is (in fact, it's good to start with chopped bacon that's a little undercooked, as it provides a more tender bite in the finished product). Once the bacon is warmed up but before it gets to sizzling, ladle over your pancake batter to cover and spread a little on the outside of your bacon circle.

❸ Let the pancakes cook and set up for a couple minutes, then gently distribute a big tablespoon of both the raspberries and the blueberries on top of the cooking batter. By waiting for the pancakes to set up a bit, you prevent the berries from sinking down to the bottom, splitting with the heat, and leaking juice throughout the pancakes to turn them into a soggy pink and purple mess (not that they wouldn't taste just fine, but looks count, too). Flip when the little bubbles start to perk on the tops of the pancakes, gently lifting the edge with the spatula to verify a good, even, toasty golden color on the bottom.

❹ As you're working through the batter (keep the finished pancakes warm in the oven on a platter), heat up the topping. I used the Smucker's blueberry dessert topping because it had a very short ingredient list, just five or six items, and none were anything different than most home preserves are made from. It was also fat-free, which I was hoping would mean it was slightly less sweet. I was not disappointed in this regard. Anyway, I combined the contents of that small jar with about ¾ cup of each of the two fruits, bringing the combination to a gentle bubble so that the fresh berries heated through and broke apart a little, their tartness and non-sugary sweetness melding with the sweeter Smucker's flavor. Keep this sauce warm and slowly bubbling until ready to top the pancakes.

❺ Out of batter, I plated my batch of Bacon Berry Buttermilk sunshine along with a heaping helping of sausage links and, well, a stack of bacon, of course. I sprinkled a little confectioner's sugar over the pancakes for the photo, but it's not necessary unless you're going to eat these pancakes without the fruit topping—to each their own. I suggest you go with my berry sauce if you're like me and don't appreciate those sickening sweet toppings in those stomach-rumbling 2:00 a.m. IHOP television ads. The fresh fruit both in the sauce and in the pancakes is such a refreshing change from those always disappointing diner dishes, and the bacon, naturally, contributes just the right amount of salty, meaty, savory goodness to downplay some of what is true sweetness in the sauce. Too, the berries both in the sauce and in the pancakes give a nice burst in the mouth, while the bacon provides a pleasantly (like bacon could ever be unpleasant) chewy bite. In all, knowing that fresh fruit and bacon can make pancakes like these, I'll stick to omelets and hash browns at my next diner stop and satisfy my craving for berries, bacon, and pancakes at home.

Note: These are not pretty, perfectly round, Martha Stewart pancakes—the way the batter runs over the chunky bacon forms irregular shapes. I don't care, it all tastes the same, but if you insist on having magazine cover-worthy, precisely round pancakes, I'd suggest using a heat-proof, handled batter mold, much like the one McDonald's uses to get its eggs perfectly English muffin-round.

BACON CHOCO PUMPKIN PANCAKES WITH BANANA MAPLE BUTTER TOPPING

Maybe it was the foot of snow on the ground, maybe it was the minus-four mark on the thermometer that seemed to only be plunging further, or maybe it was the post-holiday blues, but the thought of pumpkin pancakes was spinning around my head like a hamster on an exercise wheel. Thankfully, I have a plethora of cookbooks with a dizzying variety of pancake recipes. I scanned three of them, put them in the blender that sits atop my shoulders, and came up with this. Makes about four good-sized pancakes and eight dollar-sized pancakes.

For the Pancakes

1 cup of canned pumpkin pie mix

1 cup of buttermilk

½ cup of sugar

3 eggs

1¼ cup King Arthur white wheat flour (because this bag was already open and the my Pillsbury all-purpose was not)

Nutmeg, ginger, cloves to taste

2 teaspoons of vanilla extract

2 teaspoons of baking powder

1 teaspoon baking soda

4 tablespoons melted butter

1½ cups chopped cooked bacon

¾ cup (about) Toll House milk chocolate chips

For the Topping

1 generous tablespoon of butter, preferably unsalted

½ cup of pure, real maple syrup

1 ripe (or almost ripe) banana, sliced

❶ With the pancake ingredients mixed and ladled onto the griddle, I waited for the bottom of the flapjacks to set up a little before I added regular-sized milk chocolate chips and some crumbled bacon to the wet side. I baked them on the griddle until the top side started to bubble, and then I flipped them.

❷ By the way, I cooked this recipe on a Cuisinart Griddler, a break-open griddle/panini press combo that I think is dying on the panini side of things (probably from too many cheese overflows while making quesadillas). This was the first time I'd used the thing broken open as a griddle, and I initially set the temp at 350°F. The pancake baking was going a little slow, and the first batch of pancakes broke a bit when I flipped them, partly I think because they were a little large, partly because of the low temp. I turned the dial up to the 425°F range and, while the light never came on telling me the griddle had gotten that hot, the next eight pancakes (poured a tad bit smaller), cooked better, cooked faster, and flipped without breaking.

3 The original pancakes, a *From Morning to Midnight* recipe I based this recipe loosely on, called for the pancakes to be topped with Spiced Pumpkin Ice Cream and provided a recipe for such. However, making ice cream is not an impulsive thing, at least not in my kitchen; for me, that's like drinking a cocktail before 5:00 p.m.—it's just not right on some level (not sayin' I haven't done it, just sayin' I feel a smidge guilty if the little hand isn't on the five and the big one on the twelve). So, the idea of ice cream cast aside, at least until another time, I heated up a large tablespoon of butter and a good measure of real maple syrup in a non-stick All-Clad sauté pan, tossed in a chopped ripe banana, cooked until the works were bubbly, and poured it atop two of the most perfect bacon chocolate chip pumpkin pancakes out of the batch.

④ Wow, what a mouthful! Could easily go for dessert just as well as it did for a Sunday late-morning breakfast, and a bite with both bacon and chocolate is something no one should go through life without experiencing.

A couple points to consider when making this recipe. I think the keys to the success of this are:

- Don't add the bacon and choco chips until the bottom of the wet pancake has set.
- The milk chocolate chips are probably a better idea than using the semi-sweet morsels you usually keep in your pantry for those cookie cravings that crop up when a guy's broken your heart. Once you flip the pancakes and the milk chocolate chips start to both melt and burn

a little against the hot griddle, they kind of become semi-sweet. If you started with the less-sweet chips, they'd probably end up tasting bitter.

- I used a perfectly ripe banana, not freckled, not green, but a younger, slightly greener piece of fruit would have been a little sweeter and a bit tangy at the same time, a good offset to the sweet of the pumpkins, syrup, and chocolate. Bananas can get, I dunno, a little funky when they're really ripe and heated up, almost bitter, so a younger banana is a smarter way to go for this dish. Still, this was pretty damn good as it was.

- Do not be afraid of the pumpkin pie in a can versus solid-pak pumpkin. The former comes pre-sugared and spiced, while the latter is neither, which is why several of the recipes I based mine on called for so much sugar to be added—more than a cup in a couple recipes. I don't know that canned pumpkin pie is any less sugared than adding regular sugar to solid-pak pumpkin, but the point is my way didn't affect how the recipe turned out.

- Stick with the buttermilk. I don't think regular milk would have hurt anything at all, as far as texture and cooking go, but the tangier buttermilk seems to really brings out the pumpkin flavor.

BACONATED BREAKFAST CAPER

I love breakfast. I could eat runny-yolked eggs, sausage links, pancakes, hash browns, and sausage gravy and biscuits any time of day. But I also like more sophisticated takes on the basics, and that includes tuning up the everyday breakfast casserole.

Now, don't get me wrong, I love the kinds of breakfast dishes most are familiar with, that comforting combination of sausage, scrambled eggs, soft potatoes, and cheddar cheese. But sometimes it's heavier than what I want, especially with the oily cheddar cheese. I can never seem to get further than setting the dirty dishes on the counter after one of those heavy dishes, and a nap is nearly always inevitable. The other morning, wanting something filling but also light, I devised this pretty layered dish.

3 medium yellow (thin-skinned, waxy) potatoes	6 eggs
	2 cups of milk
10 to 12 cooked bacon slices	reserved bacon fat
1 large tomato	salt and pepper to taste
2 tablespoons of capers	

1. I started with one of my medium-sized, rectangular casserole dishes, gave a quick swipe to the bottom and sides with some reserved bacon fat, and set it aside. The potatoes were going in first, so I skinned them and sliced them quite thin, as if I was making a traditional scalloped potatoes dish for dinner. I layered them about three deep in the bottom of the casserole. Next up came the bacon slices. I halved the cooked strips, layering them thickly on top of the potatoes. On top of that went the slices of the large beefsteak tomato, and then the capers were sprinkled on top. I topped that with another two-deep layer of potatoes before evenly pouring over the 1½ cups of milk (again, just as I would when making scalloped potatoes).

2. Covering the casserole with foil and slicing the foil in several places to vent, I set the dish on a jellyroll plan (in case of a bubble over) and placed the two in a preheated 375°F oven. I went an hour, getting the potatoes just a bit shy of fork-tender, then poured in the scrambled eggs with the last ½ cup of milk and returned the dish and pan to the oven, this time, though, without the foil top. After another thirty minutes, a fork went easily into the potatoes, the top layer of which showed golden brown at their edges, and the eggs were creamy and fluffy, perfectly cooked.

3. This is a delightful breakfast dish, one quite suitable for brunch or a late dinner when you don't want to go to bed hungry, nor with a meal that feels like a rock has taken up residence in your midsection. The fresh, vinegary bite of the capers complements the tomatoes, their juices mingling with the bacon and the milk to provide a nice counterpoint to the subtle eggs. The bacon, precooked but re-cooked in a protective blanket of whole milk and eggs, is still savory, but now tenderly succulent, and the potatoes, well, you know as well as I do how mouth satisfying this most basic of foods is in such a dish. Yet without a heavy cheese to go with it, this dish didn't leave me feeling weighed down and heading for the couch for a carb crash nap. All in all, well worth whipping up next time you want something a little outside the box for your morning meal.

BACONATED PARMESAN GRITS AND EGGS

I mentioned in the recipe for "*Gumbo Ya Ya Goes Gumbo Hell Yeah!*" that I'd substituted the rice gumbo is usually served over with a baked Parmesan and bacon grits dish (you'll find the recipe for those grits in the lunch and dinner chapter). Now, I've always loved softly fried eggs over grits and cheddar in the morning and, since I had plenty of the baked grits leftover from the gumbo recipe I'd made the night before, it was a no-brainer to use them for breakfast the next morning.

I reheated a small dish of the grits in the microwave, fried two eggs over easy (in butter, because, to me, nothing highlights the egg so well; you can certainly go with cooking spray, though). Once the whites had set on the second side, I slid them onto the hot grits that I'd dabbed a little butter on and added a couple slices of fresh bacon.

I forked open the yolks, letting all their yellow goodness ooze into the grits. I don't know whether it's because I'd forgotten the Parmesan was in the grits or because my taste bud memory had wrapped itself around grits and cheddar, but, with the first forkful of this new variation, I realized the dish had evolved from morning-newspaper-fuzzy-slipper-comforting to an adult brunch dish. (I looked around for a waiter to bring me a Bloody Mary, but the dogs lying at my feet, waiting for something to drop off my fork, refused to help with that request.) These grits were also decidedly less greasy without the cheddar, and also because the grits had been baked into a custardy casserole

instead of being served in their usual melted butter and porridgey state. The bacon, both baked into the grits and with fresh slices on top, added delightful texture to the dish.

I felt so "grown up" (sometimes still a novel idea at forty-eight years) that I nearly added a salad on the side, the lyrics "Hey baby I hear the blues a-callin', tossed salad and scrambled eggs" from the *Frasier* theme song promptly running a loop inside my skull … but 7:30 a.m. seemed a bit early for vinaigrette.

BACONATED BREAKFAST ON THE GRILL

My first summer in Wisconsin, the summer of 2012, left me wondering if I'd actually left Texas. Temps soared for months, rain rarely appeared, and the humidity was sopping.

The summer I was working on crafting this book, that of 2013, was decidedly different, and maybe even typical for a state so close to Canada. To wit, the middle of June produced a drizzly Saturday morning, one that made the house cool enough that I closed the windows and doors, pulled on sweatpants and sweatshirt, and sipped my way through an entire pot of hot coffee while sitting on the couch with a blanket pulled over my lap. I shivered, contemplated making a second pot. My stomach growled.

I paced around the kitchen, ground some coffee beans, rummaged through the fridge. I was considering creating a frittata of some sort when I looked out the patio door. There stood my grill, uncovered after grilling a steak the evening before, and, for some reason, I noticed the cast-iron Lodge griddle plate, housed in its Cordura slip and sitting on the grill's bottom rack. It had been ignored in its roost there for more months (years?) than I care to admit. I had an idea. Here's what you'll need:

5 medium-sized yellow (thin-skinned, waxy) potatoes
6 to 8 sweet mini bell peppers
6 green onions
1 pound of bacon
6 large eggs
reserved bacon fat
salt and pepper to taste

1 I skinned the potatoes, chopped them in half along their longest axis, and ran them through my KitchenAid food processor with the shredding attachment affixed. (Why anyone shreds potatoes by hand, complete with the resulting scraped knuckles, is beyond me). I chunked the peppers and sliced the yellow onions, then chopped the green onions (both the white

parts and most of the green), adding them to the bowl of shredded potatoes and combined with my hands.

2. I next took the pound of bacon and, without separating the slices, chopped the pound into ½ to ¾-inch squares. This is *much* easier to do with the pound all stuck together and cold out of the fridge, by the way, as you've got more of a solid mass for the knife to work with. Individual slices come to room temperature too fast and so when you lay your knife into one, you end up chasing the bacon all over the cutting board and shredding it into useless strings—all in all an unattractive mess instead of uniform pieces.

3. My ingredients prepped, I turned to the grill and unzipped the griddle from its case, wondering what I was going to find inside, since it had been so long since I last used it. Other than a few spider egg casings and a bit of rust discoloration (not disintegration, thankfully) on the ridged side I wasn't going to use anyway, the griddle seemed otherwise perfectly fine. I gave it a quick wipe down with a wet paper towel to rid it of a bit of dust and the spider egg dust motes, then grabbed my Corning measuring cup of reserved bacon fat. Using a silicone pastry brush, I dipped it in the fat and coated both sides of the griddle, placed the ridged side down on the grill's grate, and cranked up the heat.

④ Once the grill was hot and the griddle smoking (I danced some droplets of water on it to make sure), I gave the flat, upside surface another swipe of bacon fat and spread out the potato, vegetable, and bacon mixture—and I do mean spread out. Use the whole surface of such a plate, making sure you don't have it piled high in some places and low in others. Now, once you've got that done and things are sizzling along nicely, leave it alone. I'm serious. Put the grill lid down and leave the whole dadgum thing alone.

⑤ Why do you want to leave it alone? Because if you start messing with the potatoes, which form the bulk of this dish, before they have a chance to cook about halfway through and form a crust on the bottom and get rid of some of their starch in the process, you'll end up with tiny pieces of starchy burnt potato forming a new layer of cast iron.

⑥ How long do you leave it? I don't know, but there's an easy way to find out. Take a really good flat-edged metal spatula and slide it under just the edge of the food. If it starts to lift away easily, slide it in a little more. If, as you progress, you encounter significant resistance against the spatula, pull the spatula out and let the food cook a while more. The point is to remember that the edges are going to cook faster than the middle, but you'll reach a point where the bottom of the ingredients is solid enough to lift as a whole, so once you can get

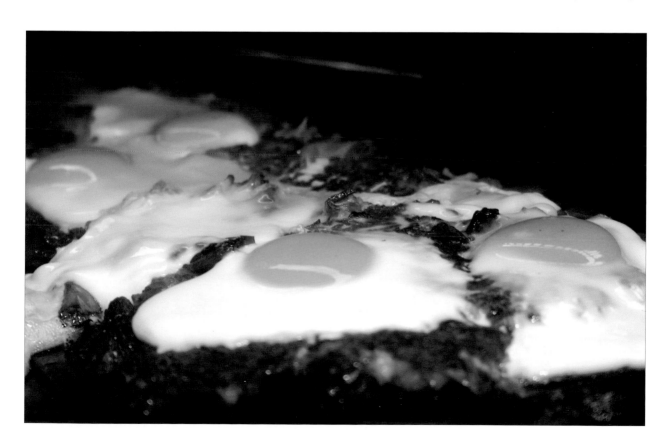

the spatuala to the middle of the pile without appreciable resistance, then you can start turning the mass over.

7️⃣ I used the edge of the spatula to cut the overall hash in half lengthwise, then in thirds across the width. There really was no practical way to flip something this big without most of it ending up off the griddle and into the grill's fire, so cross-hatching it this way made it all easier to handle. Once you've got it all flipped over, leave it alone again, following the same process just described.

8️⃣ When the hash is starting to firm up on the second side, you can start chopping at it with the spatula, getting the bacon (which will still be undercooked, as it's not making a lot of full direct contact with the griddle) down onto the hot iron surface and letting the fat render into the potatoes, much like you would butter if you were making hash browns all on their own. At the same time, the peppers and onions are getting caramelized, doing their part to add flavor as they sweat.

9️⃣ The works taking on a nice brown color and the bacon pretty close to done, I grabbed the half-dozen eggs I'd set aside. As you can see from the pictures, I cracked them open, one at a time, evenly across the top of the hash. Sure, the whites flowed one into the other, and I did have a yolk break, but, for the most part, I had a blanket of individual sunny-side up eggs on top. I lowered the lid on the grill, turned the burners down under the griddle so I wouldn't keep cooking the bottom of the hash into oblivion, and let the eggs bake in the heat. Took about 20 minutes, as they weren't in direct contact with the griddle, but I ended up with buttery, soft egg whites and semi-runny egg yolks. A sprinkle of salt and pepper, a fresh cup of strong black coffee, and I called it breakfast.

BERRY BACON CHEDDAR BREAKFAST BREAD PUDDING

Fruit goes with cheese, right? And bacon goes with cheese, too, right? Is there any good reason the three can't get along and serve up a righteous breakfast bread pudding? Not at all! Here's what you'll need for this easy early morning fix:

1 pint of fresh blueberries
1 pint of fresh red raspberries
1 12 to 14-inch soft baguette
1½ cups of cooked bacon, rough chopped
5 eggs
1½ cups of whole milk

1 cup of heavy cream
8 ounces of shredded sharp cheddar cheese
1 teaspoon salt
½ teaspoon of cracked black pepper *or* ¼ teaspoon of cayenne

1. Take your baguette or other soft type of Italian or French bread loaf and hand-tear it into one-inch pieces, placing the pieces in a large mixing bowl. Add in the chopped bacon and fruit and, either by hand or with a large rubber spatula, gently turn to mix. I say gently, because you really want to leave the berries whole for this recipe, rather than mashing them.

2. Next, in a separate bowl, scramble the eggs, then combine with one cup of the milk and all of the cream. Add in the salt and your choice of pepper; I included cayenne because I often use it in a half-dose capacity alternative to black pepper in all sorts of dishes. It's kind of like bacon—it just adds something. With cayenne, in small enough quantities, you only get the something, and not the heavily heated spice you'd get, say, when you use it in a dish of Mexican origins. There you go, my lesson on cayenne.

③ Once you've thoroughly mixed the eggs, milk, and cream, stir in the shredded cheese. I find it distributes better in a dish like this if you add it to the liquid first, rather than initially tossing with the bread and fruit, where so much of it tends to either end up on the bottom of the bowl or clumping in other places. Pour the completed mixture over the bread, bacon, and fruit. Again, gently combine either by hand or with the rubber spatula. Add the other half-cup of milk as needed to make sure all the bread comes in contact with liquid and set the bowl aside to just kind of meld for fifteen or twenty minutes.

④ I'm serious about letting the bowl sit for a while. Go clean a bathroom, dry your hair, take the dog for a walk, whatever, but let this stuff sit for a bit. Dense and crusty breads such as a baguette need time to absorb liquid in this kind of quantity. Now, some of you might be thinking you can speed this up by just adding more milk. Well, you would speed it up, but you'll be sorry if you do. You want the bread in a bread pudding to absorb all the way through, whatever liquid you're using, but you don't want it to be soggy and dripping. Ideally, when you come back to it, a piece of bread should be moistened through, but it shouldn't drip liquid, let alone fall apart, when you pick up a piece. That kind of over-moisturizing—which is the same problem I have with all those bread-based breakfast casseroles that tell you to refrigerate them overnight—is what produces a dish that has a gooey, milquetoast texture through and through. That kind of texture is only good for two groups of people: infants and the infirm geriatric, neither of which have teeth. Also, if you ove-milk this kind of dish, the dairy tends to mask all the other flavors (cayenne or not).

⑤ When your twenty-minute wait is over, give the mixture one more gentle toss with the spatula and pour into a buttered casserole dish. Into a 350°F oven it should go, forty-five minutes to an hour. The bread pudding should be moist if you stick a fork into the top and pull it apart a little, but you shouldn't see any liquid remaining. The top should also be toasty brown. If the top's brown but you still have some liquid that needs to cook, i.e, the eggs need to finish fluffing and baking, cover the dish with foil and slit it to let steam escape. Put it back in the oven and check after fifteen minutes to see how it's coming along. I did this with mine at the forty-five-minute mark, and it was done at the top of the hour.

⑥ My mouth really got a kick out of this. There was just enough cheese to play nicely with the bright, un-sugared fruit and the salty bacon, rather than make it into one of those gooey, kids'-dish breakfasts. Don't get me wrong, I love those kinds of breakfast dishes, too, but I always need a nap after one of them. This is a better way to get out of the egg-and-toast rut and get motoring through your day.

CHORIZO BREAKFAST PIZZA

Missed the word "bacon" in the title? Yes, me too, but believing that variety is the spice of a bacon-centric life, sometimes the Bacon Maven has to experiment with bacon's close cousins, including pancetta, prosciutto, ham, and all things sausage. To that end, I offer up to you this better-than-a-breakfast-sandwich dish. Here's what you'll need:

½ pound of loose ground chorizo

1 small yellow bell pepper

1 small red bell pepper

1 small sweet yellow onion

2 Kontos flatbread rounds

4 eggs

reserved bacon fat

shredded cheddar cheese for garnish

❶ Lately, I've caught a couple episodes of *Diners, Drive-ins, and Dives* that highlighted pizza joints using eggs on pizza, some for lunch or dinner, others decidedly breakfast.

❷ I make from-scratch pizza dough just fine, but you know how pizza goes—you get a *craving* for it. It's not usually something you think about at ten in the morning and think, "Yes, I'm having pizza for dinner in eight hours!" The problem with the craving is that it allows you neither the time nor the patience to make pizza dough from scratch.

❸ Flatbreads are the solution. They are pretty common in most grocery stores these days, and I've been lucky enough to find one grocery store that carries enough variety to stock three full shelves ten feet long, rather than just the one little stand in front of the deli counter of most markets. Flatbreads are also the perfect solution for someone single like me, who's through with eating the cold leftovers of a medium-sized takeout pizza before the pizza's actually gone. I also like the smooth, buttery texture of flatbreads better than the dry and roughly grainy mouth that pita breads offer and, when you treat them right, will be evenly crisp on the bottom and minus a soggy spot in the middle. More on that in a second.

❹ First up for this dish, julienne the bell peppers and onion either thick or thin. Heating a little bacon fat in a sauce pan, sauté the veggies until they are soft, the onions translucent, but the pepper strips still bright in color. Add in the ground chorizo and combine. Loosely ground chorizo, like loose sausage meat, is the way to go here, and it will usually come packaged like uncased sausage. There is chorizo that's more solid, like an un-fatty summer sausage or kielbasa, but it won't crumble and break down when cooked. If you don't use chorizo on any kind of a regular basis or have never cooked with it, you'll want to experiment with various brands. Among the ground varieties, some are *very* greasy and, when cooked down, will appear to have been reduced to four tablespoons of meat swimming in an aromatic bathtub

full of oils. Also, be sure to wear an apron or something you don't mind getting stained. The heavy red spices in chorizo are, naturally, also in the fat that renders out with cooking. Spatter it on a white shirt—hell, any piece of clothing—and prepare for the laundry fight of your life. Frankly, I think you stand a better chance of getting out Sharpie permanent ink.

5 Okay, the chorizo, peppers, and onions cooked and the excess fat drained off, get the flatbread prepped. I've tried these tasty little breads in the oven a half-dozen ways, and this is the one that gets it done correctly.

6 First, find a corrugated cookie sheet, the ones with little ridges. You could go with a pizza stone, but they take longer to get thoroughly hot and generally work better at higher temps. For me, the corrugated cookie sheet is key, as it lets a *leeetle* bit of air flow between the flat bread and the cookie sheet, and *that* is what keeps the soggy spot in the middle from happening—pretty important if you're like me and have a tendency to overload your pizza toppings. It also provides an even crispness across the bottom of the flatbread.

7 Cookie sheet procured, oven preheated to 375°F, take your pieces of flatbread and lightly brush the flattest of one side of each with bacon fat. Sure, you could use butter or olive oil, but I always have bacon fat on hand, and I think it gives just a little more *oomph* of flavor to many things, especially those that are bread-based. Place the moistened side of the flatbread down on the cookie sheet, then ladle a couple or three very generous tablespoons of the chorizo mix on top, spreading it not quite to the edge. You want a little bit of naked

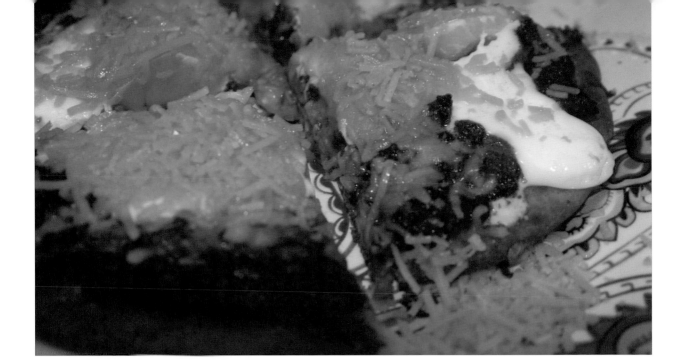

flatbread edge to keep your fingers on when you eat, without having them stuck in the hot toppings, just as you'd generally have with a traditional pizza. I also pushed the chorizo topping up higher *towards* the edge, forming a very shallow crater of topping, if you will. I did this to help the center stay firm and crispy on the bottom, and I also wanted to prevent the eggs from running over and onto the tray when I put them on later.

8. The un-egged chorizo flatbreads went in the oven for thirty minutes. Then, I carefully cracked two eggs onto the top of each of the two pizzas as I was cooking, slid the tray back in, and closed the door for about another twenty minutes. I hit the broiler for about five minutes after that to finish setting the rest of the egg whites. (It also overly cooked the yolks on the pizza at the back of the oven, so, note to self, rotate the pan halfway through the broil period if you like your yolks runny; rotate and go an extra two minutes if you like your yolks more solid.) Once done, I pulled the tray out of the oven and set it for a couple minutes on a trivet, allowing the toppings to set up a bit at room temperature. I then sprinkled on a bit of shredded cheddar cheese. A pizza wheel quartered this neat little dish easy-peasy, and I gladly dipped the pointed corner of one slice into the sunshine pool of a molten yolk the split eggs left behind.

9. Beats a breakfast "burrito" anytime.

Note: I use the Kontos brand of flatbreads. The bigger store I find them in has a huge variety of flavors, thicknesses, and shapes, but any flatbread that's not pita bread will do.

DOUBLE PORK BREAKFAST HASH AND GRAVY

It's the morning after Thanksgiving and my parents, visiting from Virginia, are up and rumbling around. None of us are Black Friday daredevils, so the plan for the day includes a few hands of cribbage, a couple old black-and-white movies, and a whole lot of nothing else. To make sure such a complicated day was fully accomplished, it was roundly agreed upon that a nap-inducing breakfast was a top priority. Here's what you'll need (even if this is the only productive thing you end up doing all day):

For the Hash

3 cups cornbread

2 cups cooked ground breakfast sausage

2 cups cooked bacon, rough chopped

3 cups potatoes, diced medium

1 large sweet onion

½ stick of butter

Reserved bacon fat

1 cup reserved chicken stock
   (boxed stock is fine)

For the Gravy

3 tablespoons reserved bacon fat

1 cup chicken stock

¼ cup flour

½ cup cooked ground breakfast sausage

1 cup cooked bacon, finely chopped

Salt and pepper to season

Up front, I used the cornbread left over from dinner two nights before. Mine is a dense, moist dish, more of a corn cake. You can certainly use a boxed quick mix for corn muffins if you want to just cut to the chase, but here's my recipe, one that doesn't take but two minutes more to whip together than the boxed stuff, and it sure does taste better:

1½ cups of yellow cornmeal or polenta

1½ cups of cake flour

4 tablespoons of sugar

½ cup of buttermilk

1 16-ounce can of creamed corn

¾ cup of sour cream

3 eggs

1½ teaspoons of baking soda

½ stick of butter, melted

1 teaspoon of salt

¼ teaspoon of cayenne

½ teaspoon of ground black pepper

① Mix together all the dry ingredients for the cornbread—flour, cornmeal or polenta, baking soda, and seasonings—so that they're well combined and evenly distributed. Holding the melted butter for last, add in the wet ingredients one at a time, including the eggs, combining each thoroughly before adding the next. Pour into a 9x8 baking dish that you've greased or buttered, then into a 375°F oven for thirty to forty minutes (check at the thirty-minute mark with a toothpick inserted into the middle, making sure it pulls out cleanly, with no wetness attached, then go in ten-minute increments until the toothpick comes out clean). The top should be toasty golden brown.

② Okay, you've got a reserve of cornbread, either fresh or leftover from dinner the night before. If fresh, let it cool while the rest of the dish gets assembled. Cook your bacon in the oven as you normally would, getting the sausage done at the same time on the top of the stove. Set both aside when done.

③ Now, heat some of the half-stick of butter and a tablespoon or so of the bacon fat in a large sauté pan. While the butter's melting, peel and dice your potatoes into nothing bigger than one-inch chunks. Make sure your dice is consistent in size so that the potatoes cook evenly and all at the same time. Into the hot sauté pan they go. Add some salt and ground pepper to season and cook until done, stirring frequently to prevent sticking and lidding the pan as necessary to help the potatoes cook through. When the potatoes are almost done, add in your diced onion. About the time the onion is translucent, the potatoes should be cooked through properly. (By the way, if you find your potatoes sticking too much, add in a little chicken broth and slap on the lid. The steam will loosen the potatoes from the pan, and the broth adds a little extra neutral flavor.)

④ Once the potatoes are cooked through, take your chopped bacon and cooked sausage and add to the pan of potatoes and onion. Toss to combine, add a little bit of stock or water to the pan—just a little, again, to keep stuff from sticking, you don't want any real liquid building up—then reduce the temp to medium-low and put a lid on the pot.

⑤ Take your mostly cooled cornbread and crumble it by raking a fork through it, breaking it up into spoonful-sized chunks. Add it to the meat and potatoes, toss to combine, add a little stock if necessary, then lid and reduce the heat to low. You're almost done now. Give the meat-and-potatoes mixture a stir from time to time, but all that's left to make now is the gravy.

⑥ This gravy comes together pretty quickly. Heat your reserved bacon fat in a small saucepan. Add the flour and whisk, making a quick blonde roux. When it smells wonderful, and before it starts to darken, add the chicken stock and continue to whisk over a medium burner until thick. Add more chicken stock if you like your gravy thinner. When the gravy is at the consistency you desire, add in the sausage and finely chopped bacon, stirring thoroughly. Salt and pepper as desired, slap a lid on the pot, and turn the burner off.

7 Service isn't any more challenging than providing a heaping helping of the meat and potato hash onto a plate and ladling over some gravy. If you want to make a bigger impression on a crowd, do as I did and put all the hash onto a big serving plate, make a hollow in the middle so that you sort of have a hash volcano, and fill the center with the gravy, making sure you let the extra pour over the sides like so much bacony-sausagey goodness deserves.

FRENCH-KISSED ELVIS

I've never been a big Elvis Presley fan. I dunno, he just never resonated with me as a musician or actor, and his kooky later days just left me shaking my head. Still, the sandwich creation most often credited to him I find pretty damned good. For the uninitiated, that would be peanut butter, bacon, and banana.

I like the everyday Elvis version on soft white bread just fine, even if I do feel like a kinder-gartner when eating one (hmm, wonder where I put that little milk carton with the straw?), but I thought I could improve on it and make a decadent breakfast or brunch treat. And that's just what I did. This makes two good-sized sandwiches, here's what you'll need:

4 thick slices of bread cut from a hearty, white, oblong artisan bread loaf

1 large banana or 3 finger bananas

2 eggs

¾ cup of whole milk

1 teaspoon of vanilla extract

4 to 6 tablespoons of smooth peanut butter

6 to 8 slices of cooked bacon

3 tablespoons of butter

½ teaspoon of nutmeg

½ teaspoon of cinnamon, plus extra for sprinkling

1 Mix up the egg bath for the bread. I put the eggs, milk, vanilla, and spices in my little Magic Bullet blender, but it's easy enough to do this chore by hand with either a whisk or a fork. However you do it, when you're done with the mixing, you want to pour it into a bowl that's wide enough to take the full flat of the slices of bread from the artisan loaf. A small, rectangular casserole dish, for instance, would work well.

2 On the stove, heat a tablespoon of butter in a large skillet. Take your one large banana, cut in half at the midsection, and then slice each half again along its length. In my kitchen, the day I worked on this, I had several small, red fingerling bananas—pretty cute, actually. I simply took three of those and cut them in half along their lengths. Into the frying pan with the bubbling butter they went, getting turned once when the downside started to brown a bit.

3 As the second side of the bananas finished browning, I took two thick slices of bread and laid them in the egg and milk mix to soak a bit, sprinkling a little extra cinnamon on the dry topside, so the sandwich would have a little extra flavor on the inside. Note that you're

only going to soak *one* side of the bread; as this is a sandwich, if you soak the topside, you're going to end up with nasty, raw egg mixture on the inside, as it's never going to see the frying pan. Blech! Also note that I chose a really dense artisan loaf of bread. Sure, you can bake your own, but most decent grocery stores these days have in-house bakeries that produce such loaves, and most are pretty tasty (and a lot less work than baking your own when you decide to make something like this on the spur of the moment). A dense loaf is required because you want the bread slice to soak up some of the egg and milk mixture in order to "French" it, but you don't want it soaking all the way through to the other side to, again, produce a spongy mess. Finally, pick a loaf that's un-herbed and un-cheesed. You really want a hearty white bread that lets the flavors of the filling come through.

4 Place your partially soaked bread slices on a clean dry plate. Spread a good tablespoon of peanut butter on each dry topside. Lay on three to four slices of bacon, depending on the size of your bread, lengthwise across the bread. Dollop on another three teaspoons or so of peanut butter, then divide up your sautéed banana halves and lay them on top of each sandwich. For the last step, take two more slices of bread and spread peanut butter on one side. Place the non-peanut butter side down into the remainder of the egg and milk mix to soak for a couple minutes (you can sprinkle some more cinnamon on the peanut butter side if you like), then place these last slices, peanut butter side down, on top of the other prepped halves with the bananas.

5 One note here: Be careful with the peanut butter, as far as just glomming it on. You want enough to add to the overall flavor profile, but, by layering it in as I've just described, you'll actually be kind of gluing the sandwich together, which will make it easier to flip without the works blowing apart or sliding apart on a slick of PB.

6 Heat the rest of the butter in your skillet until bubbly, then carefully lay each of your French toast Elvis sandwiches in the pan. Wait until the side down is toasty brown, then carefully but quickly flip each sandwich over. I have to say, I thought I was going to sorely miss having one of those special spatulas that kind of acts like a wide-mouthed set of tongs to keep delicate pieces of fish or stacked sandwiches intact during flipping. In fact, I completely expected this sandwich to fail on the flip, but it didn't. The peanut butter did just what I was hoping it would do, gluing the whole thing together. And that brings me back to what I just said about overdoing it. Had I used too much peanut butter, not only would this have been an overly sloppy treat to eat, I guarantee you the sandwich would have fallen apart on the flip (you know, like how every grilled cheese sandwich I make with tomato or avocado slides apart—sheesh).

7 Damn, these were good. I poured a little dish of maple syrup for dipping, and that was grand, but these French-Kissed Elvis sandwiches were fabulous all by themselves. Sautéing

the bananas not only meant the sandwich didn't have a cold spot in it, but it brought out a better sweetness in them than they'd had in the raw. And adding bacon and peanut butter *á la* Elvis simply makes for a fabulous flavor combination. That you get to lick a little melted peanut butter off your fingers in the end is only a plus.

PORCINE POLENTA BREAKFAST IN BED

Breakfast casseroles are crowd-pleasing and a relatively easy way to feed a group. They are filling and comforting, and they help eliminate keeping four different plates of various breakfast fare warm (without overcooking or drying out) while you juggle coffee pots, dishes, and three hot pans on the stove. The only problem is that few people tend to be really imaginative with the breakfast bake. The recipes you commonly run across are all nearly some combination of eggs, potatoes, and cheese (usually cheddar), with either sausage or bacon as the meat star. Don't get me wrong, as I've said before, I can wrap my mouth around this kind of layered morning meal and never break stride moving on to a second helping. But, again, these are *crowd*-pleasers, which means they work great for kids and the woefully picky eater—okay, I'll say it, those of the unsophisticated, inside-the-box, and less daring palates. Me being the Bacon Maven that I am, well, I wanted something different. Here's what you'll need:

1½ pounds of bacon, about 2 cups cooked and roughly chopped

2 tablespoons of reserved bacon fat

32 ounces of fresh spinach

1 pound of Johnsonville chorizo links

1¾ cups of slow-cook polenta (course ground yellow grits)

2 cups of chicken broth

1 cup of whole milk

1½ cups of water

1 tablespoon of reserved bacon fat

8 eggs

2 cups of cheese of your choice

❶ I cooked the bacon first, per my usual method in the oven, and set it aside on a paper towel-lined plate to cool and drain. While the second tray of bacon was in the oven, I slit the thin casings on the Johnsonville chorizo, removed the link meat, and sautéed it, breaking it apart and crumbling it as it cooked down. I don't have a huge number of chorizo choices here in Wisconsin, but I'm actually thankful for the Johnsonville brand. While it's not the spiciest chorizo out there, it's not dull; it definitely has the dried, smoky red pepper spice mix that sets chorizo apart from other sausages and cured meats; and it's a lot less greasy than some of the Mexican-made chorizos I used to get in San Antonio. (By the way, the Johnsonville is a loose, raw chorizo in the Spanish and Portuguese manner, rather than the dry-cured, salami-like chorizos of Europe; it does come in casings, while most loose-ground Mexican brands do not.) Once cooked through, I spooned the cooked meat into a waiting bowl, draining off the extra grease, and washed the pan.

❷ Next up was the spinach. I poured a tablespoon of bacon fat from the batch of bacon I'd just cooked into the newly cleaned pan, let it heat up a bit on a medium burner, and in went the spinach. I sprinkled with salt and pepper, tossed it all to coat, and set the lid on it for about five minutes. The lid removed, I gave it all another quick toss with the wooden spoon to get the last of the leaves wilted, let it air in the hot pan to allow just a bit more of the moisture evaporate, and then removed the cooked spinach to another waiting bowl to cool, juices and all. By the way, I didn't wilt the spinach down as far as it could have gone. I get mine tender, but still with some substance to it. I'm concerned with getting *most* of the water out of the greens, not cooking it into a black-green slime. I also want to keep as much of the vitamins as I can, as well as the bright green color—overcooking, of course, destroys both.

3 The polenta was up next. I'd chosen Bob's Red Mill Gluten Free Corn Grit Polenta for this dish, but not on purpose. I'd actually purchased two bags of Bob's Red Mill Polenta at the local health food store, the first being an organic bag. I must have grabbed the Gluten Free by mistake. And now I need to soapbox a second.

4 I don't give a rat's behind about gluten-free this or that. Yes, a gluten-free diet seems to be the only legit management of celiac disease, which, according to www.mayoclinic. com, "… is a digestive condition triggered by consumption of the protein gluten, which is primarily found in bread, pasta, cookies, pizza crust, and many other foods containing wheat, barley, or rye. People with celiac disease who eat foods containing gluten experience an immune reaction in their small intestines, causing damage to the inner surface of the small intestine and an inability to absorb certain nutrients." There are also people who claim to have been cured of everything from psoriasis to insomnia to hives to athlete's foot to mad cow disease on a gluten-free diet.

5 Yes, I'm being a little facetious here, but the whole idea of gluten-free has succumbed to a fad on many fronts. Not only am I one to decline fads, but, truth be told, I like my ingredients as unadulterated and unmodified as I can get. I'd have to consult with Alton Brown, but

my gut and my head tells me it's often just as wrong to take something *out* of a product—in this case, the complex protein "gluten"—as it is to put something *in*. (For the record, corn gluten is *not* the same gluten as that found in wheat, barley, rye, etc., that those on the gluten-free bandwagon take issue with, making much of the "gluten-free" labels you see on foods nothing more than legless marketing jargon.)The gluten-free polenta from Bob's Red Mill, according to my research, seems to have arrived that way merely by being produced in a gluten-free facility (i.e., there are no issues of cross-contamination with other products that might have the more offensive types of gluten).

6. Anyway, I had a gluten-free polenta grind—no harm, no foul, just wasn't intentional. The directions on the bag called for 6 cups of water and 2 cups of polenta. Yeah, um, no. Too dull. Thus, I put in my saucepan 2 cups of chicken stock, 1 cup of whole milk, and 1½ cups of water. I also put in a tablespoon of bacon fat. I brought the works to a boil and added in the 1¾ cups of polenta, stirred to combine and de-lump, reduced the heat, and put the lid on it.

7. Bob's Red Mill polenta is *not* quick cook (that much I did choose on purpose). In fact, the directions say this should have gone 30 minutes on the stove with periodic stirring, but, at 10 minutes, mine was nearly done. I knocked the burner down to low, kept the lid on the pot, and kept stirring for another 10 minutes, and a spoonful at that point was perfectly done. How perfectly? I almost skipped making the casserole to eat the polenta—the entire pot—all by itself. Alas, this book was calling.

8. In the bottom of an ungreased ceramic Emile Henry oval gratin dish (about 12 inches long, six inches wide at the center), I spread out the warm polenta. To that layer I added the crumbled chorizo and bacon. Next, I scrambled the eight eggs and added them to the spinach, along with the shredded cheese, in this case, the taco mix of cheddar, Colby, Monterey Jack, and manchego from Sargento. (Manchego, by the way, is a sheep's milk cheese—ain't Google just grand!) Once combined, that became the final layer on the casserole.

9. I placed the gratin dish on the same jellyroll pan I use for baking my bacon, just in case there was a spillover, and into a 350°F oven it went. I checked it at thirty minutes, coming along nicely, and with another fifteen minutes on the timer, the center had actually puffed, so I called it done.

10. My mouth got exactly what it was looking for. There was a richness to the polenta that I attribute squarely to the use of the chicken stock and milk (not to mention the crumbled bacon!). The pungent, adult spice of the chorizo was nicely matched by the spinach and cheeses, and the mix of cheeses, instead of all cheddar, kept the dish from being greasy. Add in two Bloody Marys, and you and your love have a fabulous excuse for Sunday breakfast in bed.

SAUSAGE AND BACON PANCAKE PIE

I was digging through recipe books and magazines, scrolling through Pinterest and Facebook feeds, looking for something I could work bacon into and call breakfast, but without the usual egg-based orientation. I stumbled across several that were interesting, but they all used Bisquick. Nothing wrong with Bisquick, and it's sure not a bad staple to keep on hand, especially for those impromptu pancake cravings. However, I usually find that, while I like the texture alright when I use it in a lazy-woman's shepherd's pie, for instance, overall I find Bisquick mix bread/biscuits to be overly bland. The way to fix that, of course, is to make this kind of batter from scratch and improvise. That's exactly what I did after running across several recipes that incorporated sausage into a kind of breakfast cake, a nice and lighter switch-up from the heavier baked egg casseroles.

One note: This recipe made quite a bit. Halve the ingredients if you're not feeding four and intending on leftovers. Here's what you'll need:

1½ cups of self-rising flour	2 cups of cooked bacon
1 cup of cake flour	1 red bell pepper
4 tablespoons of honey	1 green bell pepper
2 cups of buttermilk	½ medium red onion
3 eggs	1 medium sweet yellow onion
2 teaspoons of baking powder	¾ teaspoon of paprika
1½ teaspoons of baking soda	½ teaspoon of cayenne
7 tablespoons of melted butter	¾ teaspoon of salt
2 pounds of ground breakfast sausage	¾ teaspoon of fresh cracked black pepper

❶ Start with the sausage. I used a two-pound roll of Jimmy Dean regular breakfast sausage. You can certainly go with the hot, but I'd avoid the sage or maple flavors if you're going to stick with the rest of the ingredients (certainly this is an easy enough recipe to switch up with a variety of other vegetables and spices). Anyway, sauté the sausage, breaking it up as it cooks so that you end up with an even, pebble-like consistency. When it's cooked through, use a slotted spoon and remove the sausage into a large mixing bowl and set aside. Do not drain whatever fat's in the pan. (Incidentally, the Jimmy Dean tends to be quite lean in the pan, without a lot of leftover grease. Probably all well and good, but you'll be strained to make gravies off of just what remains in the pan after cooking this sausage down.)

❷ While the sausage is cooking, chop the two peppers and the two onions to a dice somewhere between fine and medium. When you've removed the sausage from the sauté pan, dump in the veggies. No need to add more oil or any butter, as there should be just enough fat

in the pan to get the peppers and onions cooking without sticking or browning. You want to cook these until the onions are translucent and without losing the pretty green and red colors from the peppers. Just when you're close, throw in the two cups of bacon (chopped medium rough), just enough to reheat it and have it become flexible again. When you can start to smell that wonderful aroma of bacon (couple minutes tops, when the pan's set on a burner a little past medium), take the pan off the heat and add the ingredients to the bowl with the sausage.

3 Time to make the doughnuts! Well, at least pancake batter, anyway. Mix together the dry ingredients to combine. Add in the honey, eggs, and buttermilk and give it a good spin under your stand mixer (you could do this by hand, but you'll have a harder time incorporating the honey evenly enough). Last, add in the melted butter and give it a spin with the mixer again, until you have a smooth batter. You want this to be just a little thicker than runny, so add either a little more flour or a little more buttermilk to get it where you want. Once you're there, pour it over the sausage, bacon, and vegetable mix, combining thoroughly with a large, flat-edged rubber spatula.

4 Pour your mixture into a deep-enough 9x13 pan that you've either sprayed with non-stick spray or greased with Crisco or butter (I used butter). I wouldn't fill it more than about three-quarters of the way up the side, depending on how fresh your baking powder, baking

soda, and self-rising flour are. As you can see from the pictures, I used a large Emille Henry deep dish pie plate, but, when I initially poured in all the mixture (which did fit), I paused to consider a puffy rise and an overflow. Not wanting my house to smell like burned food all week, I spooned some of the mix into two two-cup individual soufflé ceramics and set all three on a parchment paper-lined jellyroll tray, just in case. No matter which way you end up going, preheat the oven to 350°F and go about forty-five minutes, checking at thirty minutes with a toothpick in the middle to see how cooked you are in the center. If the toothpick comes out with any liquid batter residue, put back in the oven for ten-minute increments until the toothpick comes out clean and the top is golden brown.

5 As it turns out, I didn't need to worry about the overflow. All three, cooked together, came out perfectly, just gorgeous, with a slight puff and not a hint that I was going to have a molten lava problem during the initial baking stages. As for the taste? Wow, just awesome. Hearty without being heavy, the savory contents wrapped in the wonderful, flavorful batter for a terrific feel and taste. I ate it alone, with a little sour cream on the side, and on a quiet morning on which I figured a nap was coming sooner rather than later in the day, a leftover slice with some hot bacon and sausage gravy on top. Praise the pig and grab a second cup of coffee—you'll need it when you have a second helping of this wonderfully different break-fast dish.

SWISS SCRAMBLE WITH GRILLED STEAK TOPPINGS

When I'm cooking steaks on the grill, I generally make a large batch of caramelized onions, mushrooms, and bacon to go on top. I almost always have leftovers of both, which I generally use to make a hot cheesesteak sandwich the next day. The other night, though, I was a glutton, devouring an entire prime rib steak on one of the first cooler nights that promised the transition from summer to fall. That left me with a large cup of leftover onions and mushrooms that needed a home. Here's what I came up with for breakfast the next morning, with some beautiful help from bacon:

½ cup of caramelized onions
½ cup of sautéed mushrooms
½ cup of lightly cooked bacon, chopped medium
3 eggs
1 tablespoon of butter
¼ cup of whole milk
3 thick slices of baby Swiss cheese

1 If you don't have a mess of grilled onions, mushrooms, and bacon leftover, that's easy enough to remedy. Simply take about three-quarters of one medium sweet onion, a cup and a half of button mushrooms, and sauté in a pan with lots of butter until the mushrooms are reduced and the onions have caramelized to a sweet lovely brown. Add in your chopped cooked bacon, give it a couple stirs and a couple minutes to combine, then put a lid on your pan and remove from the heat. For the grilled leftovers (which I'd suggest, as the grilled flavor just adds that much more *oomph* to this breakfast scramble), simply reheat them briefly in a sauté pan, then cover and remove from the heat while you start the eggs.

2 Heat a large, shallow, non-stick sauté pan on medium-high and melt the tablespoon of butter, swirling it to cover the base of the pan. As the butter melts, scramble the eggs with the milk (if you don't usually use milk in your scrambled eggs, give it a whirl—I promise you will never have fluffier, lighter scrambled eggs any other way), and pour the mix into the hot sauté pan. Reduce the heat to medium after the first minute.

3 Once the eggs start to set and you can see some coagulation, lay in the Swiss slices. Give them thirty seconds or so to start to soften a bit and meld with the eggs, then evenly distribute the mushroom, onion, and bacon mix across the top. Another thirty to sixty seconds to set, then you can begin to gently scramble the mix. I prefer a flat-edged wooden "spoon" to push the eggs and filling across the bottom of the pan, kind of like a bulldozer would push a pile of dirt and gravel forward, then I can flip over a rounder mass so that the wetter

upside of the egg mix is now on the bottom. This gives me a better, more cohesive scramble—I don't have my eggs reduced to a pebble-sized kind of presentation that won't stay on my fork, nor do I end up with a silver-dollar pancake-sized mass of cooked egg that don't resemble a scramble at all. Once the wet side down starts to cook, you can get a little more authoritative with your scrambling, pushing the mix around until it's done to your liking. For the record, I like my scramble a little soft and a tad bit wet (and I hate scrambled eggs that have been browned, and that includes omelets). With such a wet filling as the onions, mushrooms, and bacon are, I'd suggest you strive for that level of doneness, too. Over-cooking anywhere much past firm and you end up with a feel in the mouth that seems like everything's overdone, including the bacon—and no one should ever overcook bacon, now should they?

THREE-PIG BREAKFAST PIE

I was randomly searching Google for a breakfasty photo with bacon for my then-new TheBaconAffairs.com Facebook page, and dug up a tasty pie from *Saveur's* online magazine. Called simply "Bacon and Egg Pie," the picture showed four stacked pieces to the pie, the egg yolks clearly intact as they would be if they were hard-boiled. Still, just bacon and eggs? The recipe, despite its gorgeous photo, needed some jazzing up. Here's what you'll need:

1 box of puff pastry (2 sheets)
12 eggs
8 slices or so of cooked bacon
12 breakfast sausage links
8 slices of Black Forest ham
1 cup of ricotta cheese
2 medium yellow or sweet yellow onions
2 teaspoons *Herbes de Provence*

① First I cooked the bacon *de rigeur* in the oven (see the first chapter of this book, "Bacon Basics"). Once the bacon was done, I decided I didn't want to spatter up the stove by frying the sausage links in a pan, so I dropped them on the tray the bacon had been cooked on (after pouring off the grease) and into the oven they went (same 385°F). I shook the tray to roll them at 15 minutes and threw in the two halved and sliced onions to the side. I rolled the sausages and stirred the onions a couple more times over the next 15 minutes in the oven and called them done.

② The original *Saveur* recipe called for twenty eggs (twenty—yikes!). It also called for a 9x13 casserole dish. Normally I wouldn't blanch at this, but with me being the only one putting this cookbook together and the only one eating the leftovers, I've made some efforts here and there to downsize my cooking creations to proportions a little more appropriate to the single life. That said, I went with a 6x9-inch dish and twelve eggs. In the end, I still could easily have provided six bacon lovers an ample serving, but if you need to feed more, go back to the twenty eggs (or twenty-four, if you're symmetrically uptight like me and hate having just a couple eggs left in the carton), and increase the other ingredients by a third to half again.

③ I rolled out the first sheet of puff pastry (Pepperidge Farm) on a lightly floured wood cutting board. A note here: I am all for scratch cooking, and part of me would like to make every ingredient in a recipe from *total* scratch—yup, deep down I'd like to grow and grind the grain, butcher the pig, milk the cow, and turn the curds into cheese, you get it—but

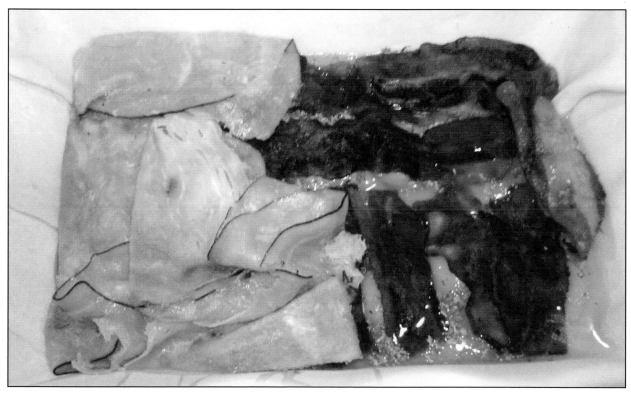

there's reality. I have a day job, the job of putting this book together, and all sorts of other things to do: I am not making puff pastry from scratch. Pepperidge Farm makes a very good and malleable product, it keeps well in the freezer, and it comes to a useable room temperature in a relatively short time, say, 30 minutes or so. How much more can you ask for? And now back to your regularly scheduled program.

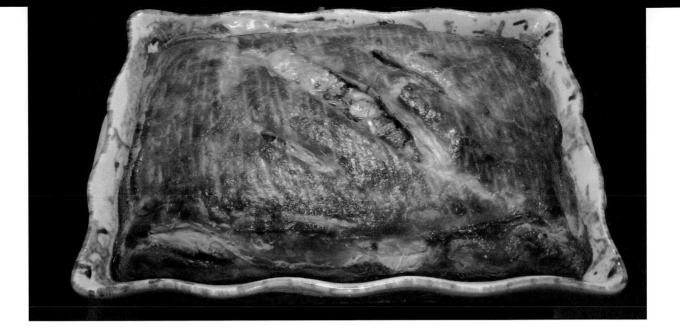

4. Once rolled out enough to drape over the edges of my casserole dish, I laid the pastry into the dish. Next, I cracked in ten eggs. I saved one and separated the yolk from the egg for the wash, per *Saveur*, dropped the extra egg white into the dish, then said to myself *What the hell,* and cracked in the last egg in the carton.

5. I next cracked fresh pepper over the top of the eggs and dusted them with *Herbes de Provence*, probably a teaspoon's worth, maybe closer to two. You'll want to see it evenly and thoroughly distributed. I love this herb combination, and it pairs well with eggs, but you don't want it to overpower everything else you're putting in, so resist the urge to get heavy-handed with it.

6. Cracking pieces of cooked bacon in half, I placed them gently on top of the whole eggs. It's okay if the pieces dip into the egg whites a little, but don't press them in or submerge them and break the yolks. Part of this dish's charm is its whole cooked yolks, instead of the scrambled presentation breakfast casseroles usually employ.

7. On top of the bacon went the slices of Black Forest ham. These were thinly sliced and came out of their package folded in half, and that's how I laid them on the bacon. I then took a soup spoon, scooped out a couple tablespoons of ricotta, and pinched pieces off to drop on top of the ham. Don't attempt to spread the ricotta, as you might with a lasagna layer, because you'll risk breaking the egg yolks below. Next came the sausage and onion layer. I sliced the sausage links in half lengthways to better distribute the bite in the finished casserole. You could just as easily chop them up, but I like this way. One more sprinkle of *Herbes de Provence*, another few twists of the pepper grinder, and I brought the hanging edges of the draped under pastry up and over the top. Do this just to lay them on top and clear the inside edge of the casserole dish; do not stretch the pastry in an attempt to have everything

meet in the middle, as you'll just end up tearing it. It won't matter a bit that you have a small double-layer of puff pastry around the square of your pan, and it's far preferable to leaking and, eventually, overcooked egg whites on the bottom of the pan if you pull too hard and rip the pastry. Ick.

8. Put on the second layer of rolled-out puff pastry. What you want to do with the overlap now, though (and per *Saveur*), is to tuck the edges into the pan, around the pulled-up sides of the lower pastry dough. Be gentle. If you rolled out your pastry far enough, there should be no need to pinch the dough onto that underneath and, again, risk a leak. You also don't want to *shove* it down the inside of the casserole and likewise risk a puncture. Just push the top dough layer easily down the side, stopping when the dough resists being pushed further.

9. Take a sharp knife and make a few slashes in the middle of the pastry top crust. Now take that egg yolk you saved, pour in a dash of heavy cream, whisk with a fork, and paint the entire crust with a pastry brush, making sure to get down into the crevices at the edges.

10. *Saveur* called for an hour at 400°F. I opted for 375 (preheated), in part because I had a downsized pie, but also because my oven smokes like a forest fire at 400, no matter what I'm cooking. I hate it, the oven, that is, but it's what I gotta live with at the moment. I checked the pie at thirty minutes—coming along nicely. I turned the pan around and set the timer for another twenty-five. At the bell, the pie was *alllllmooooosssst* right. I opted for another fifteen minutes, went back to the computer, timer in hand, and realized I hadn't actually set the timer at probably the ten-minute mark. I dashed to the oven and found—perfection.

11. I don't know how the *Saveur* recipe turned out. I'm sure it was fine, but that recipe called for a mix of ketchup and Worcestershire sauce to be drizzled over the eggs before adding the bacon (plus it didn't have the orgy of pig meats mine did). I am not a fan of ketchup and eggs. My Aunt Marty always ate her scrambled eggs that way. I'd try a mouthful, would like it, same with a second bite, but on the third my tongue would turn on me, like I'd tried to sneak something poisonous past it and my taste buds had discovered the ruse. So *Saveur's* take was out, and my *Herbes de Provence*/ricotta/ham slam was in.

12. My tongue and its suspicious taste buds were amply rewarded for the effort wrought by the rest of my being. This pie is the *bomb*. The *Herbes de Provence* pulled out the flavors of the fennel seed in particular and the other common sausage spices in general, the ricotta mated well the texture of the cooked whole egg yolks, and the puff pastry was oh-so-buttery good. That bacon meshed with sausage meshed with warm, thin-sliced ham meshed with baked egg … well, let's just say this is to die for, if only so we can go to heaven and meet and thank the pigs and chickens that gave their lives so that we may enjoy.

APPETIZERS AND SNACKS

- Bacon Beer Meatballs
- Bacon "Corndog" Muffins
- Bacon Pesto Late-Night Snack Pizza
- Baconated Pimiento Cheese Three Ways
- Bacon-Wrapped Savory Surprise Mini Pepper Poppers
- Baconated Un-Nacho Nachos
- Candied Bacon
- Elegant Bacon Bites a Deux
- Loaded Bacon Cheeseburger Dip
- Pulled Pork and Bacon Pastry Bites
- Roasted Grape and Bacon Crostini
- Tortellini-'N'-Cheese Stuffed Bacon Bowls
- Wingless Bacon Buffalo Bread

BACON BEER MEATBALLS

Guy Fieri's *Diners, Drive-ins, and Dives* is one of my favorite shows, enough so that I'll confess to watching most of the marathon run of repeats that runs on Sundays and then Mondays, leading up to his newly aired show. I love that the chefs featured rarely hold back on how they make something, almost never have a secret ingredient or process they won't reveal. It makes their food *accessible*. That said, I draw a lot of inspiration from the show—but I should never watch it when I'm hungry.

The other night, there was an episode devoted to burgers. Frankly, I could eat a hamburger every day, all day long, varying the toppings till, well, the cows came home. Watching a show like Fieri's *Triple D* doesn't help with these cravings. Anyway, somewhere along the show (or it could have been another, burgers were so deep in my brain matter at that point, I don't really remember), someone made sliders, with cold pints of dark beer in dewy glasses on the side. I was on it. Here's what you'll need:

1 pound of ground round	⅓ cup of whole milk
1 pound of ground chuck (80/20)	2 tablespoons of Worcestershire sauce
1½ pounds bacon	8 ounces of Dijon mustard
8 slices of a marbled Jewish rye bread	2 bottles of dark beer
2 eggs	2 medium sweet onions, sliced thinly
1 bunch of flat-leaf parsley	Soft slider or bratwurst rolls

❶ I cooked the bacon first, per my usual oven method. I set it aside to cool and drain, and while it did so, I took the foil off the tray, laid out the slices of the Jewish rye bread, and toasted them for about 15 minutes with the oven temp lowered to about 350°F. Once I had, well, toast, I took them out of the oven and set them aside to cool, as well.

❷ The toast cooled, into the food processer it went, and out came the breadcrumbs I needed. I followed with the bacon in the food processor, ending up with about 1½ cups of fine chop and that nice bacon fat puree that results. It's something I feel better spreads the bacon flavor through whatever I'm mixing it into. Last into the processor went the flat-leaf parsley, all but the naked lower stalks, a nice fine and uniform chop resulting.

❸ Combine everything together, meats, herbs, breadcrumbs, dairy, and Worcestershire sauce, until all is thoroughly and uniformly mixed. This should be a dense, thick mix. Add milk or an egg as you think are needed, but you don't want spare liquid here.

❹ One by one, I made 36 golf ball-sized meatballs, placing them in neat rows on my bacon-baking jellyroll pan, now lined with parchment paper. The recipe I was using as a frame wanted to cook its meatballs all the way through in a hot oven, twenty-five to thirty minutes at 375°F. But these get finished in a slow cooker for quite a while, so I wanted my meatballs to merely set enough so that they didn't fall apart in the slow cooker and the accompanying sauce. Mine cooked for twenty minutes at 350, just enough to make the set and for some of the heavier beef fat to render off.

5 With the meatballs partially done, I lined the bottom of my new Breville Risotto Plus cooker with a layer of the thinly sliced onions. I placed a layer of meatballs on top of that, another layer of onions, meatballs, onions and the last half-dozen meatballs went on top.

6 I poured one 11-ounce bottle of Guinness Black Lager in a bowl, forked in the jar of Grey Poupon Dijon mustard to combine, and poured it over the waiting meatballs in the Breville maker. It didn't seem like enough liquid to me, though   I didn't want the top half of the meatballs to merely steam—so I poured in all but two swallows of a second bottle. That

didn't cover the whole batch of meatballs in the pot, but at least the bottom of the top layer was sitting in liquid. I set the appliance on low and walked away.

7 I *gently* stirred at the end of the first hour, so that all the meatballs were getting the beer and mustard bath, and again at the end of the second hour. Still, I was thinking low was too low, and upped it to high. There it went for another two hours, the meatballs getting a stir every now and again, and at dinner time I had a steaming hot batch of slider-ready "burgers" giving off a tantalizing aroma.

8 I ate the first sliders on King's Hawaiian Savory Butter Rolls, the meatballs naked save for a spoonful of the beer and mustard sauce and some of the stewed-down silky onions. Later I tossed leftovers in a pan with some of the sauce, melting some smoked aged cheddar over them and making a meatball sub on a soft onion brat roll, a squirt of French's yellow mustard squiggled over the top and some sautéed onions added. Really, these flavorful meatballs, tangy from the mustard and beer and having good depth from good ground beef and the bacon, don't need a heavy hand with the garnishes; to go overboard with ketchup, mayo, thousand island dressing, too much extra mustard, or whatever condiment you like to slather on your burgers or sliders, would mask the nice balance of flavors already present in the meatballs. They are simply delightful bites. I'd rank them right up there as a top appetizer for football parties, or a precursor to bigger fare on the backyard grill.

BACON "CORNDOG" MUFFINS

If the snow were to stop and the month magically turn to June, I'd head for the nearest county fair and find me a corndog.

Cravings are like that. They hit you out of nowhere—like the desire for sex, a shiny tin of Altoid's in the check-out aisle, and the new car you see in the TV ad right after you tire shop for the blading Trojan in the garage—right out of nowhere. That's what happened with the corndog craving yesterday. Had to have one, but what's a Bacon Maven to do when there's six months before the Ferris wheel comes to town and she hates running her deep fryer when the windows can't be opened to get the stink of hot oil out of the house? Improvise—and to delightful results. Here's what you'll need:

1¼ cups of cornmeal

1 cup of flour

4 tablespoons of sugar

1 cup of sour cream

1 can of creamed corn

1 teaspoon of salt

1 cup of buttermilk

Fresh ground pepper

2 eggs

1½ teaspoons of onion powder

1½ teaspoons of garlic powder

2 teaspoons of baking soda

1 14-ounce package of Hillshire Farms Li'l Smokies (all pork)

8 strips of bacon

1. Start with the bacon, because you're going to go about cooking it a little differently than usual. What I did was bake my bacon in a 380°F oven on a foil-layered jellyroll pan like I always do, but I only cooked it until the fat had gone translucent and the meat was just barely starting to trend towards done. In other words, I undercooked it. I did this on purpose, and I'll tell you why.

2. My Pinterest board and Facebook newsfeed are full of a recipe for bacon-wrapped Li'l Smokies baked in maple syrup. I've made that recipe, several different ways, in fact, and while it's all tasty enough, there's just *so* much grease. Even though you only use a third of a strip on each little sausage in those recipes, because they're packed so closely together 1)

there's a actually quite a bit of bacon when you wrap the average packet of about thirty sausages, and 2) combined with whatever you pour over the top, be it maple syrup, maple bourbon, etc., you end up boiling the poor little things in this gawdawful bath of grease and sugar. Sure, you can drain them on paper towels when you're done, but they're still kind of slimy and you end up with that greasy feeling in your mouth afterwards—nothing a good beer can't knock down, but you get the point. By par-cooking the bacon first as I just described, you do away with probably half the grease, yet you still have bacon that's flexible enough to wrap around the Li'l Smokies.

❸ That's indeed the next step. When you're bacon's cool enough to handle with your fingers, break or slice each strip into thirds. Take each third and wrap it around a sausage, placing it seam-side down in your gratin dish or whatever other small, shallow-sided baking dish you'd like to use. Crowd them together—this really seems to help the bacon from drying out and getting all burnt and tough on the outside. I did mine in a 350°F oven, about 40 minutes total, though I checked at 30 minutes and decided I wanted the bacon a little more done.

❹ When the bacon-wrapped Li'l Smokies are done, remove them from the oven and set them aside to cool a little bit, then start on the corndog batter. I mixed together all the dry ingredients first, then added the can of creamed corn and sour cream, then the two eggs last. The

batter should be thick—not so thick that your spoon will stand up in it, but it shouldn't be close to cake batter, either. If you need to thicken it a bit, either add a little more flour and cornmeal, or just simply let it sit for ten minutes or so.

5 Take either a non-stick muffin tray or a silicone KitchenAid version like I did and spray it down with non-stick spray. I know, I know, the stuff doesn't always smell good when it's baking, but it does the trick and it doesn't make the food taste bad if you're using a better grade product like Pam (mine was the 100% Canola Pam). Go lightly; you don't need a lot of spray, just a touch. Next, find something small in your kitchen drawer that will let you ladle some of the batter neatly into the muffin cups. I used a gravy ladle. A quarter-cup measuring cup would work just as well. You want to fill each muffin cup about a third of the way up. Now take each of your warm baconated Li'l Smokies and place one in the center of each cup, pressing down a bit with your finger to seat it within the batter. Over this, spoon another bit of batter to cover the sausage. I got 24 muffin cups filled out of this batch (I had several Li'L Smokies left over, which I didn't at all mind finishing off in all their bacon-wrapped goodness).

6 Into that same 350°F oven, somewhere between twenty and twenty-five minutes. A toothpick inserted into the middle muffin of the first batch showed it was baked through, but another five minutes gave the muffin a deeper golden color without drying it out.

7 I served these up, once they were cool enough to pick up with my fingers, with a side of Heinz ketchup and French's yellow mustard, just like I'd dip a corndog in at the county fair. And you know what, these tasted exactly as I wanted them to, exactly as my mouth remembered a county fair corndog, but with the extra bonus of that bite of bacon. I even ate them cold, they were so yummy! Try this next time the football game's on and there's a crowd wanting something better than chips to snack on. I promise, there won't be any leftovers.

BACON PESTO LATE-NIGHT PIZZA SNACK

It's late on a Sunday evening, the last football game of the day is on, and, with an hour to go before my usual lights out, my stomach decides it's hungry. But it's not hungry for leftovers or a cold sandwich, and I don't have any bread good for a grilled cheese, my go-to bachelorette dinner. What my stomach wants is pizza, but it's 8:30, it's still snowing like mad, and my roads haven't been plowed, which means the local pub in town isn't going to be terribly willing to put one of its high school kids in their rusted-out Pinto and send him my way with a hot pie. I dug through my refrigerator, pulled out four ingredients, and reached for the giant pile of bacon I'd cooked earlier that day.

One small oval flatbread (naan bread)

1 loose cup of fresh spinach

½ cup of fresh basil pesto

4 strips of cooked bacon

½ cup of fresh mozzarella, shredded or sliced

1. Nearly all the grocery stores in my area are carrying flatbreads now. Some more than others, but if I can get them where I live, here in the middle of nowhere, I'd guess you won't have any trouble finding them either. I buy three or four packages at a time, in various sizes—the bigger flatbreads usually come two to a pack, the smaller ones three to five—and keep them in the freezer. They have great flavor and a buttery texture, and they not only make amazing foundations for pizza "emergencies" such as the one I was having last night, they work great as a substitute for other breads you'd use to accompany thick chowders and stews. I used a fluffy piece of naan with a smoked pork *pozole* I'd made the other week, for instance, a

much better accompaniment to the rich broth and hominy than a regular old tortilla would have been. Anyway, I had two ovals of naan left from the bag I'd taken out of the freezer a couple days ago (these freeze very well and thaw quickly). They're about six inches by three inches in size, perfect for fixing the growls below.

② This was so easy it almost shouldn't be included in this book, but it does go to show how having a supply of cooked bacon on hand is the solution to damned near every cooking and eating dilemma you might encounter. (That's my story, and I'm sticking to it.) Onto the flatbread went a tablespoon or two of some organic basil pesto I had stashed in the fridge, smoothed across the bread's surface with the back of a large spoon. I spread out a generous helping of fresh, organic baby spinach leaves, laid on four strips of bacon, and dolloped a little more pesto here and there across it. Last, I took of ball of fresh BelGioioso mozzarella, sliced off several hunks, and placed them on the top. I put it on a corrugated cookie sheet and into a 375°F preheated oven, and twenty minutes later I was burning my tongue and singeing the roof of my mouth on hot cheese and bacon and bubbly pesto. And that's how you do a late-night bacon snack.

BACONATED PIMIENTO CHEESE THREE WAYS

Living in Virginia post-college, riding horses and working as a secretary for a small living, I'd gone out for a night with some girlfriends, met the local bouncer at the small-town bar we'd ended up with, and promptly fell in love.

The man I'd met that night had been living in Virginia for some time, but was born and raised outside Orangeburg, South Carolina. He took me home to meet the folks before he asked me to marry him. It was in that small old house beneath the fragrant pines that I was handed a sandwich of toasted, buttered, plain white sandwich bread stuffed with what looked like shredded cheddar cheese mixed with mayonnaise. There were bits of something red in it, too.

"It's pimiento cheese," his sweet mother told me, looking up at the puzzled look on my face. "Don't you know what that is?"

I didn't, but one bite and I knew that I'd found something as Southern as magnolia trees and seersucker suits.

If you've never heard of pimiento cheese, well, you've likely never visited any of the South. It is endemic to Virginia, the Carolinas, and I've found it in Georgia; I assume it's in Florida, though I have not looked. There are several variations—some with egg, some without, some with pickle, some with cream cheese. I've never seen it done with any cheese other than cheddar. Here's how I make mine, a classic yellow cheddar and two variations.

2 cups of your favorite cheese, shredded

2 hardboiled eggs

Two 2-ounce jars of pimientos *or* one 2-ounce jar of pimientos plus a ½ cup of sweet mini peppers, roasted and diced fine (directions below)

½ cup of mayonnaise

❶ No matter what cheese you use, buy it in brick form and then shred it either using the widest slots on a hand grater or with the shredding attachment in a food processor. I always use the food processor—done in a flash and no bleeding knuckles. Set your cheese aside in a bowl and either leave on the counter to dry a bit while you work on the peppers or put it uncovered in the refrigerator if you're making this in the spring or summer and your kitchen runs warm.

❷ I took a bag of mini sweet peppers that most everyone can find in the grocery store these days, took their stems off, and spread them in a large gratin. I sprinkled them with olive oil and coarse salt. I popped them in a preheated 365°F oven for about forty minutes, giving them a quick stir halfway through. Pull them from the oven when the skins are crinkly and browning a bit, then set aside to cool. When they were cooled enough to handle, I dumped the peppers, oil and all, into a food processor and pulsed until I had a colorful relish of sorts. You don't want to purée it, rather you want some texture close to that of the jarred pimientos.

❸ Okay, so why the roasted peppers? Well, pimientos are little peppers themselves, cherry peppers in fact, a variety that's not at all spicy compared to its wide array of brethren. I have to admit, I don't ever think I've seen them in the raw. Where you usually find them is in tiny two-ounce jars, pickled. Really, each jar doesn't amount to much more than two tablespoons. That's fine if you want to halve the recipe above for a quick couple sandwiches, but if you want to make enough of this for leftovers (or to photograph for a cookbook), you're going to need to buy a goodly number of jars. Frankly, I wasn't up the raised eyebrows in the grocery checkout line as the belt rolled forward fifteen jars of pimiento, so I settled for six and the bag of sweet mini peppers. Roasted and pulsed in the food processor, those mini sweet peppers made up for any number of pimiento jars.

❹ Hardboiled eggs, you either love 'em or hate 'em. I like them just fine, and I like my pimiento cheese with them. It adds another layer of texture, plus I feel a little less guilty eating a sandwich made up of shredded cheese and mayonnaise. If you like them, great. Ten minutes in boiling water, run them under cold water so you don't burn your fingers, peel, and chop. I pulsed mine in the food processor like I do for most things when I want a really uniform dice.

5 Mix it all together—shredded cheese, diced egg, pimiento, pepper, mayo. Add more mayo if you like. Like a tuna sandwich, some like theirs sloppy with mayo. I don't. I want just enough mayo to hold mine together and make a chunky spread.

6 I made three batches for the picture and this book: regular yellow cheddar, Vermont sharp white cheddar, and a habenero Jack that was hot to trot. All of them were as different as you'd think they might be, and all were delicious. Eat it by the spoon, put it in an omelette, top a big fat burger with it, spread it on crackers or baguette slices, and stuff it in a burrito or top a taco. Oh, and you can find a pine tree in South Carolina to sit beneath and have a picnic lunch of pimiento cheese on toasted, buttered, plain white sandwich bread, a soft breeze kissing your cheek and drifting the perfume of magnolias past your nose as it can only in the South.

BACON-WRAPPED SAVORY SURPRISE MINI PEPPER POPPERS

My mother, lately, has taken to telling me when she and Dad have been out somewhere and eaten something with bacon. One of her recent texts said she'd just consumed some pre-dinner morsel wrapped in bacon, and that I *must* start working on appetizers. Can't argue with that. So I cruised the grocery store looking for inspiration.

I came across it in a package of smoked salmon that, for my local grocery store, actually looked pretty good, plus the price per pound was under the lottery winning amounts they were charging for previously frozen, raw, farm-raised Atlantic salmon. The smoked salmon, which too had been farm-raised, got an extra point from me for being a Wisconsin-raised product (buy local, stay local, blah, blah, blah). Once home, I rifled through the refrigerator and came up with this:

6 sweet mini bell peppers
3 small bell peppers
8 ounces of smoked salmon
1 cup of whipped cream cheese
4 tablespoons of capers
10–12 strips of bacon, uncooked

❶ Combine the whipped cream cheese, smoked salmon, and capers with a fork. You want to break apart the smoked salmon and really incorporate it, much like you would tuna to make tuna salad; note I said "incorporate," not "disintegrate." You don't want salmon and cream cheese mush, nor do you want to destroy the *piquant* bite from the capers by mashing them into nonexistence. Finally, you must use the softer, lighter, whipped cream cheese. If you go with a regular block, even one softened to room temperature, you'll never get the mix right. Brick cream cheese, even if you beat it in your stand mixer, just isn't going to give you the right consistency.

❷ Once you're finished with the salmon, cream cheese, and capers, move on to the peppers. With a paring knife, decapitate the sweet mini bell peppers of their bumpy tops and stems. Gently devein the inside with the same knife, making sure not to run it through and puncture the peppers, then shake or rinse out any extra seeds. With your fingers, scoop up some of the salmon mixture and insert it into the pepper cavities until full. You really should use your fingers for this. Even a narrowly designed ice tea spoon will run the risk of cutting through the peppers if you get too busy with it, plus fingers simply work better to really get a lot of the salmon mix inside, gently expanding the sides of the peppers and making them more uniformly round. Fill to the mouth.

3 A note here. I'll admit, I thought I had a bigger package of those sweet bell minis in my fridge than I did. As it turned out, I had only a package of eight. Once I finished stuffing those, I still had quite a bit of the salmon mixture leftover, so I de-capped and deveined three small regular bell peppers I'd just bought and stuffed them, too. Since this recipe was about appetizers, though, I'd say you could probably stuff close to twenty of the mini peppers. If you want to go with all regular bell sizes, you could probably stuff five to six smaller sizes to serve as a side to a meal or as a light brunch dish.

4 For each of the mini bells, wrap in a half-slice of bacon, placing them in a low-sided roasting dish, bacon end down, so they don't come unrolled. I did use one whole strip on one of the minis that was quite a bit bigger than the others–go with what works for you–I didn't *swaddle* the peppers in the bacon, just merely gave them a loose wrap. With the bigger full bell peppers, I placed two whole strips of bacon in a cross, set the pepper in the middle, and brought up the four strips around to meet at the top middle of the peppers. I also set these three in a separate roasting dish, as they would take longer to cook than the smaller peppers.

5 Into a 385°F oven, the same temp I usually bake my bacon at. Thirty minutes and the small peppers were done, another fifteen for the big bells.

6 The capsicum from the peppers mingled with the smoky sweetness of the bacon. I bit into one of the smaller mini bells, when it had cooled enough. Then another, and another. I had to force myself to photograph them before I polished them off. Yes, they were that good.

BACONATED UN-NACHO NACHOS

I like nachos when I'm tipping back a cold beer or two and watching a football game, but I hate that so many bars get the dish wrong. Too many seem to make a pile of chips on a plate, put all the toppings at once on top of the chip pile, give it a broil or bake and call it a day. That's fine, if you want one layer of eleven chips on the top with all the toppings and thirty-two chips below it that are hot, soggy, and devoid of the stuff you order nachos for in the first place.

A couple years ago, I was eating dinner at a long-established and sometimes good, sometimes not establishment in San Antonio called La Fogata. I had an appetizer that consisted of individual homemade tortilla chips that had each been painted with refried beans and topped with some mushrooms and what I'm guessing was *queso fresco*. Though they'd used bottled or canned mushrooms, the nice separate treats each had the full array of toppings and flavors. I liked that.

I had a yen for something snacky the other day, and remembered the single-piece "nachos" from La Fogatas. With a pound of freshly cooked bacon waiting for ingenuity, this is what I came up with, and here's what you'll need:

12 to 18 individual, intact triangular chips

Half a 16-ounce can of refried beans

8 ounces of fresh mushrooms

1 tablespoon of olive oil or melted butter

½ teaspoon of salt

½ teaspoon of pepper

½ teaspoon of Mexican oregano

1½ cups of Montery Jack Cheese

1 cup of crumbled cooked bacon

❶ Start with the mushrooms. Slice and dump them in a ziplock freezer bag and shake them with the olive oil or butter and the salt, pepper, and Mexican oregano until coated. Spread evenly on a jellyroll sheet lined with parchment paper and roast in a 350°F oven for forty-five minutes. This draws the water off the mushrooms so they don't turn the chips soggy, and the roasting with the minimal spices adds a little flavor. Once done, set them aside to cool. Do not chop them further.

❷ Put a fresh piece of parchment paper on the jellyroll pan and lay out your chips, leaving a little room in between each. For presentation purposes, of course, but also for ease of

making, handling, and eating, make sure the chips are of a sturdier variety and whole. Broken pieces are just too small to fuss with.

3 Heat up the refried beans until bubbly, then set your saucepan with them on a trivet next to your jellyroll sheet. Carefully dollop a generous tablespoon of beans onto each chip, being cautious of both burning yourself with the hot beans and breaking the chips while you're spreading them—which will then burn you, as well.

4 Your beans painted on, place a couple slices of mushrooms on each chip, followed by a tea- spoon of crumbled bacon. Top each with some of the shredded cheese, taking care to keep as

much on the chip as possible, and wasting as little as you can on the parchment paper. Pop the works gently (you don't want to spill the toppings off the chips) into a preheated 350°F oven and set your timer for fifteen to twenty minutes. Let them cool just enough so you can pick them up and put them on a serving plate, and dish'em up with your normal nacho toppings—guacamole, sour cream, red and green enchilada sauces, whatever you like.

5 Not only will you not be able to eat just one, I dare you to make nachos the traditional way ever again.

CANDIED BACON

I'm going to warn you up front. If you're reading this book, it's a given you love bacon. But, if you also have a sweet tooth, then candied bacon could have you in the throes of a serious addiction—and the worst of it is that this is ridiculously easy to make. Here's what you'll need:

As many pounds of bacon as you think you can handle, plus one extra
One gallon-sized ziplock bag
⅓ to ½ cup of light brown sugar for each pound of bacon

1 Like I said, this is ridiculously easy. Take one pound of bacon and, separating the strips, put them in the ziplock bag. Add in the brown sugar and massage the bag until the strips are evenly covered in the sugar. You may need to add more as you go, as the raw bacon seems to actually absorb the sugar—you'll see the loose sugar disappear almost magically as you go—but you don't want the bacon so coated it looks like it's been dipped in some sort of sugar glitter. Just a nice light coating is what you want.

2 Now, I know some of you, reading this book, have probably resisted using the foil-lined jellyroll pan and stick to your fry pan for getting your everyday bacon done. That's fine, whatever works for you, but if this describes you, put that cast iron fry pan away and make your candied bacon in the oven. This becomes really messy as it cooks, the fat melting into the melted and caramelizing brown sugar, and not only will your fry pan be a wreck that you're going to curse when it comes to cleanup, more importantly, it's unlikely you're going to get the bacon actually cooked through evenly. There's just too much "soup" of fat and sugar that, in the oven, isn't such an issue.

3 On the foil-lined jellyroll pan, line up your bacon as I've suggested you cook all your other bacon, the strips touching and tight together. Go 380 for the oven temp, but with the sugar caramelizing, the bacon, at least for me, seemed to cook a little faster than it did when plain. I think I pulled mine out at eighteen minutes, instead of my usual twenty to twenty-two. Beware, though, because although the sugar darkens as it caramelizes—in fact, it gets darn close to black—you still have to make sure the bacon is done. The darkness can be deceiving. At the same time, you don't want the sugar to start to burn, so really keep an eye on this. If you think you're getting along too far but aren't sure about the doneness of the bacon, you can take the pan out of the oven, then remove a strip to cool for a minute or so and test. If it doesn't feel quite done enough, stick the pan back in the oven, maybe lowering the temp to 375, and give the entire pan another two to three minutes, probably five at the outside.

4 And you're done. Well, sort of. Because once your first batch cools and you try the first piece—the bacon really stiffens almost literally into a candy-like treat and will be chewy, almost crunchy when fully cooled—you will promptly finish off the first batch and be sliding the second pan into the oven. This stuff is addictive in the first order. In fact, you might need a twelve-step program to get over just how good it is … nah, why would anyone want to get over bacon?

You can certainly eat this all by itself (over and over and over again), but this is a wonderful side garnish to ice creams and other desserts, especially those caramel, pumpkin, and chocolate in nature, as well as desserts with toasted nuts. You can even sprinkle a little bit of sea salt (though not the super-fine stuff) on the cooling pieces and capitalize on the sweet/salty trend sweeping palates everywhere.

ELEGANT BACON BITES A DEUX

I love appetizers, though, with really good ones, my dinner plans often begin and end with them. You eat one, then another, then eight, and you hope that, if you're at a cocktail party, no one discovers the wad of cocktail napkins you stashed in your purse.

These two little bites are like this, and a nice change from even a really good cheese platter. They're also not hard to make, which helps if you're hosting. Here's what you'll need for a small gathering of four to eight:

10 whole dates, pits in
⅓ cup of cream cheese, room temperature
5 strips of bacon, uncooked

20 dried apricots
5 teaspoons of soft, mild, peppered chévre
2 jalepeńos, halved and seeded
5 strips of bacon, uncooked

① Let's work on the dates first. I was lucky enough to stumble upon a two-pound package of whole organic dates at one of my better grocery stores, and while they were expensive, they weren't out this world, so home they went with me. You can often find them in one-pound containers, and I've seen them in five-pound containers at places like Costco and Sam's Club. What you want are dates that are whole, un-candied, and still with the pit if possible.

② Take ten of the plumpest dates you have on hand and, with a paring knife, gently make a slit in one end of the fruit and down towards the bottom. You should feel the pit as you run the knife past it. Do not poke through the other end of the date.

③ Using your fingers, take a teaspoon or so of softened cream cheese and work it into the pocket you created in the date with your paring knife. Don't be afraid to work it in. You can actually get quite a bit of cream cheese in and expand the date without stretching it to the point where it rips, if you do this carefully (and now you see why you didn't want to run the knife all the way through, and why you don't want to have pitted dates, which usually have a hole at each end). Wrap each date in a third to a half-strip of bacon and set them touching together in a small, shallow-sided casserole.

④ Next up are the apricots. I laid out two rows of ten on a large cutting board, trying to make the pairs as evenly matched in size as possible. Next I took my halved and seeded jalepeños and cut each in thirds.

⑤ The cheese I selected was a red pepper soft chévre, where the cheese itself was creamy and mild but the pepper really packed a sweet and spicy punch. Using my fingers, I took about a teaspoon and dolloped it on one apricot. I topped that with a jalapeno third, and placed another apricot on top of that. Each stack got wrapped in a third to half-strip of bacon, depending on how tall the stack was, and I wrapped from the top down, so that the two bacon ends were on the bottom and holding the little stack together. Like the dates, I put them in a small gratin dish, rather close together to keep them from tipping over as they cooked.

⑥ Both dishes went into a 375°F oven for about twenty minutes. By then I could smell the sugar from the dates melding with the bacon, and the peppery tang of sweating jalapenos. Once they were cool enough to eat, I nearly devoured them! Oh, sweet lordy, these are good! The salt from the bacon is so-so-so-so-so perfect with the dates, which are almost candy sweet on their own. The apricots, meanwhile, sandwiching that spicy bit of jalepeno, had actually taken all the capsicum heat out of the pepper, leaving it soft and fragrant, and wonderfully sweet on the tongue which, with the bacon, paired just as well as the bacon had with the date. Finally, the tanginess of both cheeses were everything you'd hope for, a perfect complement to the other flavors—and one that made me totally glad I'd skipped putting out a cheese plate or hot crab dip.

Note: Like anything else you'd cook wrapped in bacon, you want to cook this until the bacon is done. With the dates, however, done is going to look like burned, but don't worry, it's not. Dates are so dark in color that once the bacon starts to render down, and especially if you're using slices of bacon that are not thick-cut (and I recommend that you do not use a thick cut), the date is going to show through. Just keep an eye on it; if you're cooking the date treat alongside the apricot bite, judge the doneness by how the apricot treats look. Otherwise, stick to thin-cut bacon and the recommended temp and cooking time in the recipe.

LOADED BACON CHEESEBURGER DIP

There is almost nothing I like better than a cheeseburger (well, except a bacon cheeseburger, of course). I like them from the thin patty triple stack with melted American cheese and a super-soft white bun or a mushroom-Swiss with fresh Portobellos to a double-bacon with sharp cheddar or a double-thick sirloin burger with blue cheese, butter, and chives on a thick pretzel bun. The list is really endless, the beef burger a canvas of endless possibilities.

That range of possibilities includes a hundred recipes, these days, for a bacon cheeseburger dip. Yet they all seem about the same, and gooey, over-cheesed messes at that. Oh, not that they don't taste good, but I don't think you get a true cheeseburger translation. I, of course, fixed that. Here's what you'll need:

1 pound of 80/20 ground beef, preferably organic

½ a yellow onion, chopped

½ a red onion, diced

6 small spring onions, diced, whites and greens

3 cups of shredded sharp cheddar cheese

2 cups of shredded Swiss cheese

½ cup of mayonnaise (don't use the diet, olive oil, or canola oil versions)

½ cup of Heinz 57 Sauce

2 cups of cooked bacon, diced

1 cup of sour cream

8 ounces of cream cheese, room temperature

8 small sweet baby gherkin pickles, diced fine

¼ cup of hot sweet chili relish

¼ cup of yellow mustard

salt and pepper to taste

toasted baguette or Italian bread slices and/or crackers for dipping

❶ This is easy-peasy to put together. Brown your ground beef, seasoning with a bit of salt and pepper. Drain the fat off and set the cooked beef aside to cool. Trust me on the cooled beef part. If you mix all the other ingredients in when it's hot, the mix tends to get all gummy and greasy. Letting it cool first seems to let the other ingredients marry in a better manner, providing both their individual flavors and a better combined taste for that true cheeseburger flavor profile you're looking for.

2 While the ground beef is cooking, chop the onions and bacon and get your cheeses shredded, if you didn't buy them that way. Combine those ingredients, with the exception of one cup each of the Swiss and cheddar, and add to the cooled ground beef. Now you can combine all the wet ingredients, easiest to do in a stand mixer, which will better combine the cream cheese with the mayo, Heinz 57, catsup, mustard, and sour cream into a completely smooth mixture. Just when you get this smooth, add in the diced baby gherkins and give it a couple more spins to combine, then pour it over the beef and cheese mixture. Combine evenly with a spatula, making sure the cheeses don't clump up as you mix (another good reason to have the beef cooled before adding in the rest of the mix).

③ Pour into an 8x9 baking dish or an assortment of smaller gratins or other dishes, depending on how you're planning to serve, and slide into a 365°F oven for about thirty minutes. When the dip looks like it's "gelled," really melded into a thick dip, and is maybe even bubbling a little bit (after that first thirty minutes, look at it every five minutes until it's where it should be, but you shouldn't need to go more than forty-five minutes), sprinkle on the last cups (or more, if you like) of the Swiss and cheddar cheeses and set the broiler to it a bit to melt that last bit of cheese and brown the top a little. Remove from the oven at that point and let cool at least fifteen minutes before you serve—this is a true mouth-scorcher if you eat it hot out of the oven.

④ You can serve this a bunch of different ways. I used some nice wheat crackers, some warmed flatbread, and some toasted, thin-sliced artisan bread slices. Heck, I even took some leftover dip and tossed it with some fettuccine for what turned out to be a decadent dinner. But the one platform I found gave the best loaded cheeseburger taste were some warmed, soft, white dinner rolls my grocery's bakery makes from scratch. They were absolutely perfect for dipping and added that lovely, good-quality hamburger bun element to the taste.

PULLED PORK AND BACON PASTRY BITES

I didn't used to be a huge fan of barbecue. I didn't have much exposure to it in my youth, and what little I did have was some sort of overcooked meat smothered in a too-sweet-for-me sauce. Between that and the whole eatin' it with your fingers thing, it was all too messy and generally unappealing to me.

That changed somewhere along my early and mid-30s. I'd gotten passionately involved in hunting. Living in Virginia, one of the rites of passage from summer to autumn is the opening day of dove season across the state. The first Saturday in September affords the opportunity, and it's usually the one that falls on long, hot Labor Day weekend. The hunting runs from a small group of friends driving the countryside and paying a farmer $5 a head to sit in his half-cut corn field, to gatherings of 25, 50, 100 hunters, along with spouses, children, and nearly as many dogs, shooting over huge fields of sunflowers planted specifically for this day.

While to any dove hunter, opening day of dove season in the South is something special, it's these larger gatherings where it takes on the aura of a true celebration. This is the day that heralds in all the other important seasons—early teal season, general duck and goose season, quail season, grouse and woodcock seasons, and the much-anticipated deer season. It's also the day each hunter and his family have cleaned out their freezers to make way for the coming bounty. Wives make pate of Canada goose livers. Quail and duck breasts are paired with a jalapeno slice and wrapped in bacon to be grilled as appetizers. Venison sausage and marinated strips of backstrap hits the grill, too, and with the last of the summer's fresh tomatoes, chilly bowls of potato salad and sweet corn relish, salted and peppered cucumber slices, and cold peach and plum cobblers, the picnic tables heave under the weight. And yet these are just the supporting cast, for the star of the show, the thing everyone wants more than a limit of doves and the chance to see a six-month-old Lab make his first retrieve, is next to the old farmhouse, laying quietly inside two joined fifty-gallon blackened steel drums.

This is Virginia barbecue. Five men had a giant hog butchered late the night before. Working through the night to clean and prep it, they started the coals under the lovely beast at 5:00 a.m. It gets a basting of apple cider vinegar, hot chili pepper flakes, some sugar, some salt and pepper, and every hour or so, two men, one at each end of the hog and standing by with ten-gallon painter's buckets of the baste and miniature kitchen floor mops, bathe the slowly roasting pork inside and out, making short work of the task and closing the lid to the smoker quickly. Besides the one time at noon that the hog is flipped over, the marinade is all the attention it gets before legal shooting light is called and the hunters come in from the field.

That was how I was introduced to barbecue and smoking and I never looked back—for the pulled pork from that sacrificial beast, after fifteen hours on the smoker, I'm tempted to say is the best thing I've ever eaten. And it changed my mind about barbecuing and smoking forever. I *get* the slow process it takes to get it right, and while I'll always have a preference for the vinegar-and mustard-based sauces of the South over the molasses- and ketchup-based moppings in Kansas City or Memphis, this is the type of cooking I turn to when I want a taste of home.

Today, I live one thousand miles from home, and the closest I get to the pig from those Labor Day dove shoots is a smoked Boston butt on my own smoker. How I do that is a topic for another book, but let's just say that when I've had my fill of pulled pork sandwiches and leftovers for three days, there's still lots of leftover pork to deal with. One of the things I came up with over the summer was this nifty little bite. Here's what you'll need to make about six of these tasty appetizers:

2 cups of leftover pulled pork
1 cup of cooked bacon, finely chopped
2 to 3 roasted poblano peppers
1 sheet of puff pastry

½ cup of spring onions, greens and whites, chopped fine
1 egg, scrambled
Sriracha sauce for garnish or hot wing sauce for dipping

5. The easiest way to get the filling for these tidy rolls is to use a food processor. Take your pulled pork (or roasted pork loin or other pork roast) and use a knife to reduce it to a size your food processor can handle without gumming up or leaving you with an icky combination of pork chunks and pork paste. Work it in two batches if you have to, but you want to reduce the pork to an almost loose ground sausage consistency. Same thing with the bacon; you really want to get this down to a fine grind. Combine your ground pulled pork and ground bacon and add in your diced spring onions, mixing to combine. Set aside and take your puff pastry out of the freezer and let it come to room temperature while you get your poblanos roasted.

6. To roast these peppers, just like I do all my roasted peppers, I take the stems off mine, slicing through the first quarter-inch or so across the top, then lift out the seed pod. I then slit the pepper in half down its length and lay the splayed halves in a gratin dish, skin-side up. I sprinkle them with a little olive oil, sea salt, and cracked black pepper, then roast them in a 350°F oven until they are butter soft and the house smells like roasted poblanos, thirty minutes to an hour depending on how many peppers I'm roasting. I do not bother with taking the skins off afterwards, as most do when charring over a gas burner. The slow roasting with the olive oil leaves you with a beautifully soft pepper, both flesh and skin, so you won't be stuck with skin you never seem to be able to chew through.

7. On a floured wood cutting board or other rolling surface, lay out one sheet of puff pastry. Roll it out so that it's roughly fifteen inches long by twelve inches wide. Take a sharp knife and divide down the middle, then across in three even swipes to make six rectangles approximately five inches wide by six inches long.

8 Scramble the egg in a small bowl and have it next to your cutting board, along with a pastry brush. Now, take one rectangle of puff pastry and orient it on your floured board so that one of the narrow ends faces you. On the narrow end nearest you, lay in a couple tablespoons of the pork and bacon mixture against one of the narrow ends, leaving an inch of pastry exposed on either side of the pastry. Lay a slice of poblano pepper on top of the meat; you'll want less than a full pepper half, and trim your pepper slices to accommodate the roll width as needed. Roll the pastry and its filling away from you, using your fingers to keep the filling inside and folding the extra pastry in at the same time. You don't want to squeeze the pastry and filling as you roll, as you would a sushi roll, nor do you want to merely fold the pastry over the filling and have it be loose. End the roll with the seam side down. Tuck in the ends and press in toward the center of the roll, and pinching the folds together to seal the roll. Alternately, if you've left enough dough on the outside of the filling, you may be able to fold the sides and bottom in and pull the top down, stretching if it allows you to without tearing, to tuck it under the roll. Think of it as wrapping a present—whatever works and looks neat and tidy in the end. Take your completed roll and set it on a cookie or jellyroll tray lined with parchment paper, first swiping the bottom seam with the egg wash, then the tops, sides, and ends once you set it down. Repeat until your six pastry rectangles have all been used, then into the oven at 350 for about thirty minutes, but check a little before for color. The pastry should be a gorgeous and even caramel brown tops, sides, and ends.

9 Let these cool a bit before serving. Believe me when I say this is a mouth full of happiness all by itself, but you can certainly serve it drizzled with sriracha sauce or with guacamole, sour cream, or your favorite hot wing sauce on the side. In all, an excellent and really different way to use up your precious pig leftovers.

ROASTED GRAPE AND BACON CROSTINI

Have a bag of grapes hanging around that you never seem to get rid of? The Bacon Maven sure does. Tell me, why, *why*, do the grocery stores insist on selling grapes in such mass quantities? A poor single girl just can't buy a bunch or two and move on with her life. Nope, she's gotta buy enough grapes to make sure she's not going to buy grapes again for quite some time. But I digress.

You might have missed this, but I had some grapes. Flitting across Facebook or drifting through one of my cooking mags, I saw a headline that had the words "roasted grapes" in it. I didn't do more than glance at the recipe to get the gist of it, and I had an amazingly easy appetizer all planned out. Here's what you'll need.:

2 cups of red seedless grapes

3 tablespoons of champagne vinegar

2 tablespoons of rosemary-flavored olive oil

2 tablespoons of fresh rosemary

6 slices of cooked bacon

6 slices of French bread

18 short slices of brie cheese (off a pie wedge from a small wheel)

❶ Combine the grapes, the champagne vinegar, olive oil, and fresh rosemary. Toss to coat. Takes you about two minutes to do this, including taking the grapes and rosemary off their stems. Put in a small casserole and slide in a 350°F oven for about forty-five minutes, give or take. Grapes should look soft, wrinkly, steamy, and a little dulled in color, but should be surrounded by this unbelievably aromatic liquid. Sigh, I could inhale that perfume in my mind's nose.

❷ On a cookie tray lined with parchment paper, lay out each slice of French bread and drizzle a big spoonful of the hot grape elixir. Cut a bacon strip in half and lay it on top, then spoon on some of the roasted grapes. Lay three of the brie strips on top of that. Into the oven, about 15 minutes, until the brie has gone all melty-melt over the grapes and bacon. Cool just enough not to burn the roof of your mouth—or at least have a glass of really cold Sauvignon Blanc on hand to soothe the pain.

A Note: Most of the recipes I Googled for roasted grapes called for balsamic vinaigrette. Which would have been a perfect thing, had any of the six bottles of balsamic vinaigrette I was positive were in my pantry actually been there. I don't know where they are, may have left 'em behind in Texas, aliens could have made off with them. I dunno, they just weren't there. Alas, I found that out after I'd already mixed up the grapes and olive oil. When one more desperate search of my pantry turned up only champagne vinaigrette, that's the ingredient that went into the mix. Frankly, I think it worked just grand, kept the grapes light, bright, fresh. This leads me to the last sentence and the recommendation of Sauvignon Blanc.

I think most folks would have reached for a pinot noir or something similar to go with this neat little appetizer, but to me that was just too much red grape on red grape. The Sauvignon Blanc was a nice, acidic counterpoint to the sweetness of the roasted grapes and the freshness of the rosemary. I may not be a sommelier, but trust me on this one.

TORTELLINI-'N'-CHEESE STUFFED BACON BOWLS

Can you hear that commercial now? It's the lilt of every $19.99 kitchen gadget out there that the hawkers love to scream about. I never touch them. I dunno, they just seem so, um, *shady*.

My brother apparently understands my resistance to such televised tripe, probably because I launch into the script and finish the commercial for the loud-mouth announcer before they can. Kind of a running joke. Which no doubt prompted him to send me a set—"No, two, TWO sets for the price of one!"—for Christmas. I opened up the box, rolled on the floor laughing, then stashed them in a cabinet and forgot about them.

Well, I forgot about them until there was one of those days when no matter what channel you surf to, you are deluged with the same advertisement, in this case, of course, the one for Perfect Bacon Bowls. It was now or never (and, so, C.T., this one's for you). Here's what you'll need:

For the Tortellini-N-Cheese

1 16-ounce package of fresh, cheese-stuffed tortellini

2 cups of whole milk

1 cup of heavy cream

3 cups of shredded Colby and Sharp Cheddar

1 teaspoon of paprika

2 teaspoons of ground yellow mustard

½ teaspoon of nutmeg

1 teaspoon of salt

1 teaspoon of white pepper

1½ cups of panko breadcrumbs

For the Bacon Bowls

Perfect Bacon Bowl molds (As Seen on TV!)

Two to three slices of uncooked bacon per mold.

1. You can use whatever mac-'n'-cheese recipe you like. I went the extra mile and used a four-cheese tortellini, because, well, why wouldn't I? Anyway, I boiled the pasta for ten minutes, along with a little olive oil in the salted water, then dumped it in a colander to drain.

2. While the pasta was cooking, I scalded the milk, dumped in the cheeses and seasonings, and whisked until smooth. I like a fairly thick sauce on my mac-'n'-cheese, so I added heavy cream and a bit more cheese back and forth until I had the consistency and amount I needed to make the dish.

3. I buttered a small casserole dish, then dumped in the still-warm, drained pasta. I poured the cheese sauce over the pasta, giving it a quick stir with a wooden spoon. I stuck the dish in a

350°F oven for about forty minutes, then sprinkled the top evenly with panko breadcrumbs and hit it with the broiler until golden toasty brown. After that, I set the finished dish on a trivet on the countertop to setup and cool a bit.

④ I boosted the oven to 380°F and turned to my bacon molds. Surprisingly, they're pretty sturdy things, hard plastic, the centers about the size of the body of an upside down muffin tin, the slides sloping down to what I can only describe as a moat, which will hold the rendered bacon fat away from the cooked bacon.

⑤ I made four bowls, crisscrossing one strip cut into thirds over the top of the mold and wrapping two more strips, stacked, around the mold's body to form the sides of the bowl (you can go with one strip around the body, if you prefer a shallower bowl). I set the four on my regular, foil-lined jellyroll tray, and into the oven they went. I checked them at the normal twenty-two-minute mark that most of my regular, flatly laid bacon is done by, but went to just about thirty-five minutes with these molds before the bacon had cooked through and was crisp at the edges. I removed them from the oven, set the pan on the stovetop (the grease really does drain away from the bacon), then inverted them after about five minutes onto my waiting plate.

⑥ This doubting Thomasina is now a believer. For all the over-the-top hype screamed at me by an on-air announcer of dubious culinary skills (I love how they're always in chef hats and squeaky-clean chef coats, as if they've never before been in a kitchen that wasn't on a television set), these damned things work. The bacon is, indeed—and I hate to say it—a perfect bowl.

7 I took a giant serving spoon and ladled in a generous helping of tortellini-n-cheese, set the four filled bowls in a small baking dish, topped them with some fresh breadcrumbs, and set them in the still heated oven for about five minutes to toast the tops. Back out of the oven for about five minutes, until they were cool enough to pick up by hand and bite into. And again.

8 Of course, you can fill your bacon bowl with the oft-claimed dozens of recipes. You're pretty much limited by your imagination—egg salad, BLT fixin's, sautéed vegetables, scrambled eggs, beef stroganoff, whatever—but one word of caution. You *must* eat your bacon bowl and contents right when you make them. Don't even think of reheating them. I tried it, and my bacon bowl continued to cook down, shrinking into something that was more like a palm-sized bacon disc than a bowl and becoming an overcooked, jerky-tough, greasy mess in the process. Keep it fresh, eat them on the spot, and these truly are the Perfect Bacon Bowls*.

*To be honest, there are other ways to make bacon bowls. The most common way I've seen is to use an inverted muffin tin tray, molding your bacon around the cups and cooking the same way as I did with my TV gadget. I've resisted that, mostly because the thought of cleaning up the coagulated grease from all the edges and seams of a muffin tin had me running in the opposite direction. I'm not a bacon doctor—heck, I don't even play one on TV—and I'm not in the least a paid spokesperson for the Perfect Bacon Bowl, but, if you want to make these pretty darned cute bacon bowls from time to time, break down and spend the $20 for the set of four (remember, you'll get the second set for FREE!). They come clean in the dishwasher, they're really made well, and your bowls will come out perfect every time. (www.buyperfectbacon.com)

WINGLESS BACON BUFFALO BREAD

With the Super Bowl still a week away and no desire to watch the pathetic Pro Bowl game that was due to air this weekend—seriously, showing a football game taking place in Hawaii while the real world shivers in the second "polar vortex" of the year is just plain cruel—I was kind of going through football withdrawals and jonesin' for some bar food. Alas, the last dredges of the flu had me thinkin' it was best not to spread that around, so I scrounged through my larder to see if I could make something work on the scale of a buffalo wing dish. When my freezer turned up no cluck of any appropriate form, but all the other necessary ingredients, here's what I came up with:

½ loaf of soft Italian bread
8 to 10 strips of bacon, cooked
1 cup of ranch dressing
2 tablespoons of butter, softened
1 tablespoon of crushed garlic
Frank's Hot Wing Sauce
3 tablespoons of mild crumbled blue cheese, plus extra

1 Find a soft Italian loaf, one that's small-pored in the center like a good white American loaf, and also one that has a hard enough crust to hold the loaf's shape, but lacks the gum-shredding crustiness of a French loaf. Also, try to find one that's as tall as you can.

2 Cut the loaf in half across its mid-section with a bread knife, making a clean-ended half. Now, take a knife with a sharp point, insert it into the soft white part near one of the edges and about a third of the way from the top, and carefully slice to make a pocket. Do this without tearing the bread and without smushing it. Repeat with another cut-in a third up from the bottom. Next, set the loaf half on one of its edges and, taking the bread knife once again, slice the half in half lengthwise, running the knife through the bread between the two pockets you just created. Separate the halves.

3 Take your pointed-end knife and gently cut away at the edge of one of the pockets along the long side of the half and gently peel back the bread to one side, but leaving it intact on the other side. Lay in half your bacon strips and cover with the bread flap. Repeat with the other half.

4 In a small food processor, combine the garlic, ranch dressing, and butter. Spread a generous amount across the surface of the bread, covering the bacon pocket of each half, being careful not to tear the soft center bread (reserve any leftover for dipping later; I had about a half-cup left over). Drizzle both halves with Frank's hot sauce, then crumble your blue cheese (to your

liking, a little or a lot, mild or strong flavored) over the half that is the bottom of the loaf. Carefully take the other half and place it on top, sandwiching the blue cheese in between. Center on a piece of aluminum foil long enough to have the ends and edges come fully up over the side of the loaf and wrap tightly with the foil, pressing down on the top of the loaf—not enough to turn it into a panini, but enough to kind of compact it all—as you go. Into a 350°F oven, bake twenty to thirty minutes minutes or until hot all the way through.

5 When the loaf is done, let it sit on the counter wrapped in its foil for ten minutes, or even fifteen. Unwrap the foil, then cut the loaf in strips across the width. You can further make a cut down the center lengthwise to halve the strips, whichever's easier for handling and dipping. I took the reserved ranch mix, added in a little more Frank's hot sauce, and dipped away, but if hot sauce is your "thang," by all means, go all out with the Frank's. Either way, this easy appetizer will satisfy your next craving for hot wings—and bacon—even when you can't find a bar or the wings!

Chapter 4
BACONATED LUNCH AND DINNER

- Bacon, Zucchini, and Cherry Tomato Pasta Twist
- Bacon and Pulled Pork Burritos
- Bacon Buffalo Chicken Pot Pie
- Italian Love Triangle Meatloaf
- Italian Love Triangle Soup
- Bacon Mac-'N'-Cheese—the Adult Version
- Bacon Mushroom Ranch Roast Beef
- Bacon Wrapped Mini-Meatloaves
- Bacon Wrapped Smoked Lamb Gyros
- Baconated Cabbage and Dumpling Noodles
- Baconated Chicken and Rice
- Baconated Chicken Fricasee
- Baconated Rice Fritters

- Baconated Smoked Chicken Stir Fry
- Baconated Tex-Mex Mac-'N'-Cheese
- Baltic Bacon Chicken Salad
- Blanco Bacon Enchiladas Stacked High
- Bombay Baconated Pork Strips
- Flank Steak Roll with Cranberry-Bacon-Mushroom Stuffing
- Flank Steak Roll Stuffed with Bacon and Roasted Cherry Tomatoes
- Fiesta Stuffed Peppers with Bacon
- Grab a Beer Chicken-Bacon Pot Pie
- Gumbo Hell Yeah!
- Lentil Bacon Mushroom Barley Stew with Savory Sausage Meatballs
- Pork Passion Chili
- Scalloped Bacon Chicken Chowder Bake
- Slow Cooker Pork Loin
- Top Sirloin Roast with Baconated Smashed Root Vegetables

BACON, ZUCCHINI, AND CHERRY TOMATO PASTA TWIST

It's seven-thirty on Friday evening, a time that means waking hours are slipping away for this Bacon Maven, an early riser. I'm two Scotches in, contemplating a final small draught, when hunger pangs strike. I swish the last of my second cocktail, mostly just melted ice, and my stomach growls. I know that if I don't nosh something, I'll have a restless, sleepless night and a grumpy morning. My usual bachelorette fix for this kind of craving is a grilled cheese sandwich or some eggs over refried beans and rice, a little hot sauce and *pico de gallo* thrown in to make the *huevos* less breakfasty. But I'm out of sandwich bread and I'm not in the mood for premature cluck. I paw through the refrigerator, looking for a quick fix.

I uncover a recently bought container of three-cheese tortellini, spy a plastic box of cherry tomatoes, a couple zucchini, a carton of chicken stock and my glass jar of whole milk. Out they come, and I set a pot of water to boil for the pasta. Normally I'd have pulled a package of some sort of sausage out of the freezer, given it a quick defrost, and put that in, but I just didn't want to deal

with the microwave defrost where the middle is always frozen and the ends are half cooked, and I wasn't up to a grease-spattered stovetop. I was thinking I was going to be "good" and go all veggie (note I did *not* say "vegetarian"—*blech! patootey! pfft!* and perish the thought). Then, just as I'm looking for my preferred knife for slicing the zucchini, I spy the plate of leftover bacon.

The Bacon Maven has leftover bacon? WTH?

Leftover bacon I have, indeed. I do most of my cooking on Sunday, but, I'll admit, I plan bigger than I can handle a lot of the time. Let's call it striving for overachievement. Anyhow, I usually start Sunday morning by cooking the bacon I need for whatever's on the agenda that's getting baconated, three to four pounds. As it happens, that Sunday I went through only about one pound of the bacon I cooked, so I had quite a bit left. I used some here and there throughout the week on sandwiches, a slice here and there for a snack. By Friday, I had about fifteen slices of cooked bacon left.

The pasta in the boiling water, I gave the cold leftover bacon a quick, rough chop. In my large All-Clad braising pan, I heated up about a ½ cup of chicken stock and a tablespoon of butter, quickly sautéing a tablespoon of crushed garlic and about ¾ teaspoon red chili flakes (I'm guessing, I used the shaker on my jar of chili flakes instead of measuring, gave it probably six good shakes over the pan), until the aroma gave me a warm-fuzzy. Once there, in went the chopped bacon.

I let the bacon soften a little in the warm, garlicky stock, letting the flavors meld, chopping the cherry tomatoes in half while the bacon and stock simmered. When the liquid had reduced to the point where there wasn't much left and the bacon would start to refry if I didn't add something else, in went the tomatoes, and they started to release their sweet, tart liquid to the pan. By this time, the pasta was almost done, so I tipped about a ½ cup or so of the pasta water into the braising pan, then drained the pasta in a colander. I gave the sieve a quick shake, then dumped the pasta into the braiser, adding about a cup of whole milk. Stirring to coat, I topped the braiser with a lid and kept the heat at medium-low.

I quartered and sliced the two zucchini after trimming off the ends while the pasta simmered away. Ten minutes passed, and I added the zucchini, tossing to get it mixed in with everything else in the pan, then lidded it for another five minutes. Next, I added in probably three cups of shredded mozzarella and provolone (I used Sargento's this time), again mixing to combine. I lidded the pan one more time and turned the burner down to the lower range to keep the cheese from welding itself to the bottom of the pan.

I stirred everything a couple times over the next ten or fifteen minutes, liked the tightness of the sauce that was nicely thick—not Afredo-sauce thick, but not soupy, either—and called it done.

Bright and fresh from the tart cherry tomatoes and the subtly nutty zucchini, creamy and cheesy without being heavy at all, thanks to the chicken stock and dash of pasta water, the bacon you get in a bite was just a pure, moist, succulent bonus. I'll also give myself two thumbs up for the dash of red pepper flakes—the *perfect* and perfectly *right* amount and type of spice. It overwhelmed nothing, enhanced everything. Oh, and time in the kitchen? Forty-five minutes. Not bad for an impromptu grilled cheese substitution, and much better than going to bed with a growling stomach. More importantly, at least for this book, it certainly points to how easy it is to make bacon part of any meal. (The collated ingredient list is just below.)

20 ounces fresh three-cheese tortellini, such
    as Buitoni

15 slices of cooked bacon

10 ounces of cherry tomatoes

2 large zucchini

¾ teaspoon of dried red chili flakes

½ cup of chicken stock

1 cup of whole milk

1 tablespoon of butter

3 cups of shredded mozzarella and
    provolone

BACON AND PULLED PORK BURRITOS

There are several recipes in this book that use pulled pork. That's what happens when a girl gets an urge for her favorite sandwich from back home. She smokes a Boston butt, eats pulled pork sandwiches for five days, and still has plenty of delicious pig leftover. Needing a change on day six, this is what I came up with:

6 9-inch flour tortillas
3 cups of cooked pulled pork (no barbecue sauce)
2 cups of finely chopped cooked bacon
1½ cups of diced red onions
2 cups of canned black beans
3 cups of roasted bell peppers
1 small can of green enchilada sauce

1. This isn't harder than making any other burrito, with the exception of the roasted peppers. I usually keep a bag of those mini sweet bell peppers on hand. They're good chopped raw in salads, but I usually roast them and make some sort of relish with them. That's just what I did here. I decapitated and seeded the peppers, laid them out in a gratin dish, drizzled some olive oil over them, and sprinkled on some sea salt. Into a 365°F oven for about forty-five minutes. You can smell when they're done without fail. I planned to make six large burritos, so I had probably twenty-five of the small peppers in the roasting pan. When they're done and cool enough to handle, pour the entire contents of the roasting dish into a food processor (that includes the olive oil and the juices that rendered from the peppers), and give it a pulse until, well, until it looks pretty.

2. For the burritos, simply lay out each tortilla and distribute an even amount of the pulled pork, red onions, black beans, bacon, and about a third of a cup of the roasted pepper relish (you want to save about a cup of the relish for the top of the finished burritos). Roll each up, tucking in the ends as you roll so the stuffing doesn't leak all over the place, and place seam-side down in a baking dish into which you've poured your small can of green enchilada sauce (or red, green is what I had on hand). When all six are lined up in the dish, spread the remainder of the roasted pepper relish over the top.

3. I went about fifty minutes in a 350°F oven. They smelled wonderful and the tops had started to brown really nicely. I served them up over some fresh white rice and sprinkled a few scallions on top, pulled the top on a cold beer, and sat down to enjoy yet another way to use pork barbecue.

BACON BUFFALO CHICKEN POT PIE

So a couple weekends ago, Superbowl XLVII was held, and I'd grocery shopped to make a bunch of appetizers. One of those was going to be an appetizer type of thing that involved using the deep fryer, but truth be told, I hate working with my deep fryer. It's not that it's a difficult machine to use; mine is actually a fairly nice Waring deep fryer that does a really good job—but it was cold outside, I wasn't excited about the game, and I just didn't feel like standing in the kitchen all afternoon, rolling, sealing, frying, watching the timer, and draining deep-fried anything. Face it, once the fryer's going, you can't walk away.

With the deep-fried appetizer mood in the dumpster, I needed to come up with something else. Maybe it was the last hurrah of the NFL season (even if the Packers weren't playing), but I think it was more likely that, during my freezer-stocking run to Sam's Club the day before, the megastore had a full stockpile of Wright Brothers bacon, which heretofore I had *not* run across in Wisconsin (in fact, I'd only seen it in Virginia, bringing several pounds back with me after visiting my folks a couple months ago for the Christmas holidays). It is my unabashed favorite; thick and meaty, easy on the grease, and prone to little shrinkage. Sam's Club had several varieties, and I snagged two, two-pound packages of the thick-cut hickory smoked, because, at $4.14 a pound, it was about $.80 a pound less than most of the lesser-quality grocery store brands. And that's when the big "SALE" sign caught my eye—two pounds of Wright Brothers Buffalo Wing Bacon for $7.90.

Buffalo Wing Bacon? Seriously? I'd never heard of such a thing. I was a little horrified at the bright orange hue the fat edge had, but at $7.90 for *two* pounds, how wrong could I possibly go? With that in the cart and the checkout girl's assurance that I was going to love it, I decided I needed to go all the way and make a buffalo chicken something. Once the bacon-lovin' gerbils spinning the wheels in my head stopped running, I'd come up with this:

For the Pie
3 cups of cooked and chunked chicken, white and dark meat
1 pound of Wright Brothers Buffalo Wing Bacon (or make your own, directions below)
½ cup of mild blue cheese
¼ cup of chopped spring onions, white and some greens
2 8 to 9-inch pie crusts, scratch made or Pillsbury refrigerated pie crusts
1¼ cups of buffalo wing sauce (recipe to follow)

For the Buffalo Wing Sauce

1 stick of butter (½ cup)

1 12-ounce bottle of Frank's Red Hot Sauce

2 tablespoons of ground cayenne pepper

3 tablespoons of dark brown suger

1 teaspoon of garlic powder

1 teaspoon of onion powder

1 I started to bake the bacon my usual way, but once I had the package of porkbelly open, I decided it wasn't buffalo-wingy enough. I laid out the strips to cover the foil-wrapped jellyroll pan, poured a little bit of leftover Frank's Hot Wing Sauce that I'd found in my refrigerator door into a small dish, and then proceeded to paint the bacon strips with a silicone pastry brush dipped in the wing sauce. Into the 385°F oven went the souped-up tray.

2 I set the timer for twenty-five minutes, pretty much my default timer setting, but I didn't think that was going to be enough. Wright's bacon is quite thick, and with more meat than fat, tends to take a little longer. When the buzzer on my new pig timer went off, I pulled the tray out, poured off the fat, and then slid the tray back in for another five minutes. When the buzzer went off the second time, the bacon was done. Now, I wanted this a little more cooked and firmer than I usually like to eat my bacon all on its own, so that it would stand up and be both a distinct bite and flavor in the pie, so the extra five minutes helped.

3 The strips came out just a hair shy of truly crisp, and they were also dark, thanks to the brushing with the wing sauce. Eaten by themselves, they have the *suggestion* of buffalo wing flavor—a little vinegary with a little hot sauce heat, but nothing overwhelming, and nothing that overshadows the bacon flavor at all. Pretty nice, though next time I might dip the strips all the way into the sauce so both side are covered.

4 Next I whipped up the buffalo wing sauce. I Googled a bunch of recipes, and they're all pretty simple. They're also all nearly identical—butter, hot sauce, and ground cayenne— right down to the brand of hot sauce. For every one I found that *didn't* use Frank's, there were nine that did. I didn't see any reason to buck the system, but I did think that the two tablespoons of cayenne most concoctions called for was an awful lot—and since I can't leave any recipe alone, I added in the sugar, garlic powder, and onion powder. All of it in a saucepan, bring to a boil. Once it cooled a bit, I poured it in my little Magic Bullet blender; much more uniform color and consistency once my wing sauce had taken a spin in there.

⑤ Now for the pie. Playing catch-up on household chores and this blog, I took a shortcut and do something I rarely do: I used a refrigerated Pillsbury piecrust. I actually bought the package a couple weeks ago to use in a new mini piemaker I bought, but haven't yet gotten out of its box. Anyway, I next looked in vain for a pie dish (they must still be boxed up from my move to Wisconsin last year). I did find a small soufflé/cassoulet dish that I'm not sure I at all remember ever seeing before, but it looked like it would work now, and it was a much better option than digging through three three big "Miscellaneous Kitchen" boxes sitting in my 25°F garage.

⑥ I lined the soufflé dish with one of the crusts, pricked the bottom of it with a fork, and placed it in a 350°F oven to set a little. Just ten minutes took most of the fresh doughiness away. Next I cut several strips of the cooked buffalo bacon in half, lining the bottom of the soufflé with them. I dressed the chicken with my newly made buffalo wing sauce, poured the mix on top of the bacon. I topped that with a handful of chopped spring onions, the crumbled blue cheese, and then added one more layer of halved bacon slices on top before topping with the second piecrust and knifing in some vents. (I had about six strips of cooked bacon left over, which I topped the finished pie with. If you're using a regular nine-inch pie plate, you'd probably use the entire cooked pound for both the top and bottom layers.)

⑦ I boosted the oven to 365°F and set the timer for thirty minutes. When the timer went off, I took a look, and it seemed to be coming along nicely, though some of the crust edge had broken off and dropped to the bottom of the oven. (That'll teach me to take shortcuts—I daresay my own crust from scratch would not have done that.) I basted the top crust with some of the fresh bacon grease from another, but unadulterated batch of bacon I'd made earlier in the morning, and set the timer for another thirty minutes.

⑧ That's when this dish got a little, um, iffy. The timer set, I walked into the laundry room to start a load of wash. I turned on the water, poured in the detergent, and I walked out of the laundry room to go grab a towel out the master bedroom that needed a dunking. But, as I'm walking past the oven, I see flames dancing behind its glass door. Fire? *Fire!!!!*

⑨ Okay, it wasn't all *that* dramatic, but, at the same time, it is *not* a sight I'm used to. Apparently some of the fallen piecrust edge had landed near enough to the heating element that they had smoldered and then combusted. I was more disgruntled about the smoke. Nothing ruins a dish worse than smoke from food transitioning to charcoal on an oven element. Even worse are my smoke alarms, which reach decibels near glass-shattering levels. I cracked my glass doors off the eating area at the back of the kitchen to keep the smoke from drifting out to the nearest alarm, then got back to the oven and removed the bottom rack so I could spatula out the offending piecrust pieces. Sheesh.

10 Just as I was shutting the oven door again, I saw my two six-month-old Great Pyrenees puppies making a break for it. And the washing machine was still filling—without any clothes in it. *Damn!*

11 I shoved the clothes in the washer, checked the timer to see how much time I had to chase down the dogs, tugged on boots and raincoat, grabbed leashes and dog cookies, and dashed out the back door, hot on the slushy tracks of the pups.

12 Fifteen minutes later, wet dogs in hand (they'd become fixated at my neighbor's bird feeders and hadn't gotten far), said neighbors laughing at my mad dash through the snow and

impromptu Stars on Ice performance, I arrived back in the kitchen just in time to hear the timer go off.

⑬ I opened the oven door, saw the crust was close to good … . Wait. Something's missing. I can't really smell the pie. I squint at the crust, backlit by the naked oven lightbulb—was it really that much browner, any browner, than it had been thirty minutes ago? I stuck my hand in the oven—and then realized my face hadn't got slapped with the usual wave of heat when I'd opened the door.

⑭ That's it. There's no heat. What the … *no heat????*

⑮ I panicked for about five seconds, truly believing the oven, on top of everything else, had just plumb stopped working. On the sixth second, it occurred to me that, in my haste to de-smoke the kitchen, chase the dogs, and get the dirty duds in the washtub, I'd turned *off* the oven.

⑯ Grand. Just grand.

⑰ I shut the oven door, hit the temp button back to 365°F, set the timer for another thirty minutes, and opened up a Word document on my laptop to start the telling of this tale.

⑱ So how did it all turn out? Miraculously, damn good (and if you're looking for exact timing, go fifty minutes at 365°F, then for ten-minute increments thereafter until you get the crust the right color and you can see the filling bubbling through the crust's knife-cut vents. If you love buffalo chicken wings, you're going to love this even more. The chicken is completely tender, with the buffalo flavor thoroughly in every bite, just like a good batch of "wangs." The blue cheese, being crumbled fresh and without being in a salad dressing, adds the perfect flavor you expect, but without gumming up the pie and making it soupy. The bacon added was, frankly, the *bomb*—texture, salt, heat, lil' sweet—and you get that nice little bit of pie crust just when you think there might be a wee bit more hot sauce heat building up on your tongue than you want to stay comfortable with. Best of all, there's no need for a stash of wetnaps and a washcloth afterwards.

⑲ As an aside, I'm gonna pat myself on the back for the buffalo sauce. I got the constant flavor you'd expect to get when eating a basket of wings at your local pub. It was hot enough to be interesting, and money-on flavor-wise (I think the little bit of brown sugar did just the right kind of tempering to the cayenne and without the sauce having any sweetness at all), but it didn't have me reaching for a glass of water or mopping my brow. A glass of milk would have been good (though unneeded). More than anything, what I really wanted with it was a cold beer—not because of the hot sauce heat level, but because cold beer is what *goes* with really good wings. Alas, there is more bacon to be cooked, more laundry to be done, and the pups are lined up at the door again to go out. Next time … .

ITALIAN LOVE TRIANGLE MEATLOAF

As you'll see in the next recipe, *Italian Love Triangle Soup*, I had a *lot* of leftover meatball mixture. The forty-nine meatballs I'd made for that recipe were more than ample for the stockpot of soup I made (probably ten servings worth, so none without four or five meatballs in them), but they required only about a third of the total mix I'd made. What to do with the leftovers? Meatloaf, of course, was a no-brainer.

I'm not going to repeat the ingredients here, just reference the *Love Triangle Soup* recipe and adjust by half or two-thirds. I looked at the mass of ground meats and mixings I had and thought about doing one large, unformed loaf baked on a cookie sheet. The problem with doing such big and thick loaves is that the outside often gets dry before the insides are cooked through—and since this mixture contained a lot of ground chicken, that just wasn't an option. So I free-formed two loaves, each about the size of the bread loaf pan in which you'd normally cook meatloaf. And that's when this next bit of genius kicked in.

I took out the large jellyroll pan I bake all my bacon on, lined it with aluminum foil, and laid out half a package of Oscar Mayer Naturally Hardwood Smoked bacon, the strips horizontal and touching. I then set one of the loaves in the middle. I topped the loaf with a large handful of onions sliced paper-thin, then brought up the arms of the bacon on each side to meet at the top. I crisscrossed two more strips across the top so that their ends draped over the end of the meatloaf, and so that the loaf was in fact totally wrapped in bacon. I repeated the process with the second loaf.

Into a preheated 365°F oven. Normally I do meatloaf at 350°F, but I wanted the bacon to cook uniformly without either shrinking up into nearly burnt nothingness, or still being somewhat soggy at the end. As 385°F is the degree mark I usually bake my bacon at by itself, I took a stab that 365°F would be the ticket.

I'll admit, I got lucky. I set the timer and checked the loaves at an hour, gave it another ten minutes, and then I could see the finely sliced onions were actually browning at the edges underneath the narrowed slices of now perfectly cooked bacon. Out they came.

I let the loaves rest on the stove for roughly fifteen minutes before I sliced into them. When I did, I was rewarded with a meatloaf that was dense, moist, and showed not one sign of crumbling under the knife or fork. I sliced the end right between two strips of the wrapped-around bacon.

I made these loaves on a Monday night after a long day at work, after wrangling the pups through their dinner and their walks through the unending snow, and just didn't have the energy or time to whip up an appropriate side. Not a problem. One of the things my dad taught me to do with my mom's leftover meatloaf was to make cold meatloaf sandwiches with a little ketchup and

mayonnaise on good white bread. I didn't go quite that route, instead grabbing a soft mild onion bun, adding a little mayo, and then setting the juicy end slice of bacon-loved meatloaf on top to make a hot dinner sandwich.

Quite satisfying on a cold Wisconsin winter night, if I do say so myself.

ITALIAN LOVE TRIANGLE SOUP WITH PESTO POTATOES

Italian Wedding Soup is one of my favorite comfort foods. Its soothing and simple combination of flavors leaves me all warm and fuzzy inside, yet without feeling mac-'n'-cheese-with-weenies five-year-oldish. It's probably the fresh spinach that's swirled into the hot broth, certainly a more sophisticated soup element that few kindergartners would favor. Anyway, after the deep-flavored Blanco Enchilada of the week before, my tongue was wanting something smoother.

I whipped out a half-dozen cookbooks, looking for an Italian Wedding Soup recipe I could modify with bacon. I found none, and it's not like I'm lacking for Italian cookbooks. I even Googled the soup's origins, but came up rather empty-handed. Not that Wikipedia is the be-all and end-all of reliable information, but I did find its entry pretty interesting. It read:

"The term 'wedding soup' is a mistranslation of the Italian language phrase 'minestra maritata ("married soup"),' which is a reference to the fact that green vegetables and meats go well together. The minestra maritata recipe is also prepared by the families of Lazio and Campania during the Christmas season (a tradition started from the Spanish domination of Italy to the present days). Some form of minestra maritata was long popular in Toledo, Spain, before pasta became an affordable commodity to most Spaniards. The modern wedding soup is quite a bit lighter than the old Spanish form, which contained more meats than just the meatballs of modern Italian-American versions."

Ah-ha. So it seems Spain had more to do with this soup than Italy. That explained why my realm of Italian cookbooks was worthless on the subject. Wikipedia also cleared up the "wedding" part. Seems this doesn't have anything to do with white dresses and flower arrangements, but rather these soups are a marriage of green vegetables and meat in a chicken-based clear broth.

More educated on Italian Wedding Soup than I'd intended to be, I Googled a few recipes. They're all about the same: chicken stock, garlic, carrots, meatballs usually made of ground beef and pork, spinach, and orzo pasta. Now, I've made Italian Wedding Soup several times before, always with yummy results, but now the mission was to improve it with bacon. Here's my final ingredient list for the soup.

For the Meatballs
2 pounds of ground Perdue chicken
2 pounds of Johnsonville mild Italian sausage links
2 pounds of Farmland thickcut bacon, cooked
4 eggs
3 celery stalks, including leaves and hearts, diced fine
3 medium carrots, diced fine
1 medium sweet yellow onion, diced

¾ canister of Barilla Garlic & Herb breadcrumbs (about 3 cups)
Half bunch of Italian flat-leaf parsley
12 leaves of fresh basil

For the Soup
2½ boxes of chicken stock
2 cups of water
2 pounds of fresh spinach
2 tablespoons of chopped garlic
2 tablespoons of butter
2 tablespoons of bacon fat
2 3-ounce packages of pancetta slices, cut into ribbons
Half-bunch of Italian flat-leaf parsley, rough chopped

1 Gotta get the meatballs done first. I cooked the two pounds of Farmland Thick Cut slices (which is not the same as Farmland's Thickest Cut, but rather somewhere in between that more custom carving and the skinny everyday bacon) somewhere towards the crisper side. The cooked slices were a uniform mahogany in color, but without a hint of black. This is a little beyond my personal preference for eating bacon texture (I like mine a little limp and juicy), but I didn't want a lot of residual fat going into the meatballs that would not only make them greasy, but would smoke up my oven when baking them. While the bacon slices drained on a plate topped with paper towels, I mixed up the rest of the meatball ingredients.

2 A note is necessary here. I had gone to the market intent on buying two pounds of straight ground pork—no seasoning, no nothing, just ground pig. But, as is becoming the hallmark of my local grocery, the shelves were empty of what I needed, and the weary-looking butcher simply shrugged his shoulders and said he didn't have any when I asked him to ground me my needed two pounds of oink. While visions of bursting past the "Employees Only" door, finding a pork shoulder, and slamming it down in front of the apathetic butcher ran through my head, I didn't see how getting arrested was going to improve my situation. Johnsonville Mild Italian sausage links it became.

3 They really are mild, those Johnsonville links. I figured that, paired with the ground chicken, I'd get the mellow meatballs Italian Wedding Soup usually possesses. All you have to do is take the casings off the links and mix the un-sausaged sausage in with the chicken.

4 The chicken and uncased sausage innards combined in a large stainless mixing bowl, I added in the rest of the ingredients, processing the carrots, celery, onion, parsley, and bacon each by itself in the food processor for a fine dice. Last in went the eggs and breadcrumbs. I baked the gumball-sized meatballs (probably about the size of a quarter through the middle, maybe a round proper measuring tablespoon each) on a jellyroll pan lined with parchment paper, at 350°F for about forty-three minutes, until they were lightly browned in most spots.

5 Wait, back up a minute. Did she say bacon in the food processor? Why yes, yes she did, and I think this was the key to what I judged to be perfect meatballs in the end. Bacon brutalized by the high-speed blade of a food processor turns almost to a bacon paste, seems almost to separate the fat from the meat, as well (though I'd have to get Alton Brown to do some sort of official testing to verify that). What this means for the meatball mixture is that the bacon gets more evenly distributed, as does its fat—and flavor. In this manner, the bacon imparts all its bacony goodness *throughout* each and every meatball. A little sweet, a little salt, a little smoky warmth spreading consistently through each bite, all bites, instead of leaping out on the tongue here and there.

6 By the way, you can certainly give the meatballs a quick sauté in a pan on the stove with some oil. I prefer to bake mine for two reasons. First, there's far less mess with the parchment paper-lined tray; as much as with aluminum foil, if your meatballs aren't overly fat-filled, simply dump the used parchment paper in the trash and stash the jellyroll pan or cookie sheets back in their cabinet. Second, I think the meatballs hold together better, both during this initial cooking process and when submerged afterwards in a soup or sauce. I do not like to put even relatively dry meatballs directly into a soup or sauce. Too often they disintegrate, either in part or totally, and then you've defeated the purpose of 1) all that work making the dadgum things, and 2) that all-important *bite* for which meatballs exist in the first place.

7 The meatballs done and cooling on the counter, I started the broth. Into my taller Calphalon stock pot went the butter and bacon fat. Once melted and warmed up, I dropped in the minced garlic and turned the heat down to medium-low, sautéing the garlic until it was a light toasty brown, about fifteen minutes on this kind of a low temp. (I've done longer and lower, thirty minutes sautéing garlic on a quite low, barely bubbling temp, and the sweetness and nuttiness that comes out is amazing—the garlic is so transformed in aroma and flavor you almost can't believe how it tasted and smelled in the raw). Once the aroma of sweetened, lightly browned garlic hit my nostrils, I poured in the stock and water, added in the carrots and the chopped parsley. When it got to a low boil, in went the pancetta ribbons, and then the spinach. Next came a full boil, in went the meatballs, and the burner was then promptly lowered to medium-low. (And now you should plainly see that it is the bacon, sausage, and pancetta that make up the Love Triangle.)

❽ Most Italian Wedding Soups recipes call for orzo, that short, double torpedo-ended pasta that looks more like a chubby rice grain than a dried extrusion of semolina flour and eggs. I usually go that route myself, and in fact I had about a ¼ cup in a box on a shelf that I did dump in, but as it had been with the ground pork, the grocery store was also devoid of orzo—and I did *not* want to compromise with a pasta of a different shape. Wishing all sorts of horrible things on the butcher and the dry goods buyer at the Pic-N-Save, my head whisked around possible solutions. And then it came to me.

Pesto Potatoes

5 pounds of yellow potatoes
1 package of Philadelphia cream cheese
2 eggs
¾ stick of butter
1 cup of fresh pesto (usually available in stores or you can make from scratch)

❶ This begins as standard mashed potatoe fare. Boil the peeled and quartered potatoes until fork-tender and drain. The taters immediately go into the Kitchenaid mixer bowl, along with everything else. Beat slowly at first, until the potatoes are smoothed out, then up the speed to really blend in the eggs and cream cheese in particular. Pour into a low-sided casserole, soufflé (*respiro* is Italian for soufflé), or gratin dish. Bake at 350°F for one hour, or until the peaks are lightly browned.

❷ Oh, my, these are pretty potatoes! Pistachio green before cooking, they are only a slightly darker green once cooked. Fluffy and absolutely infused with pesto, much like the bacon infused the meatballs. And they were an ingenious addition to the soup.

❸ The soup finished and steaming on low, I took the potatoe *respiro* out of the oven. Spooning a tall mound onto one side of a wide-brimmed pasta bowl, I then ladled my Italian Love Triangle Soup around it.

❹ Spoon a bit of the potatoe *respire* with a meatball, with a bit of spinach and broth. Oh, oh my. Buttery smooth, the garlic and spinach were almost Valiumed in their attitude on the tongue. And the meatballs—such wonderful, sated harmony with a cloud of potatoes, or spooned with the broth and a ribbon of the pancetta. This is absolutely a dinner combination to serve on a cold winter evening shared with your best and closest friends and family.

❺ I almost, *almost*, hated eating this all by myself.

MAC-'N'-CHEESE—DEEP, WIDE, AND VERY, VERY ADULT

Smack and cheese is probably in the top three of my favorite comfort foods. I remember the little blue Kraft box of my youth that came with a can of gooey Velveeta cheese, and, in my adult life, I've often turned to Stouffer's to mend a heart broken by a guy (some women cry through ice cream and raw cookie dough, I do it through pasta and cheese). A couple years ago, I stumbled upon a cookbook devoted to only mac-'n'-cheese—and I can nearly go bankrupt experimenting with cheeses. Talk about taking it to a level as far from the little blue Kraft box as one can get.

Still, sometimes I crave a childhood food. Such a desire struck me the other day; I wanted mac-'n'-cheese with hotdogs. Seriously, it was like I was a five-year-old who couldn't be placated with anything else. Then a friend on Facebook sent me a post of a mac-'n'-cheese pie (from the blog OhBiteIt.com, if you want to see the original), with a latticed bacon top "crust." Oh. Oh *my*. I immediately set to work, altering it to make this a Bacon Maven creation. Here's what you'll need.

2 pounds of bacon
½ pound of white cheddar
½ pound of yellow cheddar
1 pound of smoked mozzarella
1 14-ounce package of Hillshire Farms Pork Lil' Smokies
2 bunches of green onions (about a dozen onions)
1 7-ounce box of small pasta shells
4 cups of whole milk
6 tablespoons of butter
1 cup of all-purpose flour
8 sheets of filo dough
Salt and pepper to taste

1 Make the lattice top first. This doesn't go any differently than it would if you were using actual pie dough. The only note of caution I'd give you is that you may want to adjust the amount of bacon, depending on the size of your pie plate. I planned to use my Emile Henri ten-inch deep dish pie plate—it's big, plain, and simple. If you use a pie plate of normal size (which I wouldn't recommend—this dish really deserves some depth), you can probably get away with one pound. I used Oscar Meyer hickory smoked bacon, just the regular cut, by the way.

② Start with a foil-lined jellyroll pan. I used my standard pan, the largest I have (and I don't think they make them larger than this for home use). I started with the long edge of the pan towards me, and laid strips, side by side, along that long side, all the way across the width of the pan. Now, I wanted a very tight weave, as I didn't want the cheese sauce from the mac-'n'-cheese part to bubble up through and over the woven strips during cooking and make the bacon soggy, so I placed the strips so they were overlapping on each edge. You may choose to do it differently.

③ With the strips laid out, now peel back every other strip. Lay in a strip of bacon vertically (the end of the strip pointing toward you and the long edge of the pan). Gently pull back the strips that you'd peeled back, so that they cover the newly placed vertical strip. Now peel back the strips in the row you had left straight for the first time. Repeat, alternating the peeling back of rows, until you have enough of a woven mat of bacon to cover your pie plate top *after the bacon has been cooked and shrunk*. Since my Emile Henri pie plate is so large, I actually pieced in additional horizontal rows of bacon at the ends of the first strips, tucking in the ends so that they didn't look raggedy in the weave, and extending my lattice work so that it covered the full length and width of the jellyroll pan.

④ Into the oven. I knocked my usual temp of 385°F down to 375°F. This was a *lot* of bacon; I'd used a full 1½ pounds, stretching the strips as I went and as they allowed without breaking. I set the timer for twenty-five minutes, but there was steam/smoke coming out of my stovetop at twenty. I took a look and the lattice was coming along nicely, but there it was already swimming in its own renderings. I poured off the excess and returned the pan to the oven. Fifteen minutes later, I repeated. Fifteen minutes after that, it was about as done as I wanted it to be.

⑤ Here's where I have to say I may be turning into my mother. Mom has always stored excess pans and whatnot in her oven. I have long deplored this habit of hers, but in acquiring extra equipment to make this book happen, it appears I've run out of cabinet space, especially for big items. The day I made this lattice top, I was also coming down with a cold. By the time it was done, I was feeling less than stellar and figured I'd put the pie together in a day or two when I was feeling better. I left the cooled lattice, still on its foiled tray, in the oven when I dragged myself to work the next day, mostly so the dogs wouldn't get to it while I was away.

⑥ Fast-forward two nights. I'm half recovered from the cold and figure I better get on with making this dish. On the oven went, while I started the prep for the mac-'n'-cheese—and 20 minutes later, the lovely smell of bacon was wafting through the kitchen.

⑦ I rushed to remove the hot tray of now twice-cooked latticed bacon. *Phew.* It had gotten a little darker, and had shrunk a little more, too, but it still looked pretty good. Heck, the reheat actually turned out to be a good thing. The lattice work, which had, of course, gotten stiff when it cooled, was now once again flexible and easy to work with, plus it came right off the foil. Let's call this accidental genius.

8 My lattice work saved, up next was the pasta. I'd chosen the small shells, rather than elbows, to better pocket the cheese sauce. You can use what you like, but I'll tell you right now, the shells worked just as planned. Texture and shape of a noodle make a difference in how a sauce clings and works with it. Frankly, I'm not often thrilled with elbow macaroni for mac-'n'-cheese, finding the insides of the tubes don't get enough sauce, often turning starchy and gummy. Anyway, shells it was. Boiled in salted and oiled water (olive oil helps keep the pasta from sticking together in a big pasty clump after you've drained it and while you're working on other components), I cooked until *al dente* and drained.

9 While the pasta had been cooking, I shredded the three cheeses in my food processor and set aside. I also dumped the two packages of Lit'l Smokies in a sauté pan, added a dash of chicken broth, slapped a lid on it, and steamed these yummy and more adult "hot dogs" to plump them up. The sausages plumped, the cheeses shredded, and the pasta cooked, I turned to the sauce.

10 Melt the butter in a stock pot and whisk in the flour to make a roux. I will say this: The original recipe called for less butter, but a full cup of flour is quite a bit, so I added more butter,

up to roughly 6 or 7 tablespoons. I whisked until the roux blonded up a bit, then started whisking in 3 cups of milk. Once lumpless and gaining heat, I moved onto incorporating the cheeses, a little at a time, whisking until smooth.

⑪ Cheese sauces like this come together and tighten up fast at this point. In fact, once I got the last of the cheese in, I could nearly stand up the whisk in the sauce without any support. Keep milk on hand and temper your sauce to the consistency you want. I wanted mine medium-thick, so that there was enough looseness for the pasta to take on and absorb some of the moisture, but not so much that the pie would be a runny mess when I cut into it. I used about another cup of milk to get mine where I wanted, and once I did, I immediately removed the pot from the heat. In a large bowl, I dumped in the drained pasta, then added the cheese sauce and the Lit'l Smokies. I chopped up the green onions, both the whites and the greens, and added them in, too.

⑫ I took my pie dish and layered in two pieces of the fragile filo dough, bushed them gently with oil, and layered in another two. I repeated this two more times, for a total of eight filo dough sheets, to ensure the bottom and sides of large pie plate were completely covered and would have an actual crust, not just a suggestion of one. Next I poured a generous amount of mac-'n'-cheese into the pie dish, the remainder in a medium casserole dish (yes, I made too much).

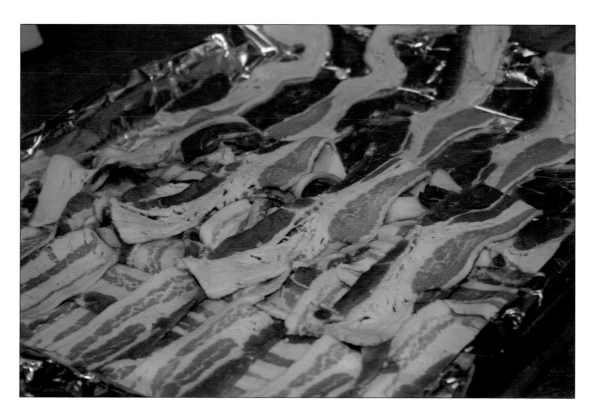

⑬ Into a 350°F oven went the pie, sitting on a jellyroll pan in case of overflow, for forty-five minutes. When the timer rang, I gently peeled back the foil from the bacon lattice and placed it over the top of the pie, "sealing" the edges with another six slices of bacon I'd cooked in a partial bend, so that the entire top was covered. Fifteen more minutes, looking good, and I put a lid of foil over the bacon to keep if from cooking/browning more, and gave it another fifteen minutes.

⑭ So how did this turn out? Well, it's not that a child *wouldn't* eat this, but the bite of the green onions, and the smokiness of the smoked mozzarella and Lit'l Smokies combine to take your kindergartner mac-'n'-cheese with weenies into something very, very adult. That it's all topped with a lattice of smoky, succulent, wondrous bacon, well, that's what the Bacon Maven is all about, now, isn't she?

BACON MUSHROOM RANCH ROAST BEEF

My Facebook newsfeed features a conglomeration of food ideas. I get regular excerpts from *Food52*, *Bon Appetit*, *Saveur*, and others. These professional sights are interposed with the posts from individuals, so I get granny's favorite batch of cookies and best-ever pie, lots of wild game recipes (a majority of my fans there are hunters, just as I have been), and *Taste of Home* type of stuff: macaroni and cheese from scratch, but with Velveeta, desserts made with box cake mix, that kind of thing. I usually don't pay a whole lot of attention to the latter, not because they're recipes that don't taste good—on the contrary, many are absolutely fabulous!—but I prefer not to use mixes and pre-packaged foods, that type of thing. Still, one recipe caught my eye, and I thought I needed to give it a whirl.

The recipe was for a chuck roast that had been rubbed with a package of dry ranch dressing mix and a package of brown gravy mix. Set in a slow cooker, it gets six banana peppers set on top, plus a stick of butter. That's *it*. The poster swore that, despite its simplicity and lack of liquid, this was one of the best roasts she'd ever had. Hmm. I thought I'd give it a whirl, but the Bacon Maven way. Here's what you'll need:

3 to 4-pound beef chuck roast

12 ounces of mushrooms

1½ tablespoons of veal *demi-glace*

7 strips of bacon, uncooked

2 tablespoons of dry buttermilk

3 tablespoons of a combination toasted onion flakes, salt, dried garlic, Worcestershire, dried parsley, and dried chives

1 stick of butter

1 cup of Hidden Valley Ranch Dressing

❶ Commercial ranch dressing? I know, I know, I just got through saying I don't like using pre-packaged foods. Here's where I'd normally *mea culpa*, but I like the stuff, and I'm not a health food junkie or purist. As I get older, I try to eat more organic, that kind of stuff, and while my dreams are often punctuated with the pretty chicken coops from William Sonoma and the gorgeous orange yolks I'd get from my own chickens, I still gotta deal with reality, and for me that's a shortage of time. Plus I just like Hidden Valley Ranch Dressing. So there.

❷ Okay, I took my roast, hit it with the Jaccard, and marinated it in the Hidden Valley Ranch Dressing. It went twenty-four hours in my fridge, and then I rinsed off the roast and patted it dry. I can tell you that the marinade really did its work—that roast was loose as a goose in handling it.

3 I combined the dried cultured buttermilk (which consists only of sweet cream churned buttermilk, sweet dairy whey, and lactic acid) with the combination of herbs. By golly if it didn't smell exactly like ranch dressing—only I had it without all the preservatives and extras in the pre-packaged stuff—and rubbed the roast from horn to hoof, as it were. I next wrapped it in the bacon strips—nothing fancy, just lay out the strips, set the roast on top, and bring the ends around to cover.

4 Meanwhile, in the slow cooker, in this case my Breville Risotto Plus, I lined the bottom of the pan with half the mushrooms I'd purchased. *Mushrooms?* You must be thinking. *Didn't she write something about banana peppers?* Well, yes, yes I did. However, on the visit to a newly discovered and heavily stocked grocery store to gather up the makings for this dish, I'd found it completely devoid of the huge bin of banana peppers I'd seen there the week before, so I had to rethink this recipe mid-store. Thus, I went with the mushrooms, in this case a mixture of shitake, oyster/pleurote, and mini bellas. To the 'shrooms, I dolloped over the solidly thick veal *demi-glace* I keep on hand (mine is from William-Sonoma and, yes, it's another packaged product, which is making me look like quite the hypocrite at the moment, but I have about much time to make *demi-glace* as I do to take my car engine apart and put it back together again for grins). I put in the roast on top of the mushrooms and *demi-glace,* ringed it with the other half of the mushrooms, and set the stick of butter on top of the works, just as I'd seen in the post on Facebook.

5 Three hours on the high setting, five on the low. I stuck a fork in it and called it done.

6 Okay, I wasn't actually quite done, but I did stick a fork in it and it fell apart. Oh, oh my. By this time it was fairly late, 8:00 p.m., and I couldn't take any more real kitchen work. So I took out a soft onion brat roll, spooned some of the mushrooms on top, then laid on some provolone. On top of that I forked some of the easily shredded roast onto one side, then spooned on some Chinese hot chili sauce on the other. A quick toast in the oven to firm up the soft roll, and I had an awesome hot sandwich, perfect so late in the evening and close to bedtime.

7 The next evening, I got a better start on the full dinner presentation I'd intended. I'd refrigerated the slow cooker's insert overnight, which allowed the heavy fat from the bacon to solidify on the top. Easy to pluck off, I now had some really flavorful liquid underneath and no longer needed to call my cardiologist. I set a pot of salted water to boil for a 16-ounce package of whole wheat organic farfalle pasta I'd snagged at the store, then pulled the roast out of its pot and shredded it on a cutting board. With the pasta boiling away, I poured the mushrooms and broth into a large sauté pan to heat and reduce a little. I drained the

pasta of most of its water (I left about a quarter-cup in the stock pot) when it was close to al dente, then immediately put it back in its hot stock pot with a half-stick of butter, a quarter-cup of whole milk, the leftover pasta water, and a handful of fresh rosemary, with some salt and cracked pepper. I tossed to coat, then put the lid on to let it all thicken and sauce up a bit. I turned back to the simmering mushrooms and put in the shredded beef, plus a little more fresh rosemary. The meat heated through, I poured the pasta into a large serving dish, then spooned the shredded roast and mushrooms into the middle.

8 I loved it! Reminiscent of beef stroganoff, but without the heavy cream sauce, the fresh rosemary lightened this wonderfully tender dish without losing any of the depth and complexity imparted by the bacon, *demi-glace*, mushrooms, and the ranch/buttermilk marinade. I judged it to be excellent fare for a cool spring evening supper. Pair it with dry rosé or a light ale, and you have a winner.

BACON-WRAPPED MINI MEATLOAVES

Meatloaf is one of my all-time favorite dinners. My mom makes bangin' good meatloaf, and my dad taught me all about cold meatloaf sandwiches on good white bread dressed with a little ketchup and mayo. As many points as it scores on the comfort-food scales, though, it's a stretch to call it sophisticated. I fixed that, with a little help from bacon, of course. Here's what you'll need:

1 pound of lean ground beef, preferably organic
1 cup of finely diced sweet onions
1 cup of finely diced carrots
1 cup of finely diced celery
1 cup of sourdough breadcrumbs (directions below)
2 eggs
1 teaspoon of onion powder
1 teaspoon of garlic powder
1 teaspoon of salt
1 teaspoon of ground black pepper
18 strips of bacon, uncooked
1 tablespoon reserved bacon fat or butter

1 Heat a sauté pan on medium and melt your bacon fat or butter. As the pan heats, get the onions, carrots, and celery diced fine. When you're done dicing (I ran mine through a small Cuisinart food processor, so that the dice was consistent in size all the way around), add the vegetables to the hot pan, and sauté until tender and the onions are translucent. Do not brown the vegetables. Take them off the heat when they're done and remove the vegetables with a slotted spoon to a waiting mixing bowl.

2 While you're sautéing the vegetables, you can get your breadcrumbs made at the same time. I took a half-loaf of sourdough bread I had leftover from a loaf I'd purchased from the grocer's bakery (a whole artisan loaf, not pre-sliced sandwich bread), tore it into chunks, slapped them on a cookie sheet, and popped them in a 365°F oven until they were a light toasty brown, about twenty minutes, give or take. Once they'd cooled a bit, I put them in my big KitchenAid food processor, added in a little bit of garlic salt and ground black pepper, and pulsed until I had breadcrumbs. Ta-da!

3 Bring your ground beef to room temperature. You can certainly do this while you're sautéing the vegetables and working on the breadcrumbs. I've said it before, but try and find grass-fed organic beef if you can. Especially for hamburgers and meatloaves, organic beef has a texture that holds together better than ordinary ground beef, one that won't crumble when you stick a fork in the finished product. Once your beef is less than refrigerator chilly, add it to the bowl with the cooled sautéed vegetables. Add the breadcrumbs, spices, and eggs, and mix by hand until everything is evenly combined.

4 Time to prep the meatloaf mold. I used a fancy-schmancy oversized muffin tin that has a design in the mold. It wasn't the design I needed (though it does make a pretty presentation for baked-again mashed potatoes), rather the size. Any large muffin tin will do, and I say large, because everything you just mixed up will divide between six molds of this size for a decent, dinner-sized serving in the end. You can certainly go with a regular muffin tin, but you'll probably want to serve two for each adult serving.

5 I laid three strips of bacon in a starburst across each of six muffin tin molds. After that, I scooped out a handful of meatloaf mixture and pressed it into the molds on top of the

bacon, evening out the meat at the top of the mold to make a flat surface. I pulled the ends of the three strips of bacon up over the flattened meatloaf mixture to meet neatly in the middle of each. Into a 365°F oven, about forty-five minutes. Like you would with any other meatloaf, you'll want to see the "loaf" pull slightly away from the sides of the mold, plus the bacons should look done where it's crossed over the top of the meat. If your mini loaves have pulled substantially away from the sides of the mold, you've likely overdone it (easy to do with really low-grade beef, and yet another reason to use organic or at least grass-fed ground) and will be eating hockey pucks for dinner.

6 I made the Bacon Maven's Bacon Cheddar Garlic Mashed Potatoes (in the chapter on side dishes) to go with this. I took that out of the oven with the meatloaves (cooked at the same

time), let both of them sit on the stovetop for about ten minutes. To plate, I gave myself a generous helping of spuds, then took a large serving spoon and gently slid it down the side of one of the meatloaves and lifted it out, inverting it so the flat side was down on the spuds. See? Told you there was a way to make this a comfort-food classic a little more sophisticated! But don't let all these good looks fool you. These little meatloaves, bacon wrapped as they were, were downright succulent, and not the least bit greasy from the bacon (in fact, there was very little rendering moisture at all left in the muffin tins. I'm going to give props again to the organic beef for this, but I think that the meatloaf mix actually absorbed some of the bacon renderings. The bacon on what was now the bottom of each little loaf was certainly crispier than that on the side and tops. Those areas were absolutely cooked, don't get me wrong, but they were juicy and tender, because they were never exposed to the open heat the topside of the loaves were when they were in the oven.

7 Give this a whirl the next time you've got a craving for meatloaf. I think you'll be pleasantly surprised at just how elevated this blue-plate special can become.

BACONATED CABBAGE AND DUMPLING NOODLES

Most people reserve cabbage for Easter's corned beef dinner or for cole slaw. The Bacon Maven felt the need to change that, with a hearty, comforting dish for the first cool evening of fall.

When the first cool evening hits after the long hot summer, I instantly desire something on the order of "stick to your ribs." When I came across a dizzying variety of Amish-made egg noodles at the Woodman's supermarket, I knew I had the foundation for a hearty first-dinner-of-autumn dish. Here's what you'll need:

1 9-ounce bag of thick, wide egg noodles, preferably Amish type
1 small head of red cabbage
1 small head of green cabbage
1 pound of bacon cooked and chopped
¼ cup of butter plus one tablespoon
2 tablespoons of bacon fat plus ½ tablespoon
½ cup of chicken stock
¼ cup of heavy cream
1 tablespoon of olive oil
1 teaspoon of dried red chili flakes
Salt and pepper

❶ Take both heads of cabbage and core and quarter. Shred three-quarters of each cabbage head and set the other two quarters aside for the time being. In a large sauce pan or stock pot, melt half the butter and half the bacon fat. Add in the shredded cabbage and sweat until silky and tender, adding in the other half of the butter and bacon fat as the cabbage starts to dull in color. Add the bacon in at the end, toss to combine, slap a lid on the pot, and take it off the heat.

❷ Boil the noodles in a pot of salted water with the olive oil. Take my word for it and search out these super-thick Amish-type noodles. I used Harrington's, which had no added preservatives, but a quick Google search of "Amish noodles" turned up several brands that are easily ordered; some were even stocked at Walmart. Sure, you could go the Barilla or Cremette route, but those noodles are really too thin for the desired results in this dish. The Amish noodles are, for all intents and purposes, dumplings that are flattened out. They take longer to cook than other noodles—my pot took more than fifteen minutes to get the noodles past gummy and into *al dente*.

❸ When you've got the noodles cooked to the proper doneness, drain in a colander and transfer to a large oven-proof bowl or casserole. Add in the still-warm cabbage and bacon, the red chili flakes, the warm chicken stock, and the heavy cream, tossing to combine. Salt and pepper to taste, then cover with foil and move to an oven set on warm. The noodles will soak up most of the liquid as you keep this dish warm, the rest melding with the other ingredients to form its own sauce. Sweated, reduced cabbage is a tasty thing, but it sure isn't pretty. Oh, the green cabbage isn't so bad, but the red cabbage loses all its gorgeous purple color and becomes a rather unattractive shade of its former self. I solved that by taking the last quarters of both the red and green cabbage, shredding them, and giving them a quick sauté in a hot pan with the ½ tablespoon of bacon fat and the extra table-spoon of butter, along with a little salt and extra ground black pepper. When the colors of the cabbages got really bright, I removed the noodles and cabbage from their warming spot in the oven and added in the cabbage I'd just flash-sautéed, again tossing to combine.

❹ Wonderful! There were three great textures, between the still-crunchy sautéed cabbage, the buttery sweated cabbage, and the dense, chewy noodles. The bacon, softened by the heat of the reduced cabbage, spread its lovely flavor throughout, and the little bit of red chili flakes served to add just the right amount of zip to this lovely dish to keep it from being boring. Best of all, the whole dish was ready in about forty-five minutes, and it's perfectly suitable as either a side to grilled or roasted meat or served on its own as a main course. Simple, fast, delicious, and baconated. How much more could you ask for?

BACONATED CHICKEN AND RICE

It's late, I'm hungry, but I've had a less than wonderful day, and I'm not in the mood to put a ton of effort into making dinner. A rummage through the refrigerator produces a couple chicken breasts that need something done with them, a head of fresh broccoli, a pound of fresh spinach, and about three cups of leftover jasmine rice. There's a lone can of cream of mushroom soup in the pantry, offering a quick fix. *It won't be exciting, but'll be mostly healthy and quick to fix*, I thought to myself. It was a quick-fix dinner I'd made a hundred times before, edible, but boring. Then, on the counter, I spied the last cup of bacon ends that I'd cooked a couple days before.

I heated up a large sauté pan to a bit more than dead-middle medium, melted a tablespoon of bacon fat, and then chopped up the cooked bacon ends and tossed them in to warm. Next I took the three small chicken breast halves and cut them into sixths, adding them to the pan once the bacon ends had softened, a couple minutes or so. Once the chicken breasts had browned a bit on each side, I added in the can of mushroom soup, a cup of chicken stock, and a cup of whole milk and covered the pan. When the liquid got to mildly bubbling (five to seven minutes), I stirred to combine it all, getting all the chicken and bacon evenly coated.

In went the rice next (a 16-ounce package of smoked basmati and wild rice I'd picked up at a health food store). The rice quickly soaked up most of the liquid, so I poured in another cup of chicken stock and set the lid back on the pan. A few minutes to get it all warmed through and I dashed in a bit more stock, then in went the two heads of chopped broccoli, with the spinach on top of that, but I did not stir the veggies in. Instead, I set the lid on the pan again to wilt the spinach down to a workable mass (uncooked, fresh spinach, of course, has a lot of volume for little weight, making it tough to work into dishes until it's wilted down), as well as steam the broccoli sitting under the spinach but atop the rice and chicken.

I gave the lidded pan about five minutes, saw that the spinach was reduced in mass and coming along nicely, and took a wooden spoon to the dish, gently folding the spinach and broccoli into the now-sauced rice, chicken, and bacon. Once all was incorporated and evenly combined, I let the pan simmer without the lid for another five minutes, giving the broccoli a chance to cook through, then dished up my dinner once the broccoli was just fork-tender and still bright green.

Like I said, this is one of my standby, too lazy to really cook dinners. It's always edible, always filling, relatively healthy, but hardly a culinary masterpiece. Easy, sure, but mundane, *meh*, humdrum, ho-hum, shoulder-shrugging so-whatified. But that one simple addition of a cup of bacon ends made an *enormous* difference in this otherwise plebian dish. That little bit of smoky goodness brought out, I dunno, just something *more* in every other component in the pan, taking it if not to "Wow!" status, at least to, "Yes, yes, I will have a second helping!"

I cook three or four pounds of bacon on the weekend to work into these various recipes, but I rarely get to everything I want to cook. That means I have a plate of leftover bacon sitting on my counter more weeks than not, waiting for inspiration to strike me. Turns out that inspiration doesn't have to happen—a cup of bacon here, a cup of bacon there, and *voilá*, your everyday dish has a new take, a makeover, a zip and a zing to it, and sometimes even a different and unexpectedly pleasing flavor profile it didn't have before.

You don't have to cook three or four pounds of bacon on the weekend if you're not writing a cookbook, but cook up just one pound and add it here and there to your mid-week comfort meals. It's the surest way I know to turn a meal that yawns into one that has no leftovers.

BACONATED RICE FRITTERS

I'm a little nuts for basmati and jasmine rice. I love their perfume as the rice is cooking in my steamer, and the texture to me is far better than everyday long-grain white rice. In fact, I love it so much, I almost always make extra and use it throughout the week in a variety of dishes.

Recently, I noticed my Pinterest page was filled with a variety of rice fritters. Most were pretty simple in construction—rice, a couple eggs, a bit of cheese, and maybe some onion. Too simple for me. Here's what you'll need:

3 cups of cooked white rice

2 cups of finely chopped bacon

1½ cups of shredded cheddar cheese

1½ cups of frozen sweet corn (thawed and drained)

8 green onions

3 eggs (scrambled)

Salt and pepper to taste

1 teaspoon of sweet curry (optional)

1 teaspoon of dried red pepper flakes (optional)

1½ cups of panko breadcrumbs

1. Let's start with the "or not" version. I put my leftover rice from a dinner the night before in a large mixing bowls, breaking any clumps that had formed during cooling. Next I dumped in the chopped bacon and cheese and mixed lightly by hand to combine.

2. For the corn, I took a package of frozen corn and dumped about a cup and a half in a mesh sieve. I ran the corn under some warm water to thaw, then let it sit in the clean sink to drain. Once drained, I added it to the rice mix, along with the onions, scrambled eggs, and the salt and pepper. I combined all of this by hand until thoroughly and evenly combined.

3. I rinsed off my hands and poured a measure of panko breadcrumbs onto a small plate. Taking a tangerine-sized scoop of the rice mixture in hand, I formed it into a ball and lightly flattened, but not too much, as the ball will break apart before you can get it into the proper fritter flatness. I laid the slightly flattened ball on the spread of panko crumbs, and *then* I pressed it out a little flatter, the panko holding it together. I flipped the fritter—gently, it's still a bit fragile—so that the other side became coated in panko, and flattened it out a little more. My fritters ended up about the size of a coffee mug mouth.

4 I laid each fritter on a jellyroll pan lined with parchment paper—or at least I did until I remembered that I'd pulled out the sweet curry and red pepper flakes to use. I had eight patties done at that point, and when I finished muttering "dammit" under my breath, I added in the curry and pepper flakes to what was left of the rice mix. That gave me four more patties, for a total of twelve. Into the oven they went, 365°F preheated. I peeked at them at thirty minutes, gave them another ten, and they were starting to toast up nicely, so out they came.

5 Honestly, I can't believe I've never made these before. You can snack on these all day, they were so yummy. I made sandwiches with them (sure, carb-overload, I know), put some fried eggs over them, and ate them all by themselves with a little ranch dressing. And, oh, the curried ones! These were *fantastic!* But the weird thing about them was they tasted almost identical to a crab cake, both in seasoning *and* in texture. I can't tell you why and I can't tell you how, but if you get a yen for crab cakes and can't find the crab (and you're like me and refuse to use that imitation garbage), then this is the way to rock it.

BACONATED SMOKED CHICKEN STIR FRY

Food of the Asian persuasion is, perhaps, the one type of cuisine I've had trouble wrapping my head around when it comes to adding bacon. But the other evening, I smoked a chicken slathered in sriracha sauce, ground ginger, and an Asian grill rub, the intent to make a stir fry when the chicken was done being smoked. But once I got the chicken out of the smoker, I got to thinking, *Well, bacon's smoked, how much could it hurt?* Here's what you'll need:

1 smoked chicken, about a four-pound fryer

2 red bell peppers or ancient sweet reds

2 zuchinni

1 8-ounce package sweet snap peas in pods

½ pound bacon, raw and chopped

1 8-ounce package roasted and salted cashews

2 cups of bean sprouts

3 to 4 spring onions

sesame oil for the wok

1 teaspoon of soy sauce or a tablespoon of hoison sauce to taste

Jasmine rice to serve under the stir fry

❶ The chicken was easy. I quite literally slathered all over and inside the body cavity of a regular-sized fryer chicken probably half a cup of sriracha sauce, several tablespoons of crushed/pulverizied raw ginger, and a couple tablespoons of some Asian grill rub spice mix. I set the bird upright on a beer-can cooker from Williams-Sonoma (see the note at the end about this particular can cooker). Three and a half hours in a 225°F smoker with hickory, and I had a gorgeous bird. Now, I realize not everyone has a smoker or wants to go to the extra time it takes to get a piece of meat properly smoked. For you, a few options. First, roast a chicken in your kitchen oven, slathering the chicken in the same way, and you could probably put a grill smoke box in your oven for short periods at a time, so long as you were cautious and didn't smoke up your kitchen. You could do the same, of course, on your grill, and that way you can leave a smoke box on there and not worry about the in-house consequences. Finally, if you've got a really good butcher or grocery store, it's not impossible to find a chicken that's already smoked, and, if so, you've just cut your work for this dish down to half (though I'd also say I get pretty jazzed smoking my own meat, so I'd miss half the fun, too).

2 Once the chicken was cooled and the meat pulled off the carcass, I heated up my wok. I have a Breville electric wok. (I have to tell you, after years of dealing with a traditional cast iron wok, once I used infrequently because I just didn't like the damn thing, I would be hard-pressed to go back to the other kind. This is a brilliant appliance. It gets wicked hot—

meat-searing hot—fast, it's non-stick and it holds an ungodly amount of food. Feeding six out of this one isn't close to a problem.) Once the wok was hot, I dumped in the cashews. Yes, they were already roasted and salted, but you want to toast them up a little bit, get them coffee-and-cream caramel-colored. Not only does it bring out the flavor of the nuts, it keeps them firmer once you add them in with the other ingredients and their liquid (and helps keep them firm in leftovers, too, so they don't turn to mush). Once they're toasted, scoop out the cashews and set them aside.

3. Next, I heated up a couple tablespoons of sesame oil, then in went the bacon, which was chopped in the raw. Just as the bacon was done but not crisp, in went the red peppers. Once their color got bright, I added the sugar snap peas and zucchini, just a couple quick stirs to get them going and for maybe ninety seconds—remember, I told you, stir fry in an appropriately hot wok should go pretty fast. Into the wok next went the chunked-up chicken, another few stirs and a minute or two to get it heated back up, and last in went the bean sprouts, cashews, the chopped green onions (both greens and whites), and a couple shakes of the soy sauce bottle.

4. This was amazing! Despite a mix of vegetables that was maybe a little off-beat (sugar snap peas instead of snow peas), the mix really did have a distinctive, dedicated Asian flair. But oh, what the smoked chicken and bacon did to it! The chicken was phenomenal. There was just a hint of the sriracha to it, but it was all the way through every hunk of chicken, as was the smoke flavor. In fact, when I took the lid off my wok to serve up a second helping, that gorgeous smoked chicken aroma greeted me like a best friend. The bacon, being smoked itself, of course, might as well have just walked down a church aisle and said "I do" to the chicken—each was the perfect complement to the other. Best of all, the smoked flavors really just *added* something to the dish, rather than overshadowing or diluting the Asian flavors I was wanting in the first place.

5. Then again, isn't that what bacon's all about?

Note: Williams-Sonoma's "beer can" cooker is probably the best of its kind I've ever used. For one, the wide, fry pan-sized bottom provides a rock-steady base for even a really large Perdue roaster, so no more tipped-over chicken, spilled liquid, and a huge mess to clean up. Second, that same pan bottom doubles to roast vegetables as you cook the chicken, or it can be used by itself as a fry-pan on the grill. Third, there's no need to find a tall-boy beer can anymore to set your chicken on. The "can" is integral to the cooker base, attaching/detaching with a simple twist that locks/unlocks the can's two little studs in the base's half-circle screws. Simply fill it up with your beverage of choice (I used about ¾ can of ginger beer for this smoked chicken), then twist it off when you're done cooking and throw both pieces in the dishwasher.

BACONATED TEX-MEX MAC-'N'-CHEESE

I l-o-v-e *love* macaroni and cheese in almost any iteration, from the simple to the complex, from on the cheap with Velveeta (don't be a hater—I know it's a cheese "product," but it has a melty creamy goodness that's hard to duplicate, and sometimes you just plain want that), to a dish with a mix of cheese that would keep Wisconsin's dairy farmers in business for a long time to come. I also love mixing in other ingredients, as was the case with the super flavorful Tex-Mex Mac-'N'-Cheese I came up with. Here's what you'll need:

1 pound Delallo Organic Whole Wheat Pasta Shells

24 ounces Queso Fresco

16 ounces of salsa Jack or pepper Jack

12 ounces of soft chorizo

2 cups of smoked spiced chicken thighs

1½ cups of roasted sweet mini peppers

2 4-ounce cans of diced chili peppers

5 small sweet onions

1 large red onion

8 ounces of frozen sweet corn

2 cups of cooked bacon (about 1½ pounds pre-cooking)

3½ cups whole milk

1 cup of whipping cream

½ teaspoon of nutmeg

½ teaspoon of cinnamon

2 cups of French's fried onions

1½ cups cooked diced bacon

1 Roast the peppers and cook your bacon, get them chopped when they're cooled, then the rest of this dish comes together pretty easily.

2 Get your chorizo cooked, drain it, and set aside. Next, in a clean saucier or sauté pan, sweat your onions down, adding the frozen corn once the onions are translucent, and letting it sweat off some of its moisture. Add in the chopped mini peppers and chili peppers, combine with the cooled chorizo and the chopped bacon in a large mixing bowl, and set aside for a moment.

3 While you're working on the chorizo, you can get the chicken thighs cooked at the same time (you can also cook them when you're roasting the peppers and save some time).

Now, I actually smoked mine. I did a dry rub of cumin, cayenne, a little salt, and black pepper, three hours in my smoker at 225°F. If you don't have a smoker or don't want to take that kind of time, you could certainly either do the dry rub applied to the thighs and roast them in foil packets for about forty-five minutes or so at 350°F in your oven. Either way, they'll be moist and nicely spiced along the lines of the chorizo. Chop the thighs

into bite-sized chunks once they're cool enough to handle, then combine them with the chorizo mix.

4. Get a pot of water set to boiling for the pasta. Once you dump the pasta in, you can get another pot working on the cheese sauce. Wheat pasta takes a little longer to cook than straight white pasta, closer to twelve minutes or so, rather than the eight or nine for regular white pasta. This time will get your sauce started and finished at just about the right time.

5. For the sauce, take a large sauce pan or medium stockpot and add the milk. Bring it to scalding over a medium-low to medium heat, being careful not to burn ('cause there's nothing like the smell of burned milk in your house to keep your nostrils curled). Once you've got those little bubbles around the edges and steam is apparent, start whisking in your cheeses, adding in the chopped green chilies and the nutmeg and cinnamon at the same time. If your milk's hot enough, this should take no time at all. Add the heavy cream to get a consistency you prefer—I like mine thick, but not so thick it's like wallpaper paste, because I want it to be able to spread throughout the dish and cling to the pasta in the right way. Take it off the burner as soon as you get it where you want it.

6. Back at your bowl with the chorizo mixture, add in your pasta and toss to combine evenly. Pour the cheese sauce over the works and combine one more time, thoroughly but gently—you don't want to break apart the pasta—then pour it all into a waiting casserole dish. I ended up using a deep-dish lasagna pan.

7. Into the oven at 350°F. I was pretty close to being done at the fifty-minute mark, but wasn't super happy with the bright red chorizo fat bubbling along the surface. Chorizo's like that—you think you've got all the fat drained off it, but it continues to give its all-in whatever dish you put it in. Now, don't get me wrong, there wasn't a lot of grease, but it wasn't pretty, so I dug through my cupboard, found the bag of French's fried onions, tossed a couple cups together with the other cup and a half of diced bacon, and instantly had a crunchy, tasty topping that made the whole thing prettier when I took it out of the oven ten minutes later (so, to recap, a full sixty minutes, adding in the fried onions over the top for the last ten minutes or so or until they're toasty brown).

8. This was a really rich mac-'n'-cheese, just loaded with flavor. The shells, by the way, were an excellent choice, hanging on the sauce and little pockets of meat, corn, and peppers like little ladles. I ate it plain, and I also double-carbed and served it over rice with some extra shredded cheese for garnish. You won't regret it either way.

BALTIC BACON CHICKEN SALAD

One of my favorite guilty pleasures when I lived in San Antonio, Texas, was indulging in a pint of the curried chicken salad made by the onsite chefs at the southern grocery chain in that state, H.E.B. I'm not sure why they called it "curried." It didn't taste a bit like curry powder—or turmeric or garam masala* or any of the other exotic spices to be found in India. What it did taste was delicious. Creamy, a warmth to the taste without anything approaching heat, and the chicken obviously finger-shredded and oh-so-tender. Okay, so they made a great chicken salad. But why an indulgence? Well, if I remember correctly, the calorie count was sky-high.

I'm about as far away from San Antonio these days as you can get without crossing over into Canada, but a healthy amount of leftover chicken and a plate of bacon made me want to try to recreate some of that wonderful flavor from the H.E.B. deli counter chicken salad. Heck, chicken salad is such an easy thing to dress up, and I don't imagine there's much you *can't* combine with it to make either a salad or sandwich filling. Here's what I came up with on this go-round.

4 cups leftover Sunday dinner chicken chopped into one-inch cubes	1 cup golden raisins
1½ cups shredded carrots	1½ cups chopped cooked bacon
1 medium yellow onion diced	1½ cups mayonnaise
	1 tsp Penzeys Balti seasoning

1 Y'all know how to make chicken salad. Dump all the above into a large enough bowl, mix to combine, adding more mayo (or less) to suit.

2 The question to be asked and answered here is why the Balti seasoning (and just what the heck is it?). To be honest, I picked up this jar on a whim. I'd headed to the Penzeys in Appleton, Wisconsin (they're headquartered in the Wisconsin town of Wauwatosa), over the summer, committed to working through more than one favorite recipe in a stunning book of curries I own and needing a pretty wide array of uncommon spices. I'd been in Penzeys once or twice before, but hadn't really dawdled there, so on this trip, looking for some very specific and oddball seasonings, I was pretty blown away to find that Penzeys had each and every one of them. They also had one that wasn't on my list, and that was the jar called "Balti."

3 Balti is a mix of spices. In order on my jars ingredients list were coriander, garlic, ginger, cumin, dundicut chilis, Ceylon cinnamon, brown mustard seeds, cardamom, cloves, fennel, fenugreek, charnushka, star anise, ajwain, black cardamom, cilantro, anise seed, and bay leaf. Since I knew it was the flavor of actual curry powder I was seeking for my San

Antonio-remembered curried chicken salad, and since the Balti mix seemed to cover just about every other escape route, into the salad it went.

④ I went cautiously, just a scant teaspoonful. Good thing, because a little goes a *very* long way.

⑤ So how did this mix come out? Pretty damn good, the best part being the sweet side of the bacon and the golden raisins playing hand in hand with the warmly exotic mix of seasonings the Balti provided. The carrots and onion were a nice textural balance against the tender chicken.

⑥ Four cups of chicken goes for a while, so I've tried this salad a couple ways. I went oh-so-bland eat-at-your-desk Monday fare and put a big scoop on a soft onion bun. It was okay, but freshly made, was a little too cold and the onions, supposedly a sweet variety, left me unkissable. Last night I tossed a big dollop into a non-stick sauté pan and heated it a bit before putting it on a semi-soft and short type of sub roll that I'd prepped with cold mayo and chili relish. Now that was more like it. In the heat of the pan, the onions and golden raisins had mellowed, the carrots had softened just a bit and sweetened, and the flavors from everything in the "salad" became more tightly woven together for a more consistent taste bite to bite. Cold, you get a pop of sweet here, savory there, which isn't a bad thing, but I sure did enjoy the hot salad sandwich. In fact, I've been thinking of it almost in the manner of a pulled-pork sandwich and think a really creamy coleslaw with a dash of vinegar would be fantastic under this hot salad. Ah, next time …

(By the way, I did a quick Google of "H.E.B. curried chicken salad," not expecting anything, and waddayaknow. The store has an online recipe for curried chicken salad, and while I can tell from the ingredient list it's not the exact formula for the one it prepares for the store's deli counters, it does contain garam masala—that'll teach me to speculate.)

BLANCO ENCHILADAS—STACKED HIGH AND BACONIZED

I traveled to Las Vegas last week to attend a trade show related to my day job. Foodwise, I'm fickle about Sin City; I've had just as many bad meals as good at my share of high-end restaurants as I have dishes of excellent fare. But since I live in rural Wisconsin, where being a "foodie" is a challenge, due to a lack of resources and higher-quality ingredients, I'd particularly looked forward to this annual trip.

I got lucky this time out and had only one dinner that disappointed (at Envy, which seems to have gone to pot since I and the group I dined with were there last year—the food was merely mediocre and the service was absolutely abominable, inexcusable when a steak costs $95). The unenviable Envy aside, I found very good Dover sole and truffled raviolis at Il Mulino, and was overjoyed to make a return visit for the Thai food at the stupendously good Lotus of Siam (absolutely worth repeat trips, even when one only gets to visit Vegas once a year). Unfortunately, I left without getting to one of the restaurants that's been on my must-eat-at list for a while.

Bobby Flay's Mesa Grill has long called to me. I much admire Flay's style and creativity, his intensity, and his grasp of things grilled and Southwestern in flair. Alas, I never seem to get Mesa Grill crossed off my to-do list, and the more I thought about this yearly regret on the long flight home, the more I was craving something *en las formas de* Bobby Flay-Rick Bayless-Aaron Sanchez (*olé!*). But after a week away from home and my two sweet puppies, along with the whopping 4°F that greeted me when I got off the plane, I also needed my craving to be satisfied with something comforting—bacon added, of course.

Tex-Mex running through my head, I was naturally thinking casserole or lasagna in structure, and I had corn in a cayenne cream sauce floating around my gray matter, as well. I did a little Googling and came up with *rajas con crema,* roasted poblanos in a cream sauce, to which I could easily add sweet corn. Now, when I think comfort food, I think Alfredo sauce, mac-'n'-cheese, anything gone all white and creamy so, for the protein part of things, chicken seemed the way to go. Here's the full ingredient list:

For the Chicken Layer
1 whole chicken, in this case a 9-plus-pound Perdue roaster that could have been a pterodactyl for its size (and price tag)
1 bunch of cilantro
1 teaspoon of ground cayenne pepper
1 teaspoon of Mexican oregano
1 teaspoon of cumin
¼ teaspoon of nutmeg
½ teaspoon of cinnamon
Salt to taste
2½ cups of buttermilk
¼ cup of green salsa

For the Poblano Layer
12 poblano peppers
12 to 15 slices of cooked bacon
1 16-ounce bag of frozen sweet corn (yellow or white)

1½ cups of whole milk

1½ cups of sour cream

1pound of Monterey Jack cheese, shredded

1 bunch of cilantro

2 tablespoons of butter

½ teaspoon of ground cayenne pepper

¼ teaspoon of nutmeg

¼ teaspoon of cinnamon

Salt to taste

To Separate the Layers

25-30 corn tortillas

2 cups of canola oil

1 I slid the Perdue roaster of pterodactyl proportions (and price—at $1.79 a pound, this particular cluck slid across the grocer's scanner at more than $14!—when did cluck get this big and expensive, sheesh?!) into the oven at noon. I had water in the pan (to use as stock for later), the chicken sprinkled only with large crystal sea salt and fresh ground black pepper, but I don't really need to tell y'all how to roast a chicken that's going to be used in another dish, do I?

2 Next into the oven went the tray of halved, deveined, and seeded poblanos. Gotta admit, these were not the best-looking poblanos I've ever seen, but seeing as how I'd already cleaned out the Waupaca Pic-N-Save, it wasn't going to get any better. I placed the peppers cut-side down on a foil-lined jellyroll pan, the same one I'd be using next for the bacon. I drizzled the tops with a little light olive oil and a bit of regular Morton's table salt, and into the oven at 350 they went. I checked them at forty-five minutes in, and they were as done as they needed to be.

3 Now, most of the *rajas con crema* recipes I found online called for the poblanos to be roasted whole over a flame until the skin is charred. Convention then calls for them to be put hot into a plastic bag to steam as they cool, and then the blackened skins can be removed and the peppers themselves seeded and deveined. That's all fine and dandy if 1) you could get your patio grill above 100°F when it's 4°F outside, or 2°F) you are fortunate enough to have a French gas oven or other such extravagant cooking range with a set-in grill such as a La-Canche or the beauty that graces the kitchen on Paula Deen's show. Nonetheless, I plunked

my hot pre-prepped and oven-roasted peppers into a gallon ziplock bag to sweat. Cooled, I started to remove the skins, but it hardly seemed worth the effort. I'm guessing I'd have a different opinion with a truly charred pepper, but the skin on my peppers, thanks to the less-intense environment of the oven and probably the drizzle of olive oil and salt, were as tender as the pepper meat itself. In the end, the sweating and skinning was less than purposeful. Moving on.

4 The chicken cooled, I quickly rid the skeleton of its meat, cutting the bigger breast and thigh pieces into uniform one-inch chunks. That chore done, I looked for a way to dress it so it wouldn't dry out in the *lasagne.* Searching my refrigerator, I found a half-quart of buttermilk that hadn't given up the ghost, and a jar of organic green salsa that was three-quarters finished. I'm trying to rid my refrigerator of all the half-finished jars and bottles of this, that, and the other, so into the blender went about 2½ cups of buttermilk

(maybe 3 cups) and about ¼ cup of the green salsa. I mashed in a full bunch of cilantro, and churned it in the blender until I had a pretty pale green and cream mix.

⑤ Next, I turned to the stove and dumped the spices for the chicken layer into an All-Clad nonstick sauté pan and toasted them for a couple minutes on medium-high, until the cinnamon and nutmeg aroma became pronounced. I dumped the hot spices over the bowl of chunked chicken, then poured over the buttermilk and cilantro mixture, tossing it all to blend.

⑥ Back to the poblanos. Into a large hot sauté pan went the butter and the long sliced (not chopped or diced) onions. They sizzled along until translucent, then in went the poblanos, which had been sliced into strips, and the bag of frozen sweet yellow and white corn. (Again, it's winter here in Wisconsin, and fresh corn is nonexistent. You can certainly substitute fresh corn when it's seasonally available if you like the extra work, but truthfully, a bag of brand-named frozen corn—and *just* corn, none of those frozen quick-steam options or those that come in some sort of frozen sauce—isn't bad at all, and a far sight better than corn in a can.)

I let the corn unthaw a bit, then added in the chopped bacon, sour cream, milk, and spices. I brought the pan of all this stuff to a bubble, poured it into a big stainless bowl, and stirred in the chopped cilantro bunch (all but the barest portion of the stems included), and shredded Monterey Jack cheese.

7 By the way, most of the *rajas con crema* recipes I found called for Mexican *crema* or *crème fraîche*, neither of which are available where I live. Wisconsin, for all its cheesy history, is decidedly unworldly in its production views of milk products, i.e., no *queso fresco,* Mexican *crema*, *crème fraîche*, or Devonshire clotted cream to be found. I used Daisy sour cream, pretty much the only kind besides its own store brand my market stocks.

8 Working quickly to get them done before the poblano mixture could cool, I heated the oil in an All-Clad braiser and dipped the white corn tortillas in two at a time for a quick bath. Probably no more than sixty to ninety seconds in the hot oil, the tortillas took on a light golden color. I drained them briefly on paper towels, then began layering them in my favorite 9x13x4-inch lasagna pan (yup, that's 4 inches deep, a bigun). I put twelve gently fried tortillas in the bottom of the pan, three across the width of the pan, four along the length, making sure there were no exposed gaps to the pan bottom. I spooned over a little more than half the poblano mixture, layered on another nine fried tortillas, then layered over all the chicken mixture. One more layer of nine tortillas, the rest of the poblano mixture, and I topped the works with the contents of one can of green enchilada sauce.

9 A note here. Sure, I could have made the enchilada sauce by hand and undoubtedly will at some point. I am fairly devoted to scratch cooking, and with the exception of making my own mayonnaise and grinding my own flour, I don't use a lot of ingredients that aren't in their original or near-original form. I'll even admit to being a bit of a purist snob about it (enough that I feel guilty about not making my own mayonnaise), to wit, I despise *Semi-Homemade* with Sandra Lee—"semi-homemade" my ass. Using a can of beans, a can of soup, and a package of pre-cooked meat to make a "meal of love" for your treasured family is no more "semi-homemade" than serving up a bucket of the Colonel's finest after you've thrown away the container so no one knows. And *no one* changes the décor of their kitchen every day to match the "theme" of their semi-homemade meal. There, I've said it. *Pfft!* to *Semi-Homemade.* That rant over, *my* definition of semi-homemade is using a can of Campbell's soup or a jar of enchilada or salsa or a box of Jell-o every now and then, every once and in a long while, as a singular needed component in an otherwise natural ingredient-rich list. I also try to make those pre-packaged things as organic and preservative free as can be found (Campbell's soup the one exception, because seriously, its mushroom soup is nearly indispensible for quick dinner fixes). Okay, rant and self-justification time over.

⑩ Into the oven at 350°F this monstrous, unrolled, double layered enchilada went, forty-five minutes uncovered, forty-five minutes with foil on top. Done.

⑪ I let it sit on the cooling stove top for fifteen minutes before I sliced into it and served it up for dinner, and after a full three hours of cooking (not counting the two to roast the cluck), I was pretty damned pleased with the results.

⑫ The poblano layer was awesome. I'd make that portion of it as a dish all by itself. The peppers had an earthy sweetness, deeper and less sugary than roasted red or green bell peppers. The bacon's smokiness was a perfect complement, a light shadow of flavor to the peppers, corn, cream, and spice combination.

⑬ The chicken layer was equally delightful. The buttermilk, though a last-minute addition on my part, proved to work as a marinade, even though the chicken had already been cooked. It imparted not only a slight tanginess, great against the sour cream tang of the poblano layer, but also served as a tenderizer. The chicken has the most wonderful bite to it, like chicken breasts that get pounded with a tenderizing mallet before cooking for something, like chicken picatta. Finally, toasting the spices for this layer was absolutely the way to go (though I might have reduced the amount of Mexican oregano, which comes on really strong when heated this way), giving the chicken layer a deepness and complexity of flavor to match that the bacon and poblanos gave the other. I'm also giving myself points and props for quick-frying the tortillas. I'll admit, I find corn tortillas difficult to work with, and steaming them never seems to give me more than a broken, crumbled heap of ruined cornmeal. With this dish, I not only didn't want them breaking, I also didn't want them mealy and soggy when the dish came out of the oven. The quick minute and a half in the oil prevented both, and the texture was almost fluffy cornbread-like after baking between the layers.

⑭ Two things I'd change. First, I'd add a little more salt to the chicken layer. I have a tendency to be overly cautious with salt, primarily because it's one of those things that makes a dish unsalvageable if you go too far, but also because I figure you can always fix it with the salt shaker on the table at serving. In this case the shaker worked just fine, but I've made other dishes where it seems I've used half the salt shaker and still have a dish bland beyond words. Better to taste as you go. The second thing I'd change would be the cilantro. While the bunches I had were a pretty green, they lacked in both flavor and perfume. I've noticed this every time I've bought cilantro in the year and a half I've lived here, probably because it's in such stark contrast to the cilantro I used to get in San Antonio. It's one of my favorite herbs to work with and I use it frequently, but it seems I'm going to have to grow my own this spring and/or add in a good dried cilantro (like that from Penzeys Spices) to enhance.

BOMBAY BACONATED PORK STRIPS WITH GINGER BEER COUSCOUS

Digging through the freezer the other day, looking for four cowboy steak-thick pork chops I thought were on my "Pork/Bacon" shelf, I found only four regular everyday pork chops. They were okay, nothing special. Not thin enough to be cheap-seat pork, not really thick enough to stuff with anything. What to do, what to do. Then I remembered the bottle of Crown Maple I'd spied at the liquor store and couldn't resist. When I saw the bottle, I was thinking that pork chops should be at the top of the list for some sort of drunken combination, the pork the one to be intoxicated, not necessarily the cook (though that's certainly a possibility). Alas, the Bacon Maven's soberness (at least at the time she was staring at the hundred bottles of spices on her walls and in her pantry) managed to whip up something that brought on warm thoughts of an Indian spice market, sultry aromas wafting through the air, their exotic combinations waiting for fruition. Whether through good skill or good luck, that is indeed what she came up with. Here's what you'll need:

4 medium, ½-inch thick pork chops

⅓ cup of Crown Maple Bourbon

¼ teaspoon of cayenne

¼ teaspoon of cinnamon

¼ teaspoon of nutmeg

4 red bell peppers, long enough to hold a half pork chop end-to-end inside

1 cup of golden raisins

16 ounces of Israeli pearl couscous

1 tablespoon of bacon fat

1½ cups of chicken stock

12 strips of bacon

1 small onion

1 tablespoon of sweet curry

1 16-ounce can of ginger beer

1½ cups of chicken stock

Salt and pepper to taste

1 Slice each pork chop in half, lengthwise. I took a Jaccard tenderizer to mine next, to help with the marinating. Skip this if you don't have a Jaccard or similar tool. You don't want to pound these strips to flatness. While a Jaccard, used heavily enough, will reduce the height and increase the width of whatever it is you're Jaccarding, it won't smash it down to chicken picatta levels as a mallet-type meat tenderizer will do.

2. Mix up the pork marinade next. This includes the Crown Maple, plus the cayenne, cinnamon, and nutmeg. I mixed mine up in my Bullet Blender, which does a great job of really combining things like this. Then, placing the pork in a large enough plastic container, I poured over the marinade, slapped the top on it, shook to make sure the pork was coated on every surface, and sent it all to the refrigerator. I'd go a minimum of six hours; longer, even several days, can't hurt it.

3. The night I assembled the complete dish, I took the pork out of the refrigerator and brought it to room temperature. When it was cool to the touch but not cold, I heated up my Staub grill pan to searing temperature, took my tongs, and placed each strip in the pan, reserving the marinating liquid. A couple minutes each side, no more, put nice marks on the outside without cooking them all the way through. I removed the strips from the pan and set them on a cold plate to set.

4. The couscous was up next. I usually use the couscous from RiceSelect. It cooks up fast and reliably and I like it just fine. Alas, a perusal of my pantry, much like that of my freezer, failed to turn up the container of pearl couscous I thought was there. I intended to braise the pork, which I'll get to in a minute, over a bed of couscous, and wanted the larger pearl-sized instead of the really fine-textured, pinhead-sized traditional couscous, of which I found two containers. Still looking for the container of pearl I thought was somewhere, I stumbled upon a small bag of Israeli couscous, a brand called Osem that I'd grabbed somewhere, sometime, to have on hand. Which is exactly what it became, on hand, that is.

5. The Israeli couscous takes a little more cooking than the RiceSelect. RiceSelect generally takes no more than two cups of boiling water, a little butter, stir in your couscous, slap a lid on the pot and reduce the heat to low, and five minutes later you're done. With the Osem, you start with butter—or in the Bacon Maven's case, a tablespoon of bacon fat—and sauté the finely diced small onion until translucent. I also diced up a spare red bell pepper for some color, tossing that in the initial sauté, too. Once the veggies are sufficiently sweated, dump in the couscous—no liquid! This works much like Rice-a-Roni does—you must brown the small pasta, which is what couscous is, before adding liquid. This takes some time and attention, i.e., don't leave the pot at this stage and walk into another room for a long conversation with your special someone (or the dogs, in my case). You don't have to stir it constantly, but you'd be amazed how fast something like this can go from toasty, nutty brown to burnt nastiness. So keep an eye on it, get the couscous toasty, nutty brown, and then pour in your chicken stock.

6 Frankly, the package called for two full cups of liquid. I took off half a cup, though, undercooking it a bit, as there was going to be liquid added when I braised the full dish and I didn't want couscous mush. The liquid in, I stirred briskly, lidded the pot, and took it off the heat.

7 Take the remaining three bell peppers, core, deseed, and devein them and cut them in thirds. Laying the pepper thirds on their backs, put in a handful of golden raisins. Don't *fill* the pepper hulls, just spoon in a couple tablespoons' worth. Next, lay your seared pork chop halves on top, then wrap the works in bacon. I used two strips per pepper/chop arrangement.

8 Spoon the hot couscous into the bottom of a braising pan, distributing evenly. Do not pack it down. Arrange the eight pepper/chop packages in a circle on top of the couscous.* Gently pour over the reserved marinade (nothing wrong with this, it's all gonna get cooked, so get the idea of raw pork juices out of your head), then the can of ginger beer. Lid on the braiser, into a 335°F oven it went, one hour, five minutes under the broiler (lid off, of course) to crisp up the bacon a little.

9 The Bacon Maven would give herself an enormous pat on the back for this dish, if she could stop eating it. You know how every once in a while you get a dish infused—yes, yes, "infused" is the right word here—with a variety of spices, yet none overwhelms the other? This, *this* was that dish. I could taste it all, every spice, from the ginger in the ginger beer and the maple in the pork marinade to the sweet curry and the oh-so-perfect sweet-salty-smoky bacon, and on and on, all in harmony, none struggling to beat the others down with a whip to my taste buds. Can't go wrong with this one, it's not hard, and other than locating sweet curry (I got mine at Penzeys, www.penzeys.com, where you can certainly order online) and ginger beer (I've seen several liquor stores here in Wisconsin carry it, and a Google turned up), and the Crown Maple (for which I recently saw a television commercial, and for which you could probably just as easily substitute your own regular whisky, some maple syrup, and some maple extract), this really isn't an ingredient list to scare anyone. A really nice, slightly exotic spin to weeknight dinner or a really special weekend supper with friends.

*I arranged four of my bacon-wrapped packages of pork chop-side up and four of them bell pepper-sideup. The pork chop halves that had been belly-up were a little dry. Flavorful, and certainly not anywhere near desert-dry, but in comparison to the ones that had been cooked with the bell pepper-side up, were missing a tenderness and succulence. So a note, do this dish red pepper-side up.

FLANK STEAK ROULADE TWO WAYS

I think I've mentioned this before, but I have a voluminous cookbook collection. They range from the classics of *Fannie Farmer, The Joy of Cooking,* and Julia Child's omnipotent *Mastering the Art of French Cooking,* to a small collection of *Southern Living* annuals, a pair of books dedicated to tangine cooking, and a random but thorough assortment of titles like *Luscious Lemon Desserts, Elegant Irish Cooking, Around the Southern Table, The Meatball Bible Cookbook, The Old World Kitchen, Glorious French Food,* and the four-volume (meat, vegetables, fish, and desserts) from Larousee (though woefully, not an original set). Some I've cooked out of not at all (or, rather, not yet), while others wear drops of olive oil and a dusting of pastry flour throughout their well-turned pages. In all, I have more than two hundred volumes and yet, like Imelda Marcos with her shoes, I have trouble resisting adding to my burgeoning bookshelf. I am an addict, one who hopes only to live long enough to cook, significantly, out of every single treasure.

One volume I recently acquired was Williams-Sonoma's *Sunday Roasts, A Year's Worth of Mouthwatering Roasts* by Betty Rosbottom. A *year's* worth of roasts? Clearly, this was a necessary addition to my library if for no other reason than I don't tend to roast a lot of meat; large pieces of meat are hard for a single person sometimes. There are, really, too many leftovers even for someone dedicated to remaking said leftovers into soups, sandwiches, and casseroles. However, the minute I stumbled upon this title, I was overcome with a craving for a thinly sliced, rare roast beef sandwich. Clearly, this was the universe telling me this book had to go home with me.

With other things on the kitchen agenda the day I took this lovely book home, well, naturally I got sidetracked. Still, I remembered the book the next weekend, grabbed it, looked for something both affordable (i.e., not a prime rib roast) and manageable size-wise, and headed to the butcher. There I snagged the last flank steak in the case, a good looking two-pounder, then grazed the grocery store for inspiration and went home to cook. Here's what you'll need:

16 ounces of Portobello or white button mushrooms

1 pound of bacon, cooked and minced fine (about 1 cup)

5 ounces of soft, mild chévre

3 cups of day-old bread, preferably a hearty loaf of wheat or oat, cubed and toasted

1 cup of dried cranberries

1 cup of chicken stock

1 tablespoon of veal demi-glace

½ stick of butter

bacon for wrapping roast

1 tablespoon of olive oil

2 tablespoons of *Barolo e Tartufo** or 2 tablespoons of port with a teaspoon of truffle olive oil

Salt and pepper to taste

1. I know that some of the above might seem like an odd combination of ingredients, but I tend to have a knack for putting things together, so stay with me here for a bit.

2. Start with the bread. I actually had on hand a half-loaf of an artisanal whole wheat and oat bread that had cranberries in it. Now, I don't expect you to scour your region's grocery stores for such a thing, nor make your own, which is why I said to go with day-old bread of whole grain and have on hand a cup of dried cranberries, which I'll get to in a second. Take your bread and cut it into crouton-size chunks or slightly smaller, spread on a cookie sheet (I used my jellyroll pan that still had the foil on it from the last batch of bacon I'd cooked, just for that little extra flavor), and pop it in a 350°F oven for ten to fifteen minutes, until toasty brown all over.

3. Empty the toasted bread into a mixing bowl and set aside, then start the mushroom prep. Take your pound of mushrooms and dump them in a ziplock freezer bag with the table-spoon of olive oil and a pinch of salt and a little ground black pepper. Toss to coat, then spread the dressed mushrooms on your cookie tray, though this time lined with parchment paper. Same oven, same 350°F, probably about thirty minutes, until most of the water has drawn off the 'shrooms and they smell all roasty-toasty mushroomy. Set them aside in their own bowl.

4. Make the stuffing. Bring to boil the cup of chicken stock, the butter, and the teaspoon of veal demi-glace. You can leave the demi-glace out if you want—it's available from Williams-Sonoma, but quite expensive, or you can make your own, but who has that kind of time, including me, which is why I have the jar from Williams-Sonoma. If you don't want to do either, swap out the chicken stock for beef stock. Anyway, bring all that stuff to a boil, add the toasted bread cubes and dried cranberries, take it off the heat. Add in the *Barolo e Tartufo** or port and truffled olive oil mix and stir until the bread has absorbed all the liquid and looks like, well, warm stuffing, just like you would making stuffing from a Pepperidge Farm bag of stuffing mix.

5. Get your flank steak prepped. Lay it out on a cutting board, cover with wax paper, and take a tenderizing mallet to it. You won't get it to pound out to any kind of thinness, after all, it's a flank steak, which is definitely a more muscular cut, but pounding on it a bit will help break down some of that inherent toughness. After tenderizing, trim what you need to make it a generally uniform rectangle of meat.

6 Run your bacon and the mushrooms in a food processor until finely minced, then spread the mixture across the open flank steak end to end and side to side, but leaving about an 1½ inches of one end unadorned. Top the mushroom and bacon mix with the stuffing (you'll likely have a little stuffing leftover). Now add the soft goat cheese (chévre), dotting teaspoons of the lovely stuff evenly across the stuffing mix. Starting with the end that has the stuffing mix all the way to the edge, begin to roll the steak away from you and towards the end that is unadorned with stuffing. This won't be a tight roll, like sushi, but it should be a compact roll—you don't want gaps between the stuffing and the meat. Don't be skittish with stuffing that oozes out the sides, just push it back in as you roll forward. When you're done rolling, wipe away stuffing that's oozed out of the long edge of the end and push back into the roll

as much as possible. Now, flip the roll over so that the seam sits on the cutting board and tie the roast with kitchen twine to hold it all together when it cooks. I used about three pieces, one on each end and another in the middle. Take your final tablespoon of *Barolo e Tartufo* (or port wine and truffled olive oil), and rub it over the outside of the roll.

7. On a separate cutting board, lay out side by side six or seven strips of raw bacon. Place the rolled and tied roast in the middle of and perpendicular to the rows of bacon, seam-side down. Bring the ends of the bacon up so that they meet at the top and overlap, then wrap two more pieces of bacon around each end—it'll stick on its own to the other bacon.

8. I went to the oven with this one, setting the tied and bacon-wrapped roast in a small, shallow casserole dish and giving it about ten minutes in a hot, preheated, 425°F oven. I then lowered the temp to 350°F, gave the roast about another twenty-five minutes, until a thermometer came back with a reading of 130°F. Because ovens vary so much in their true temperature readings and in their regulation of the temperature, check the roast at the twenty-minute mark and then monitor every five until you get the desired temp with a thermometer plunged to the dead center of the roll.

9. This was so good I may never use a flank steak for fajitas again. Not only was it fabulous as a hot main entrée, it made spectacular cold sandwiches with some fresh baby spinach, a little mayo, and, of course, a couple extra slices of bacon. The mild creamy chèvre played wonderfully against the Barolo e Tartufo and the cranberries in the mild stuffing, and there's the added bonus of a whole other layer of complementary flavors, thanks to the bacon and roasted mushrooms, whose saltiness and earthiness were a super counterpart to the tartness of the cranberries and chèvre.

Note: The Williams-Sonoma store is a dangerous place for me, its shelves stocked with all sorts of wonderful and non-mainstream things. Case in point, Le Bontà's Delizia al Barolo e Tartufo truffle and Barolo wine glaze. At $34.95 for a scant 3.38 fluid ounces, it seems nearly as pricey as the truffle itself from which it derives, but I had to have it. A thick mixture of grape must ("must" as a noun, not a verb, is a component of authentic—and expensive—balsamic vinegar), sugar, Barolo wine, and summer truffles, the label indicates its use as part of a dressing for salads, grilled meats and fish, and even cheeses and potatoes. It's luxuriously dense in flavor, so a little goes a long way, and, despite its cost, I'm not one bit sorry I bought it.

That first roll turned out so well, I decided another variation was in order, so I headed back to the butcher the next weekend and ordered up another flank steak. You'll find this one much simpler, as far as the ingredient list goes, but you'll not find flavor has gone missing. Here's what you'll need:

1 3 to 4-pound flank steak
1 pint sweet cherry tomatoes
6 slices of lightly cooked bacon
1 tablespoon olive oil
Salt and pepper

1. Prep the tomatoes first. Pour a pint of the best cherry toms you can find into a small gratin dish, so that they fit cozily in one layer. Drizzle with the olive oil and sprinkle with the salt and pepper. Into a 350°F oven, about thirty minutes or so, until the tomatoes have burst and the juices are bubbling and thickening up.

2. While the tomatoes are roasting, prepare the flank steak in the same manner used for the first roll; put it on a cutting board, cover with wax paper, give it a sound beating with a meat tenderizing mallet, and trim what's necessary to make a mostly uniform rectangle. Season the steak both sides with salt and pepper, then place your six softly cooked bacon slices (you don't really want it super crispy) to cover one side. Once the cherry tomatoes are cool enough to handle, ladle them on top of the bacon, then roll and tie the roast as before, pushing any of the tomato goodness that leaks out back into then roll as you go. Wrap the roast in bacon as you did for the first recipe.

3. I went with the grill on this one, using a ventilated round-bottom pan from my chicken can cooker. Any vegetable grilling tool of the aerated type will do. I set it on direct flame, searing the bottom until the bacon easily came away when the roast was picked up with tongs, then the top side, and then briefly on each long side, just enough to get the bacon about halfway to crispy and with the lid down in between turns. Once that's done, roast the roll on indirect heat until a thermometer stuck through to the center of the roast hits about 130°F, probably another twenty minutes or so, depending on how hot you're running your grill. As an alternate to the grill, you can certainly go the oven route, do as I did with the first version; preheat the oven to 425°F and put the roast in for ten minutes before dropping the temp to 350°F to finish it out to the desired 130°F internal temp. Either way, remove from the heat, tent with foil, and let it sit for fifteen minutes before slicing.

4. This roast was every bit as good as the first, though its filling was substantially different. A little lighter, this was a great dish for a last warm summer evening, and the leftovers made for rockin' BLT sandwiches the next day. I give myself a pat on the back for these two dishes, but the applause, of course, really goes to savory, salty, sweet, wonderful bacon.

FIESTA STUFFED PEPPERS

Stuffed peppers are one of those comfort food favorites, and I'm fond of making them when the cool days of autumn set in. When I ran across a bevy of colorful summer peppers, though, I rattled my brain molecules for something a little brighter, a little different, and a little more in tune with the warmth of the days. Here's what you'll need for this wonderfully different take on a classic:

8 large yellow, green, orange and red bell peppers

4 chicken breasts

3 cups of cooked rice

1½ cups of crumbled cooked bacon

1½ cups of frozen corn or fresh corn cooked and taken off the cob

1½ cups of crumbled queso fresco cheese

1 8-ounce can green enchilada sauce

1 8-ounce can of red enchilada sauce

1 large bunch of fresh cilantro

1 Frankly, I had the chicken breasts on hand from dinner the night before. I'd seasoned them with cumin, salt, pepper, and cayenne and grilled 'em up in the waning heat of the day, taking the pressure off the air conditioner in the house and fighting off the gnats outside with the smoke from the grill at the same time. I took the four breasts that were left over, laid the knife to them, and diced them up medium.

2 The rice was also left over from dinner—I always make extra, just so I can make something else with it the next day—so I gave it a quick re-steam in the microwave to loosen it up and separate the grains, then mixed it in with the chicken. Next in went the corn (I used the frozen, which I actually prefer, since fresh corn can get mushy if you let it boil too long and then cook it in something else), and then I spun the cilantro, stems and all, in my small Cuisinart food processor and mixed that in, too.

3 Call it a split personality, call it having my cake and wanting to eat it, too, but I just couldn't make up my mind between red and green enchilada sauce. So I didn't. I took my chicken mix, put half in another bowl, then added the green sauce to one, the red to the other. By the way, I just wanted the enchilada sauce to moisten the rice and chicken mix, not saturate it, so the small 8-ounce cans you find in the Mexican food aisle of the grocery store worked out just fine for these proportions.

4 Now it was time to prep the peppers. I'd taken care at the market to choose peppers that stood up flat and true on their bottoms, so that they wouldn't tip over when cooked. Except for the red pepper, one of which I desperately wanted for its color, despite its ounce-of-gold price. Unfortunately, every single one at the grocers lacked a stand-up shape. For the yellow, green, and orange peppers, I sliced off just enough top to give a level edge and allow remov-

al of the seed pod inside. For the red pepper, I de-stemmed, then sliced it in half lengthwise and deseeded.

5 Into the bottom of each pepper I laid a couple tablespoons of chopped bacon, then some queso fresco. In went a good-sized serving spoon of the chicken mix next, and I pressed it down with a coffee-cup teaspoon to spread it into the corners of the peppers and make a really full pepper. Another dose of bacon and queso, then a last heaping serving spoon of chicken mix to top, piling it high and mounding it with my hand on top. (The red peppers got just one layer of each, having just a third of the depth of its upright cousins.) I placed them all in an oval Emile Henri ceramic gratin dish, and popped them into the oven. Ran them at 350°F for about an hour, taking a sharp knife and slicing just a little bit into the top of one of the peppers to test for doneness. Just between off the vine firm and soft as butter, I called them done.

6 What a nice change these were from the traditional, sloppy Joe-like ground beef-tomato-onion mix usually stuffed in green bell peppers. Lighter, full of flavor, the bit of smoky bacon and the taste of grilled chicken shaking tastebuds with sweet roasted pepper and corn went beautifully with the fresh cilantro and enchilada sauces (both!) adding the south-of-the-border flair I was looking for. And oh-so-pretty with the different colored peppers. All around a great use of leftovers and a super weeknight dinner when the heat of July and August are getting to you and you just can't face another cold salad.

GRAB A BEER CHICKEN-BACON POT PIE

I love chicken pot pie. It is one of those comfort foods I could eat any time. The thought of that creamy sauce, succulent chicken, and sweet summer peas and carrots … well, it sends me.

I was kind of jonesin' for chicken pot pie last weekend, spring continuing to elude us here in Wisconsin, but I didn't want to simply add bacon to the classic. It's not that you couldn't, but I don't always want to mess with a particular taste that my mouth craves. So I came up with something else. Here's what you'll need:

1 8 to 9-pound roasting chicken

2 pounds of sliced button mushrooms, roasted

1 pound of bacon, cooked and rough chopped

½ pound of smoked cheddar

2 teaspoons of ground sage

2 teaspoons crushed rosemary

3 tablespoons of butter

⅔ cup of all-purpose flour

1 cup of heavy whipping cream

2 pie crusts (one each top and bottom) for the full-size pie plate of your choice

Salt and pepper to taste

1 Whenever possible, which is usually, I roast the chicken I'm going to need parts for in whatever dish I'm concocting. There is something about that time in the oven, bones sweating out their goodness, fat rendering and basting at the same time, that imparts flavor not to be found when using deboned chicken breast and thigh cutlets (and don't get me started on frozen parts). Still, once again, my grocery store stuck it to me.

2 I went in looking for a Perdue roaster. Yes, I know these are not organic chickens. Yes, I know that this is big agri-business. However, Perdue's chickens are now cage-free and have an all-vegetarian diet. I also find Jim Perdue kind of sexy, but I digress. To me, these are the best-tasting, meatiest roasting chickens on the market, bar none, and my only choice without a reliable and nearby source for whole organic cluck. Perdue's pop-up timers work *perfectly*—it's almost impossible to screw up one of these birds. The part I like best? Simply sea salt and peppering the skin before roasting gives you a decadent, don't-tell-your-cardiologist treat when done: perfectly crisped and seasoned skin. It's like eating Lay's potato chips, but better, and with a slightly modified tag line: "Betcha can't eat just some of it." I walked over to the chicken case in the Waupca Pic-N-Save,

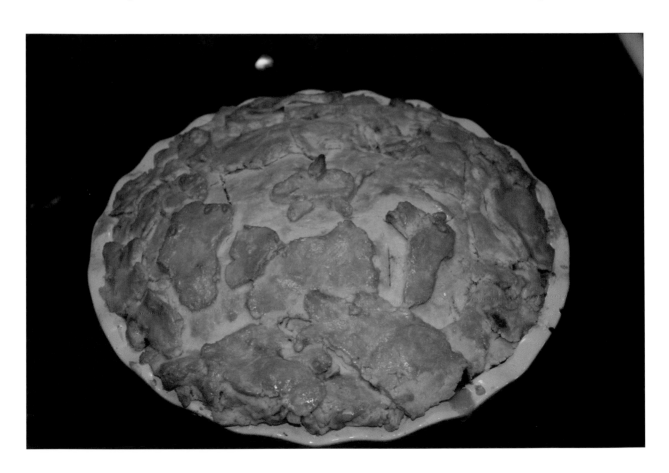

and discovered there were none. Oh, there were roasters all right, but they were the store brand. I don't mind a store marketing its own stuff, but enforcing a monopoly on product is wrong on more levels than I have time for here. I snagged one and left the market in a huff.

③ This cluck had a pop-up timer, at least. I combined some sea salt, ground black pepper, and a teaspoon each of the sage and rosemary, rubbed the bird inside and out, stuck it in the oven. It came out all right, but it wasn't perfect, a little underdone at the joints and just missing some of the pizazz of the Perdue. I looked at it sadly, let it cool, and pulled it apart.

④ My favorite pie plate, if you can call it a plate, is a coated ceramic Emile Henry deep dish that seems a foot wide, but is closer to ten inches across. While the chicken cooled, I worked on pie pastry. I started with the standard pie crust recipe from my standby for cooking basics, *The Fanny Farmer Cookbook*, by Marion Cunningham, but instead of using shortening, I used bacon fat. I'd been talking to a pastry chef at Williams-Sonoma a couple weeks ago and asked her about doing this, and she'd said she didn't see why not. After all, pie crusts back in the day (and still the best ones today) use lard, and bacon fat wasn't that far off. She advised I freeze the bacon fat first, which I'd done. I made a double batch for a nine-inch crust, and I wasn't thrilled. It was quite a bit of work to work the frozen bacon fat into the flour and, upon rolling out, the dough was cantankerous about sticking together as I attempted to roll it into a round, the edges splitting and refusing to be rolled and melded back together. I got the first crust rolled out enough to cover most of the bottom and sides of my pie dish, but not all. So I swiped some dough from the top crust, rolled it out, and patched in the sides that didn't come quite to the top edge.

⑤ This, of course, left me short of enough dough for the top crust, so I whipped up a second single crust. The bacon fat now not quite so frozen, it cut into the flour *much* easier, which gave me hope for a better rolling out experience. Alas, that was not to be. But back to the pie for the moment.

⑥ Next up were the mushrooms. I dumped each pound in a ziplock bag, put in half the remaining rosemary and sage, plus a little pepper and salt, then half the butter, shaking to coat evenly. I lined my largest edged cookie sheet with parchment paper, set the oven to 375, spread both pounds of mushrooms evenly on the sheet, set the tray in, and cooked them down for about forty minutes or so. What you want to do is get most of the water out of the 'shrooms, so they don't sweat out during baking and make everything soggy.

⑦ I hand-tore the chicken into fork-size pieces, using about two-thirds of the meat available from this chicken. Next I mixed in the chopped bacon, then the roasted mushrooms. I had pre-baked the bottom crust, and once cooled, I put down a layer of the cheese, then spooned in a good measure of the chicken-bacon-mushroom mix. I placed roughly eight slices of the smoked cheddar cheese on top, then repeated the layers once. Back at the stove, I took the renderings in the pan from the roasted chicken, began to heat it up, and whisked in probably 2/3 cup of flour, a little at a time, to start a roux. Then went in about a cup of heavy whipping cream, again, a little at time, whisking until it was thick, but pourable. Hot and bubbling, I poured it over the pie innards.

8 Now for the second crust. Just wasn't my day for bacon fat pie dough. I barely got the second crust to roll out, so I mixed up about another half-crust worth of dough, rolled it out, and pieced it over the gaps. Fork-whisking the egg, I then sealed the pieces and glazed the top crust in a few broad strokes with a pastry brush (pretty sneaky, eh?) and called it a day. Fifteen minutes at 425°F to set the crust, reduce to 350°F and let it do what it needs to for an hour (at least with a deep dish like mine—adjust accordingly for smaller, normal-size pie plates). Frankly, I don't think it turned out that bad, looks-wise, I mean. The glossy shine on my patchwork crust looks homey and is actually pretty yummy. As is the pie. It was a good medley of flavors, solid and filling. This is not a kid's pie. Which brings me to the "Grab a Beer" part of the recipe name.

9 I add very little salt when I'm cooking, usually just barely what's necessary (in fact, I often find myself salting things at the end of a cook prep or at the finished dish, so cautious am I about over-salting). Still, for all my care, this pie was a little salty.* Not "Oh my god, where's the water?!" salty, but still. Salty. Like pretzels with crystal salt are salty. So, while I wasn't reaching for the pitcher of water, this very hearty, very *adult* pot pie lacked for only one thing. A beer. To that end, I grabbed a Guinness Black Lager out of my wine fridge and, ta da! A filling slice of pub fare, pub beer included, right from my own kitchen.

Note: Turns out the cheese was the culprit, when it came to the deeper (again, not unpleasant, just deeper) salt presence. I'd bought about a quarter pound of this smoked aged cheddar the week before from my butcher and found it absolutely delicious. In fact, I was surprised; while I like smoked cheeses, some are so overpowered by either smoke or salt, you can't even taste the cheese. This one was just great, with a mild smokiness that truly complemented the mild, aged cheddar flavor, and being a drier cheese than un-aged cheddar, I thought it would be less greasy in the pie. As it turns out, apparently the cheddar I bought for this recipe—same brand, from the same butcher—came from a very different batch at the cheesemaker's. I grabbed a slice for a quick snack a couple days after I made this pie, and the most prevalent taste was salt. Not unpleasant, but absolutely distinct. Lesson learned? Taste your components individually, especially when they come from artisanal crafters. Things can and will change from batch to batch.

GUMBO HELL YEAH!

After driving back from Virginia and spending the winter holidays with my parents, cousin Mara, my brother, and his son, I unloaded the five pounds of bacon and four pounds of crab meat, unpacked my luggage, got the pups settled back into the four more inches of snow that had showed up in my absence, and hit the cookbooks.

I said early on that the intent of this blog was to take recipes I stumbled upon on the web, as well as the thousands of recipes that occupy the hundreds of cookbooks I have in my own kitchen, and work bacon into as many of them as possible. Let's face it, bacon as a standalone item only goes so far. So this will be about creating with bacon—bacon as an add-in all on its own, as well as bacon fat as a substitute for other oils and fats and as a glaze and basting material. To that end, I'm going to use bacon variations, the pancettas and prosciuttos, and it also makes sense to extend some of the experimenting with sausages and hams. No, this is not the all-*pork* book (that one's coming next). The focus will remain on bacon, but with the periodic addition of other seasoned, smoked, brined, and otherwise cured pork pieces. And with that caveat in place, here we go.

For the mirepoix

½ of a full bunch of celery, chopped

2 medium sweet Mayan onions, chunked

½ a small bag of organic baby sweet carrots found about mid-way down the depth of my refrigerator's vegetable drawer, about a cup

1 cupped palmful of sea salt, probably about a tablespoon

generous sprinkling of ground organic black pepper

½ cup of bacon fat

½ cup of unsalted butter

⅔ cup of all-purpose flour

For the gumbo

1 5-pound duck

2 medium onions, chopped

1 medium green bell pepper, seeded and chopped

1 medium red bell pepper, seeded and chopped

2 garlic cloves, minced

2 14-ounce packages of Johnsonville Andouille sausage links, sliced

2 cups of cooked bacon, chopped rough

4 bay leaves

1 teaspoon dried oregano

1teaspoon of dried thyme

1 teaspoon salt

Cayenne pepper to taste

4 tablespoons filé powder

One recipe of baked creamy cheese grits (below).

➊ I truly had intended to follow a recipe I'd wandered across in one of my 200 cookbooks and merely substitute bacon fat for the vegetable oil, add a cup of chopped bacon, and end of story, bacon infusion accomplished. But my Monday morning New Year's Eve trip to the Waupaca, Wisconsin, Pic-N-Save undid that plan in a hurry. There were no chickens. Okay, there were three embryonic-puny store brand (Roundy's) chickens among the stacks and stacks of boneless chicken breasts. And there was the smell, somewhere among those cellophaned packs, of a chicken gone outlaw. I walked around the case three times. No Perdue roasters. No Perdue fryers. I don't like the taste of Roundy's beef and, with the smell of a spoiled chicken coming from somewhere near the infant cluck carcasses, I sure as hell wasn't going there. Damn. One more walk around the case and a frozen 5-pound duck went in the cart.

➋ With the chicken out the window, I just wasn't feeling kielbasa. I like kielbasa just fine, but I wanted something more gumbo-ish. Johnsonville to the rescue, and two five-packs of Andouille (can you believe that? No chickens, but Andouille!) joined the quack.

➌ Back home, I thawed the duck mostly through the day on the counter, then the rest of the way overnight in the fridge. This morning, into the pot it went, along with a mirepoix.

➍ It's funny. The recipe I was kind of using as a foundation was absent a *mirepoix*, instead merely calling for the chicken to merely be disjointed, submerged in a pot of water, brought to a boil, then simmered for thirty to forty minutes at a lower temperature. Really? No *mirepoix*? I am a devotee of Guy Fierri's *Diners, Drive-ins, and Dives* airing on the Food Network, as well as a few other show on that station and the Food Network featuring a range of chefs and talent, and I gotta tell ya, I think I've seen just one instance where a chef simply boiled its fowl

in water and nothing else. So, my thinking is that a *mirepoix* not only makes culinary sense, it should be *de rigeur*. Duck and *mirepoix* it was.

5 Despite how uptight I was about the celery, carrots, and onions going into the pot, I was terribly disinterested in disjointing the duck. For one, the bird I purchased had been tightly compacted before it met its heavy plastic freezer wrap; prying the legs and wings away from the body and then running poultry shears around the works looked to be an angst-ridden and laborious process. So I put the duck whole and intact into my largest Le Creuset stew pot along with the *mirepoix*, poured in water not quite to cover so I wouldn't have a boil-over mess, and dialed up to medium-high. Once bubbling along nicely, I lowered to just below medium, turning the duck over in its now-glorious broth after one hour, and simmering another hour more until it was abundantly clear the meat would fall away from the bones.

6 I let the duck cool on the cutting board for an hour. While it was doing so, I poured the duck stock through a colander and into another stockpot, separating the *mirepoix* from the liquid. I then chopped a full green bell pepper and a full red bell. Then I came to the onion part. I knew I had a half-dozen Mayan sweets at home, but, while at the grocery store the day before, I'd snagged a bag of pearl onions, thinking they'd go well with the chicken that turned into a duck. I also grabbed them because the last two times I'd needed pearl onions, the market was devoid of them.

7 Oh, grocery market inspiration, the devil that you are. Pearl onions, which I can't recall working with in their primitive state before but which I have often liked in a creamed sauce, beef stews, and other such dishes, turned out to be a bitch to work with. Worse than peeling garlic, because you can't crush the little bastards and still call them "pearls," they also made me cry like a girl. I was not amused. Too, after all the work, it looked like I only had about one regular onion's worth of pearls (about a cup), and so I ended up chunking up one of the Mayans anyhow.

8 The duck cooled, I took to de-meating it. Hmmm. Good thing I went with Daffy. That five-pound duck yielded about 2½ cups, maybe 3, of cooked meat. Had the two-pound chicken the "Ya Ya" recipe had called for been available, I think I'd have had only enough for a chicken salad sandwich.

9 Now for the roux. I looked twice at the foundation recipe, not believing my eyes. Vegetable oil for the fat base? In a *southern* cookbook? *Pfft!*

10 The only answer to this blasphemous roux route was to go the bacon route. I took a half-cup of the bacon fat from the thick-cut hickory smoked Smithfield bacon I'd bought in Virginia and cooked earlier the day, added a half cup of unsalted butter (unsalted seemed to make sense, given the salt in the bacon), since the recipe seemed to be doubling itself on its own, what with the whopping five-pound duck, and whisked in ⅔ cup of King Arthur white wheat flour. (And, yes, I have regular ol' everyday white Pillsbury flour, but the King Arthur bag was open, the Pillsbury wasn't). Just under six minutes of constant whisking later, I had the roux at the milk chocolate color "Ya Ya" asked for. I dumped in the onions and diced bell peppers a second before the aroma from the roux went from that delightful nuttiness to "damn, screwed it up." Next came the Andouille, two fourteen-ounce Johnsonville packages of five links each, sliced, followed by roughly a half-pound of diced, Cure 81 pre-cooked, pre-sliced dinner ham and the spices.

11 I stirred this all around, the Andouille and veggies releasing their juices, the roux mixing with it all nicely, for about ten minutes. Then I added 3 cups of the duck stock, the hand-torn duck meat, then 2 more cups of stock and a cup of water (the duck really is greasy), and turned the burner up to medium-high.

12 Washing up bowls while I let the gumbo come to a boil, I spied the colander of mirepoix. I hate to waste stuff like that, but I didn't want chunked celery and carrots in a gumbo. Into the blender it went, with just a little of the leftover stock, and once pureed, I dumped it into the gumbo. I was a little alarmed at first. The puree had a pretty orange hue to it, thanks to the baby carrots, but once I got the whole pot of gumbo up to a boil and everything was well combined, the color of the gumbo had returned to that milk chocolate so desired. After simmering on low for about an hour, I stirred in the filé powder, added the chopped bacon, and kept the pot on low for several more hours, until the dinner hour arrived.

***

I'm all for gumbo over rice, but I was so far gone from the foundation recipe that baked creamy cheese grits sounded more than right with my new Gumbo Hell Yeah! I took Quaker instant grits ('cause here in Wisconsin, that's a foreign substance, and real grits are simply not to be had) and made it as follows:

2 cups of water
2 cups of whole organic milk
1 cup of grits
¾ cup of Parmesan, give or take

¾ cup of chopped cooked bacon (in this case, the Smithfield bacon I'd cooked two days before)
4 eggs, scrambled.

1 I heated the water/milk until bubbling but not boiling so as not to burn, stirred in the grits, and cooked about the required five minutes until it was thick, but not solid. I poured it into an oval casserole, dumped in the chopped bacon and cheese, and then quickly the eggs, stirring briskly to keep the eggs from cooking prematurely. Into a preheated 350°F oven for forty-five minutes and *voilá!*

2 I ladled over the reheated duck and Andouille Gumbo Hell Yeah!, which had been sitting in my refrigerator "marrying" for two days. (I usually marry a stew or some such more than twenty-four hours before I attempt a main course presentation. In this case, the forty-eight hours was pure laziness.) It was wonderful. The gumbo, thanks to the duck and the bacon fat and butter roux, was rich and complex without being overwrought. The custardy grits played a nice balance game of texture with the smooth gumbo, and while most cheesy grits recipes call for cheddar, the parmesan was a better pairing with the duck and Andouille. I topped the dish with chopped green onions, which I really feel almost made the whole dish; their peppery bite bridged the silky gumbo and the custardy parmesan grits that might have been a little too rich without the onions (plus the green looked pretty before the spoon went in). Finally, and thanks to the Andouille (and probably the filé powder, which can certainly be increased as desired), the concoction *did* taste like a gumbo. No, it didn't taste like you imagine a seafood gumbo should taste, that oh-so-*distinctive* gumboness that only shrimp can bring to the arrangement, but the foundation recipe I'd used never intended this to be a seafood gumbo. Consider it mission accomplished.

3 The only thing I'd change is that I'd chop the duck meat, rather than finger-shredding it. Stewed down, chopped meat would have been a definite "bite" between the teeth, something that was a little absent with the shredded meat. But this is just a texture thing. Regardless, I'd serve this combo for a winter dinner to a table full of guests any time.

LENTIL BACON MUSHROOM BARLEY STEW WITH SAVORY SAUSAGE MEATBALLS

Yep, that's one long recipe title. That's what happens when the Bacon Maven flips through too many cookbooks on a Saturday morning, while she's hungry, and before she heads to the market. I can tell you that this recipe is part German, part Italian, part good all-American stick-to-your ribs winter fare, and all Bacon Maven. Here's what you'll need:

For the Meatballs

12 mild Italian sausage links

1½ cups of carrots, diced fine

2 small sweet onions, diced fine

1 bunch of flat leaf Italian parsley, minced fine

4 cups of breadcrumbs

1 tablespoon red pepper flakes

2 teaspoons salt

For the Soup

23 ounces of white button mushrooms sliced

½ pound of dried lentils

1½ teaspoons of crushed rosemary

½ teaspoon of salt

¾ teaspoon of cracked black pepper

1 tablespoon of olive oil

3 32-ounce boxes of organic chicken stock

¼ cup of flour

2 tablespoons of bacon fat

8 ounces of medium pearl barley

2 heaping cups of chopped bacon

2 tablespoons of cracked black pepper

Salt to taste

1 Get the meatballs started first. Take your sausage links (I used Johnsonville mild Italian) and strip the casings off. I find this works easiest if the links are cold from the fridge. I simply take a paring knife and run it in a straight line down the length of the link, then peel it easily away and drop the meat directly into my mixing bowl. Add the rest of the ingredients and mix by hand until the ingredients are evenly combined. I then form the meatballs about jawbreaker size and set them in evenly spaced rows on a jellyroll tray lined with parchment paper. Into a 365°F oven, about forty to forty-five minutes. They should have a toasty brown crust to the outside and smell heavenly when they're done. Do not burn your tongue trying one before they're cool enough to handle. Also, this batch makes a lot of

meatballs, more than you'll likely want or have room for in the pot. The smart thing to do is add them, reheated, to leftover bowls of the soup later in the weak—and you can't tell me you won't want to do this, because, if you're anything like me, you always end up with more broth and less content as the leftovers are consumed.

2 Mushrooms are up next. Take about two-thirds of your stash and dump them in a gallon ziplock bag, adding in the crushed rosemary, the ½ teaspoon of salt, ¾ teaspoon cracked black pepper, and tablespoon of olive oil. Gently massage the bag to coat the mushrooms, then spread them evenly on another parchment paper-lined jellyroll pan. Up the oven to 375°F and go about thirty minutes. The mushrooms should be dried down and starting to golden up.

3 While the mushrooms are roasting, start the soup base. I melted the two tablespoons of bacon fat in a stockpot, added the flour, and made a quick blonde roux. Once I had the roux a darkening yellow, I added in the chicken stock, plus a little water to bring the level up in the pot. To this I added the lentils, brought the pot to a boil, then reduced and simmered for about thirty minutes, enough to let them start to break down and thicken the base. Once that first thirty minutes had expired, I added in the meatballs, chopped bacon, the roasted mushrooms, and the remaining uncooked mushrooms (I kept some of the mushrooms unroasted to mix up the texture). An hour on simmer and I added in the barley (I used Quaker medium pearl barley, not the quick-cook type), topping off the pot with more water as needed to keep at least some viscosity in the stew. You'll need to do this periodically as the barley cooks and releases its starches, as well as when reheating after the leftovers have been refrigerated (you could also add in additional both/stock).

4 I tested the soup after an hour, added a little salt, but thought it also needed some pepper. I looked at a jar of organic ground black pepper I had, though it looked like it had a couple teaspoons left in it, and upended it into the pot. Should have been wearing my glasses—I had more like two *tablespoons*! I mixed it in, swore, sneezed, threw the lid on the pot, and let the whole thing think about what I'd done to it for another hour on low.

5 Dinner time, I have some crusty bread hot from the oven, and it's the moment of truth—and I got away with murder (murder by pepper, that is). The overload of pepper absolutely *rocked* this dish, playing off the meatballs, the bacon, and the rich lentils perfectly! Make the same mistake I did and prepare your rumbling tummy for seconds with this one. Truly a grand dish for dinner on a cold night.

PORK PASSION CHILI

A friend on Facebook asked me not long ago about chili recipes. I gave her some general suggestions, but when the forecast here in Wisconsin, on April 17, called for daytime temps in the 20s and still more fresh snow to add to the bazillion inches on the ground, I thought it was a fine weekend to make a new recipe.

I'm generally a kitchen-sink type of chili cooker. I like a lot of stuff in mine—green and red bell peppers, jalapeños, corn, beans (and, yes, I'm aware that beans deny a chili its authentic origins), stewed tomatoes, etc.—and I also like mine thick, almost stand-by-itself-in-the-dish thick, rather than the really loose and soupy and highly tomato-based chilis some like. However, in recent years, I've begun to wean off the ground beef I've always used, gradually adding in more pork (and a couple other things I'll get to in a minute). I've been at about a 2:1 pork-to-beef ratio, but this time I decided to go, um, whole hog, as it were.

2 pounds ground pork	1 teaspoon nutmeg
2 pounds Johnsonville All-Natural Sweet Italian Ground Sausage	1 tablespoon Spanish paprika
	3 tablespoons dried cilantro
1 pound Johnsonville All-Natural Hot Italian Ground Sausage	2 bunches fresh cilantro
	6 large red bell peppers
4 tablespoons cumin	2 medium sweet or yellow onions
1 tablespoon Mexican oregano	2 jars Bertoli Arrabbiata Spicy Tomato and Red Pepper Sauce
3 tablespoons chili powder	
1 tablespoon ground cayenne	½ cup masa flour
2 tablespoons onion powder	14 ounces organic creamy peanut butter
2 tablespoons garlic powder	2 cups cooked bacon, bacon fat reserved
1 tablespoon cinnamon	Salt and pepper to taste

❶ Using my huge All-Clad slow-cooker, I took the removable insert and set it, with all the ground meats in it, on the large burner of the stove. I browned the meat until done, breaking up the large chunks of stuck-together grind as I went. Surprisingly, there was little fat to drain off, so I didn't, and just plunked the insert back in the body when the meat was cooked through. Next I dumped in all the ground and dried spices, both jars of Bertoli tomato sauce, and stirred to combine, set the cooker to high, and put 4:30 on the time.

❷ At this point I turned to the bell peppers. Topped and seeded, I sliced them into quarters and placed them in a gratin dish to roast. (You can certainly use any roasting pan you want, just don't overlap a second layer too much). I drizzled the peppers, very lightly, with the warm bacon fat, then sprinkled with salt and ground black pepper. Into a 350°F oven they went for an hour. When the timer went off, I hit them with the low broiler for about ten minutes and called it good. Once the peppers were cooled and the timer was down two hours on the slow-cooker, I rough chopped both the peppers and the two onions and swirled them into the now-bubbling meal. I also poured in the juices/salt/pepper/bacon fat that was left in the dish; it was so roasted red pepper sweet when I stuck my finger in it to taste, I couldn't resist.

3. When thirty minutes were left on the slow-cooker's clock, I pulsed the fresh cilantro through my small food processor, minus only the lowest parts of the stems. Into the chili they went, but I don't know why I bothered. My grocery store's fresh cilantro is nearly odorless and tasteless. I guess I keep trying because I keep hoping the heavenly aromatic cilantro I used to get in San Antonio will one day show up. Sigh.

4. I added another hour to the slow-cooker timer at this point, but reduced the setting to low. When the ninety minutes was gone, I stirred in the masa flour and peanut butter.

5. Peanut butter. Yup. I was fortunate enough to know the late Matt Martinez, Jr., of Texas culinary fame. He wrote a food column for a magazine I edited for a couple years, was an avid country-wide chili competitor, and ran Matt's Rancho Martinez, a six-generation eatery in Dallas, until his passing in early 2009. Now, Matt advocated just a little peanut butter (and no masa, finding it gritty sometimes—the one I use lacks grit, which is why I use it here and for making tamales), but as it is with the bacon, I've found that more is better.

6. Why PB at all? I can't really explain it. It seems to gather the ingredients together, almost like a kindergartner teacher having her class of young charges hold hands to go out to recess or cross a road. It smooths the texture of the sauce surrounding the elements, calms an overly tomatoed sauce, and evens out spicy heat. Note I did not say it takes that spicy heat down. Not at all, in fact. You can make your chili as rip-roaring yippy-yo-kai-ye cayenne hot as you want—the peanut butter is simply going to make your preferred heat level uniform in a way that mixing by spoon, regardless how thoroughly or how often, simply cannot do. Take my word for it (and Matt's). Peanut butter is the way to go.

7. The recipe as I've listed here fills my eight-quart All-Clad slow-cooker, i.e., it's a big batch. Since this is always the way I tend to cook (though I'm trying harder to reduce the size of my concoctions), I've used most of a small jar of creamy in the past. This time I used my local store's organic creamy peanut butter, which is wonderfully smooth, dense, and does not separate. It came in a fourteen-ounce container, and I put in the whole thing. Last, I added about two cups of cooked bacon that I'd chopped to fineness in the food processor.

8. This is the first time I'd used this PB in a chili. It's *much* thicker than commercial brands, even the pretty good natural PB from Planters (which also doesn't separate and has the consistency

of every other national brand, natural or otherwise). This thickness nearly undid my chili. I had a bit of a tough time getting it to meld in and "become one" with the rest of the meal. Several times over the next hour I stirred the pot with a flat-paddled wooden "spoon," actually smearing some of the peanut butter around the surface to disconnect it from itself, as it were.

9 At 8:30 p.m., with bed time not too far around the bend, I scooped a couple small ladles into a bowl. Not bad. A little bright, but I expected that. A chili—or a soup or a stew—cooked this short a time rarely pleases my tongue. So here's the next secret "ingredient," if you will, one that will probably have the ever-so-uptight food police coming after me with handcuffs, a search and seize order for all my kitchen pots and pans, and a court mandate that says I should be allowed only a platic spork for eating. Are you ready?

10 Here it is: I turned the slow-cooker off and merely left the chili, in its cooker body and with the lid on, sitting out on the counter overnight. That's right. No refrigeration. Oh, the horror, the *horror*.

11 Or not so much. I do this with all my stews and soups, and for a couple reasons. One, I once put a not quite cool-enough pot of something in my refrigerator and shattered the glass shelf (and seriously, the pot wasn't *that* hot). Second, I think the gradual cooling down and *then* refrigerating the next morning does the creation better. I can't prove this, and I do not have Alton Brown's technical background or expertise to begin to prove it, so you're just going to have to go with me on this one. It works. Hot or cold weather, air conditioning or heat, rain or sun (or this damned snow that won't go away)—it just *works*.

12 I refrigerated the slow-cooker insert first thing in the morning. Home for the last couple hours of the workday, I put the insert back into the cooker's body and set it to high to reheat.

SCALLOPED BACON CHICKEN CHOWDER BAKE

After making the "Grab a Beer Chicken-Bacon Pot Pie," I had a good measure of hand-pulled chicken left over, about a third of the meat from the roughly nine-pound roaster I'd cooked. I'd been telling a friend recently that I had a small, oval Le Creuset cassoulet that I hardly ever used. The pile of chicken seemed the perfect excuse to remedy that situation. Here's what you'll need:

2 cups of cooked chicken, rough chopped or hand-pulled into fork-size pieces

5 medium red-skinned potatoes

8 to10 slices of cooked bacon

1½ cups of frozen corn

4 tablespoons of butter

1 cup of heavy whipping cream

Salt and pepper to taste

1. Slice the potatoes very, very thin. They don't need to be see-through, but not far from it. The last thing you want is a bite of raw potato from the middle of the casserole.

2. I placed two thin layers of potatoes in the bottom of the cassoulet, dotted it with thin slices of butter, sprinkled lightly with salt and fresh ground black pepper, and drizzled a little of the cream over this layer.

3. I next took the frozen corn, put it in a mesh strainer, and ran some warm water over it to quickly thaw it and remove all the extra water from the ice crystals. Combining the chicken with the thawed corn just so they were uniformly mixed, that became the next layers. Another few dots of butter, salt and pepper, and another drizzle of heavy cream.

4. Two more thin layers of potatoes were next, but this time I skipped the butter, salt, pepper, and cream, because the bacon came next. Fully layered on top of the potatoes, I *did* drizzle whipping cream on top of the bacon layer. One more layer of potatoes, with butter, salt, pepper and cream on the top to keep if from becoming a layer of leather in the oven, the build was done.

5. The *casssoulet* went into a 350°F oven for an hour with the lid on. I took a sharp knife and pierced the layers to see if the potatoes were cooked through at the buzzer. They were, but I like the top of a dish like this browned a bit. Thirty more minutes with the top off, then five minutes under the broiler at high, and this bubbling dish was done.

6. If you love scalloped potatoes and love the chicken-corn chowder take on the New England clam classic, then you are going to swoon for this one. Silky with cream and butter (how could it not be?), the bacon was the highlight of this dish. Call it accidental genius, but the cooked pork belly strips, treated to a second cooking dressed in cream and sandwiched between tender layers of potatoes became so tender, such a wonderful bite between the teeth, I was tempted to eat the entire contents of the cassoulet in one sitting. I didn't of course, but you get the point.

7. Make this. Spend a extra couple hours in the gym if you have to justify it, but make this.

TOP SIRLOIN ROAST WITH GRILLED AND MASHED BACON POTATOES AND ROASTED BACONATED ROOT VEGETABLES

I had probably watched too many episodes of *Diners, Drive-ins, and Dives* and its ilk on the Food Network and Travel Channel, because I was jonesin' for roast beef. *But how to get there and get bacon worked into it*, I wondered, half in my head, half out loud. The dogs cocked their heads at me as I pawed through my cookbook shelves. I opted for one of my newer books, *Sunday Roasts*, from Williams-Sonoma, flipped to the beef section.

Prime rib? Well, sure, that would always be my first choice, but I wasn't exactly working on a lobster budget this week. Standing bone-in prime rib? Sure didn't have a lobster-for-20 budget, either.

A chuck roast seemed a little low-brow for what my mouth wanted, and visions of the dry, overcooked pot roast so many of us are unfortunately familiar with flashed through my brain. There are those awful roast beef dinners at old diners, two drab pieces of rubbery meat between two slices of Wonder bread, some thin brown gravy ladeled over the top—you'll always need a steak knife to wrestle off a bite, and you'll chew on each mouthful like the cow it came from chewing its cud. Then there were the pot roasts of my youth. My mother, unless I'm wrong, when I was a kid, used to do her pot roasts in the pressure cooker (a device I'm still terrified of to this day). That dreadful, hissing

appliance produced a roast that, in my memory, still makes me wrinkle my nose and turn away. Don't get me wrong, my mother is a very capable cook—our heritage includes no Italian, yet she makes a from-scratch spaghetti sauce that would make all of that boot-shaped country weep with joy—but I don't recall pot roast being one of her better meals. No doubt she was working on a skimpy budget and with cheap cuts of meat, but that gray, almost chalky in texture and nearly flavorless mass of cow has never made me want to endeavor on a journey to recreate it. Well, at least until one of those damned TV shows visited my living room, its juicy pink slices just calling out my name … .

The last recipe I checked in the W-S book was one for a top sirloin roast. *Okay, now maybe we're on to something*, I mumbled. The dogs looked at me funny again, and I grabbed my car keys and headed for the butcher, visions of succulent beef and roasted vegetables dancing through my head. By the time I got home post-butcher and grocery store visits, I had dinner as a three-part adventure. Here's what you'll need.

For the Sirloin Roast and Baconated Root Vegetables
1 3- to 4-pound top sirloin roast
2 parsnips
4 to 5 medium turnips
1 8-ounce package of baby carrots
5 beets
3 tablespoons of crushed garlic
2 teaspoons of pepper
2 teaspoons of sage
4 teaspoons of veal demi-glace
½ pound of bacon, chopped

For the Baconated Mashed Potatoes
6 to 8 medium yellow, thin-skinned potatoes
½ pound of bacon, uncooked, chopped
½- to ¾-pound of bacon cooked and chopped small (about 1 cup)
salt and pepper to taste
1 stick of butter
1 8-ounce package of cream cheese
1 cup of whipping cream

① I have to say right off that the slab of meat the butcher handed me wasn't like the one in the W-S book. That picture, of the finished product, was of a neatly rolled and tied round roast. My roast was tall and narrow; with the fat cap on top, it probably stood five inches tall and about two inches across the width. I dunno, maybe the picture in the book went with a different roast, but there wasn't any rolling and tying to be done with the cut I had. Hmmmm.

② I dressed the roast as suggested, slitting both sides all over with the end of a sharp knife and rubbing in the garlic that I'd mixed with the pepper and sage, making sure much of it made it into the slits. I stood it on the end opposite the fat cap in a big roasting pan. Raw and firm, it stayed upright, but I didn't think it would stay that way once the heat hit it. I wondered if the root vegetables would help.

③ I peeled the turnips and parsnips, chopped them roughly. I took the beets, which were organic "Love Beets" already peeled and in a vacuum-sealed pouch, and quartered them. I piled them around the standing roast, then spread the package of baby carrots around, too. I evenly distributed the chopped bacon, then dolloped on the veal demi-glace here and there, including a couple or three dots on top of the roast for good measure.

4. The roast wasn't going to take that long in the oven, so I started on the potatoes next.

5. I half-skinned the yellow potatoes I had, taking off just enough to remove any deep eyes and other rough spots. I like some skins in my mashed potatoes, provided a thin-skinned potato like reds or yellow-gold are used (skins from russets are just too thick and mean to work). Semi-peeled, I chunked the potatoes evenly and laid them onto a big piece of aluminum foil. Pulling up the sides of the foil to make a kind of basket, I then topped the potatoes with the chopped raw bacon and gave the works a good sprinkle of salt and pepper. Onto the preheated grill—that's right, the grill!—the packet went, indirect heat (my two left burners were on, the two right off, and I set the foil packet on the right). I threw in a small smoker box of hickory chips for good measure, figured it couldn't hurt, left the top of the foil pack open, and closed the lid on the grill.

6. At thirty minutes, the potatoes were about halfway there, so I preheated the oven to 425°F. Once at temp, the roast went in, fifteen minutes at the high heat, and then the temp got lowered to 350°F. I turned on the interior light when the fifteen-minute timer rang, and I was disappointed but not super surprised to see the roast had fallen over on one side and was now sitting cockeyed over half the vegetables. It was clear it wasn't going to stand up again, so I merely flipped it after fifteen minutes to lay on the other side.

7. Now, I like my roast beef rare, and my gut said that, when I flipped over the roast to expose at the fifteen-minute 350°F mark (now twenty-five minutes total), I was just a few minutes of having it where I like it. Still, I was pretty far off from the recommended time in the W-S book, which called for a total of forty to fifty minutes at the 350°F setting. I pulled the roast out at a little over thirty minutes at 350°F (now forty-five minutes total), and felt I'd probably gone too far even then. I was going to see in a bit, but now it was time for the roast to stand, twenty minutes per *Sunday Roasts*.

8. While the roast rested, I left the root vegetables in the still-hot oven, giving them a stir first, then turned back to the potatoes. I'd added about a cup of chicken stock when I flipped the roast over, also stirring them and gently lifting up the ones that were sticking and browning at the bottom (you want to do this carefully and not rip the foil), and now the potatoes and their bacon bits were perfectly cooked. Into my KitchenAid stand mixer they went, along with the chopped cooked bacon and the cream cheese. I added the whipping cream a little at a time, alternating with tablespoons of the butter, until I had a stiff, thick, and creamy batch of grill-roasted mashed taters.

9. For service, I mounded the potatoes on one side of a serving platter, hollowing the middle. Into that middle I spooned the perfectly roasted baconated root vegetables, loving the splash of color from the beets, then sliced the roast and laid it alongside. My gut had been

right—the roast was somewhere between medium rare and medium, but it was still tender and full of flavor, thanks to the garlic rub in the slits and the demi-glace I'd added. The roasted vegetables, all of them, had fully benefitted from their two different cooking methods and the incorporation of bacon. I tend to use the word "depth" when describing ordinary foods to which I've added bacon, and the root vegetables and mashed potatoes shouldn't be excluded from its use. I don't know what it is, but bacon just *adds something* that brings out, extends, enhances, *enriches* the flavors that are already there.

10 There's a saying that bacon is the duct tape of the kitchen, that it "fixes" everything. I disagree. This wonderful, succulent bit of cured and smoked meat and fat is not a Band-Aid, will not repair a dish you've otherwise screwed up. But it absolutely will make anything you've already cooked well and correctly *exponentially* better.

Note: Some of you are probably wondering at the sanity of adding beets to the assemblage of root vegetables. Frankly, I kind of bought them on a whim and mostly because adding white rutabagas (which I did not use) to the white turnips and white parsnips and the cream-colored mashed potatoes didn't seem so eye-appealing to me. Sure, I had the carrots, but I wanted a little more pop. The beets provided that, but roasted as they were alongside the other vegetables and with the bacon and demi glace, also imbued a wonderful twist to the flavor profile of this classic medley. They retained a sweetness that complemented the same in the roasted carrots, but the roasting had beautifully mellowed that sharp, bright flavor beets cooked otherwise usually have. Try them this way (especially with the bacon). I promise, you'll be pleasantly surprised at how well this colorful little root veggie plays with others.

BACONATED VEGETABLES AND SIDES

- Bacon Antipasto Rye Loaf
- Bacon Corn Cake
- Bacon-Lovin' Gravy
- Bacon-Wrapped Tex-Mex Green Beans
- Baconated Grilled Hasselback Potatoes
- Baconated Kugel
- Baconated Refried Beans
- Blanketed Asparagus and Bacon
- Broccoli and Bacon Ricotta Cassoufflé
- Candied Bacon Brussels Sprouts
- Cumin-Spiced Twice-Made Potatoes with Bacon
- Double Cabbage, Rice, and Bacon Ends Pie
- Maple Pecan Bacon Date Wheat Loaf
- Pork Lovin' Portobello Caps
- Roasted Poblano and Bacon Relish
- Spaghetti Squash and Bacon Stuffing
  (with Smoke-Roasted Chicken)

BACON AND ANTIPASTO RYE LOAF

I get in cooking moods, sometimes. I get a theme running through my head or even just a desire for something and, like a terrier with a tennis ball, I can't let it go.

The other week was a perfect example. Bitter cold, already too much snow on the ground, I wanted a blanket warm from the dryer, a glass of cabernet—and fresh-baked bread good for dipping in olive oil and balsamic vinegar. My cloche baker was still on the countertop, I having succumbed to this same craving for the warm smell of fresh-baked bread just two days earlier. I scanned my pantry, glossed through a couple or five dozen bread recipes, and came up with this decadent, almost antipasto bread just perfect for dipping. Here's what you'll need:

1½ cups of water, warmed to 90°F
1 tablespoon of active dry yeast
1 tablespoon of sugar
1 tablespoon of honey
2 tablespoons olive oil (preferably a very sweet extra virgin)
1¾ cups of rye flour
2¾ cups of bread flour
2 teaspoons of sea salt, ground fine
1½ cups of cooked bacon, chopped fine
8 ounces of soft, dry-cured salami, chopped ¼- to ½-inch dice
1¼ cups of black olives, pitted and rough chopped
3 tablespoons of fresh rosemary leaves
2 teaspoons of fresh cracked black pepper
½ teaspoon of cayenne
Coarse sea salt for sprinkling

❶ Proof your yeast. Put your yeast in a small mixing bowl along with the sugar, honey (warm it a bit in a microwave to help it mix with the other ingredients, but don't get it scalding hot), and olive oil, then add in the warm/hot water. Stir to mix, though the olive oil will separate some. Set the mixture aside for a moment.

❷ In a large mixing bowl or in the bowl of your stand mixer, combine the two flours and the fine sea salt. If you only have coarse salt, run it through a spice/coffee mill to grind down. Of course, you can certainly use everyday Morton's table salt. All you want to do at this stage is spread the salt around so that it doesn't kill off the yeast when it comes into contact.

3 Chop your salami, olives, and bacon and have them ready to go, along with the rosemary leaves you've stripped from the stems. It's important that the salami is a soft variety. Now, I didn't go looking for this ingredient when this recipe was forming in my head, but I wandered across these lovely packages of Busetto Classics Dry Salami Nuggets in my grocer's specialty cheese section, I could feel through the packaging that the little discs were quite pliable and thought they'd be a really great, chunky, meaty addition to this bread. I found some good black pitted olives in the same area, and, that's when the antipasto idea really took shape.

4 Back at your bowl of flour, add in the yeast mixture and combine using a bread hook, or work in by wooden spoon or hand until the dough starts to come together. If it's looking a little shaggy and dry, add in a drizzle of olive oil here and there, alternating with a tablespoon of warm water until a better consistency starts to form. Before it becomes one cohesive ball of dough, though, you want to add in your olives, bacon, salami, and rosemary leaves.

5 With all the heavy ingredients added, give it all several good turns with the stand mixer and bread hook, but this is a chunky-monkey loaf, and the dough's going to need more help than your dough hook can provide. Though a lot of the hard ingredients will have been incorporated into the dough at this point, there's going to be a decent amount in the bottom of the bowl, and now it's time to work those in by hand.

6 Take a large wood cutting board, flour it, and put your dough bowl on it. Scoop out some of the olives and other ingredients in the bottom of the mixing bowl and start working it into the dough by hand, kneading as you go. Again, you can add a little olive oil if needed to keep the loaf pliable, and while you may have an olive slice or a bit of bacon or salami fall out as you turn and massage the dough, once the majority of it comes together and the dough texture is relatively smooth, you've gotten it as far as it will go.

7 Time for the first rise. Put your dough into a large oiled bowl, cover it with plastic wrap to make a tight seal, and place the bowl in a warm place. You want it to double in size, and that's going to vary, depending on your kitchen temperature, general weather, etc. I was cooking with outside temps in the single digits, and my house is pretty cool, so I preheated my oven to 250, turned it off, and left the door cracked for five minutes before I put my bowl in, then shut the door and turned on the oven light. With my cold weather, I went nearly four hours before I felt the dough had risen enough. If you're in a warmer clime, it could be half that, or even less. Check the dough's progress at the hour mark, but don't take the plastic wrap off. Check every thirty minutes or so until you get the dough to the double mark.

8 When the dough has doubled, lift it out of the bowl and massage it into a tighter ball. I saw a tip in a couple recipes that said to poke a hole into the center of the ball and kind of stretch the dough into a wreath shape, and I thought that was kind of cool, so that's what I did. I then placed the working bread in my cloche base that I sprinkled a little bit of flour across, put the cover on it, gave my oven a quick reheat back to 250, then turned it off and repeated the first rise. If you don't have a cloche baker, use a focaccia baking stone dish (again, with the flour sprinkled across it), regular loaf pans (you'd want to skip the wreath thing and likely divide the dough into two, and you likely want to both grease and flour loaf pans, if they're not nonstick), and maybe even a pizza stone sprinkled with a little corn meal, and put a towel over your dough. This second rise, about back to double the size you started with, went two hours for me; you could easily expect to go half that or less in a warmer location or weather.

9. At the end of the second rise, I preheated the oven to 450. While it was warming, I brushed a little warm bacon fat across the surface of the dough and sprinkled on some coarse sea salt, pressing it into the dough lightly. I put the top back on the cloche baker and into the hot oven it went. Forty-five minutes later (less if you're not using a covered cloche baker—check at thirty minutes and then every five minutes from there until the crust is a deep brown and a long toothpick inserted in the middle comes out clean), I pulled it out, removed the baking top and moved the loaf with potholders to a wire rack. Five minutes after that, I was singeing my fingertips pulling off hot chunks of this wonderfully fragrant, flavor loaded bread and dipping it in a dish of excellent olive oil and rich, real balsamic vinegar—and the sore fingertips were totally worth it.

BACON CORN CAKE

Not long after I cooked up my first batch of bacon ends—and after making a dedicated effort to use most of what I cooked in a recipe, instead of picking a piece off the pan every time I walked by it—I smoked a large, bacon-imbued pork loin. I'll be posting that in the next couple days, but let's just say that the cute "little" roast I took home from the _butcher_ wasn't as little as I thought it was going to be, when I had the lady behind the counter cut it off the much bigger whole loin (and I don't know where they're getting their pigs from, but this one had to be as long and big as a hippopotamus). I had a lot left over. What to do, what to do. Hmmmm. The thought of soft tacos came to mind, but I wanted something other than my usual spiced rice under the pork. Cornbread? _Bacon_ cornbread? How about Bacon Corn _Cake_? I usually work off one of the basic recipes in the "Quick Breads" chapter of my trusty _The Fanny Farmer Cookbook_, when I whip up cornbread, though I never stick to it exactly. I didn't in this case, either, looking to come up with a really moist, cakier corn bread—I hate the dry crumbly stuff that won't hold a pat of soft butter without falling to pieces. Think super-moist like your most decadent devil's food cake (but obviously withouth the lightness of a dessert cake). Here's what you'll need:

1½ cups of yellow cornmeal

1½ cups of flour

1 cup of sugar

2 tablespoons of baking powder

½ teaspoon of salt

1 cup of whole milk

2 eggs

1 16-ounce can of creamed corn

2 cups of cooked, chopped bacon ends

1. None of this is rocket science. I combined the dry ingredients in my Kitchen Aid stand mixer, the 16-ounce can of creamed corn, enough milk to make a batter somewhere between stiff and not-so-stiff. Finally, in wentt the bacon ends. The bacon ends, already cooked, of course, had been run through my food processor to get them down to a uniform size that would distribute evenly through the batter and provide a consistent texture in the bite. Trust me, that made all the difference, and those couple pulses in my smaller Cuisinart processor worked _brilliantly_ to effect exactly what I wanted.

2. I swiped down one of my Emile Henry medium-sized oval gratin dishes with some bacon fat, poured in the batter, and set it on a cookie tray in a preheated 375°F oven, in

case of run over. (I'm an admittedly sloppy baker when I'm multitasking in the kitchen, and admit to sometimes losing count of the teaspoons and tablespoons of things that make batters and dough rise, such as baking powder, yeast, and baking soda, to predictable overflowing results.) Forty-five minutes later, the top set and starting to brown, I stuck a toothpick in to find a solid center.

3 The Bacon Maven's going to give herself a pat on the back here and say this is potentially the best batch of corn cake she's/I've ever made. And I'm giving full credit to the bacon ends, which spread their beautiful, fatty decadence through the whole dish. I almost could not stop tearing off chunks while it was still warm, adding a pat of butter here and there (and, yes, the added butter was also worth it—make a call to your cardiologist for a therapy session if you need to alleviate the guilt, but I promise you I didn't). Nothing crumbled, super moist and thick, sweet from the creamed corn and sugar, with just the right amount of smoky salt from the bacon ends. When I stopped eating it out of the pan, I did indeed make soft tacos with it, nestling the warm sweet bread against a soft flour tortilla, some of the smoked pork with some more bacon ends atop it and a little spicy barbecue sauce (that recipe's coming later, too). One of the real winners, though, was yesterday morning's breakfast, pictured here. Last two wedges of bread, a couple soft-boiled eggs (should have gone six minutes, not seven, but still good), and a small helping of glistening, make-your-stomach-growl bacon ends hot out of the oven. The green dollops on top of the corn cake wedges are some slow-roasted *poblanos* that I pureed with a little butter in my Magic Bullet blender.

BACON-LOVIN' GRAVY

As it had been with the Italian Love Triangle Soup, I had a *lot* of leftover meatball mixings, which I turned into Wrap Your Bacon Arms Around Me Meatloaf. Now, I like to dress up my meatloaves. Sometimes it's just a mix of ketchup and mayo on the side or some ranch sauce for dipping. Other times it gets a dollop of sour cream on the top, or even some basic white gravy ladled on.

Gravy. I'm not a huge fan of gravy, actually, especially not the brown kind made from giblets and such. But every once in a while I get a hankerin' for white sausage gravy, the kind a good diner would ladle over hot biscuits. Since Wrap Your Bacon Arms Around Me Meatloaf was concocted by half with Johnsonville Mild Italian Sausage, but was a meatloaf that also had plenty of bacon to it both inside and out, that got me wondering: could I make bacon gravy? As it turns out, indeed I could! Herc's what you'll need:

1 pound of thick-sliced bacon, cooked and rough cut

½ a medium red onion, rough sliced

1 medium sweet yellow onion, rough sliced

2 to 3 tablespoons of bacon fat

1½ cups of half-and-half

⅓ cup of white flour, plus extra as needed

Whole milk to thin the gravy to preference

Salt and pepper to taste

1 Once the bacon was done baking in the oven via my usual method, I removed the tray, forked the cooked bacon onto a paper towel-lined plate to drain, and poured the remarkably little hot bacon grease (I like the Farmland bacon more and more) into a waiting sautée pan. Looked to me to be about 2 to 3 tablespoons worth. I heated the pan until the grease was lightly popping, then slid in the rough-sliced onion combination.

2 While the onions were sweating, I chopped the cooled bacon, then fork-whisked the flour into the half-and-half, making sure there were no lumps, making a cold roux of sorts. Once the onions were translucent (not browned in the slightest), I poured in the flour/cream mixture.

3 Working quickly, I fork-whisked the onions with the cold roux, then tossed in the chopped bacon. This tightened up very quickly—in fact, you could knock back the extra tablespoon or two of flour if this kind of mixture binding so quickly intimidates you. Regardless, keep the milk at hand, because this is what you'll splash in, a quarter-cup or so at a time, until you get the gravy to the consistency you want. I like mine about hot-lava thick, still loose enough to pour, but able to stand on its own on a fork and just slowly drip through the tines.

4 I'd foil-wrapped the almost-whole Wrap Your Bacon Arms Around Me Meatloaf leftover from the night before and had stuck it, nesting in a small casserole dish, into the oven when I started cooking the bacon. When the bacon came out at the twenty-five-minute mark, I dropped the oven temperature down to 350°F and let the meatloaf continue to reheat while I worked on the bacon gravy. All told, once the gravy was where I wanted it, the meatloaf had been in the oven another twenty-five minutes or so. I pulled it out and set it on the stovetop, then threw a lid on the pan of gravy and turned off the pan's burner, letting both rest for about ten minutes.

5 The resting, of course, was more for the meatloaf than the gravy, but it worked out fine for both. I sliced off a slab of the perfectly reheated and juicy meatloaf, ladling over a generous amount of the hot Bacon-Lovin' Gravy.

6 Winter comfort food? Oh yes, yes indeedy

BACON-WRAPPED TEX-MEX GREEN BEANS

Green beans. I love them steamed with lots of butter, and I love a greenie-beanie casserole made with mushroom soup and those French's fried onions on top for the crust (and, I'll admit, that's one dish that needs the soft green beans from a can, not fresh ones—and before you say, "*Ewww*, canned grean beans," read the J.V. Anderson's article, "You're Doing it Wrong: Green Beans," on Slate.com). But that's about my limit of creativity with this veggie. I dunno, it's a good standalone dose of green healthiness (*sans* the butter I usually encourage, of course), but what else do you do with them?

If you're the Bacon Maven, you wrap your head around the project, dig through your pantry, clean out your refrigerator, and come up with this dandy side dish. Here's what you'll need:

2 cups fresh green beans

1 teaspoon of ground cayenne pepper

1 tablespoon of fresh crushed garlic

1 tablespoon of brown sugar

½ teaspoon of salt

½ teaspoon of ground black pepper

1 teaspoon of lemon juice

2 cups of spiced, cooked white rice

6 strips of bacon, partially cooked

1 cup of cooked black beans

1 cup of salsa

½ cup of queso fresco cheese

1. Combine the brown sugar, crushed garlic, cayenne, black pepper, salt, and lemon juice. Put the green beans, ends trimmed, in a gallon freezer bag. Add in your "dry rub," as it were, and shake/massage until the green beans are properly covered. Refrigerate at least two hours, but several days doesn't hurt a thing.

2. When you're ready to make the dish, start with the rice. I did mine in my new Breville Risotto Plus. I washed two cups of jasmine rice until the water ran clear, then added one cup of chicken stock and one cup of water, then sprinkled in some hot paprika, red chili flakes, a bit of salt, and some cayenne pepper, probably a teaspoon of each.

3. Next I prepped the bacon. I only partially cooked it for this dish. I wanted to render out the heaviest part of the fat, but still leave the bacon flexible enough to wrap around the green beans.

4. When it was that way, I took my dry rub-marinated green beans, about a third of a cup at a time, laid them lengthways on a cutting board, and wrapped each little bundle in a half-cooked bacon strip.

5. The rice done and still hot, I spooned about a cup of it into the bottom of a Le Creuset small oval gratin dish. Added to that was a half-cup of the black beans. In this case, I used Bush's canned black beans, but you could certainly make your own black beans from scratch—which I'd've done had I thought that far ahead of time—the liquid in the can drained off. I didn't want this to be a soupy dish. On top of each of the two gratin dishes I was working with, I placed three bacon-wrapped green bean bundles, then spooned a half cup of salsa

over each (*pico de gallo* would work just as well, if you like the jalapeño bite), then into the oven they went, 375°F, for about forty minutes. I then sprinkled on the crumbled queso fresco and gave it another five minutes to melt.

⑫ This is a beautiful and flavorful dish! The green beans were cooked through but still crisp, and they went surprising well with the salsa and black beans. And *oh!* the bite with the bacon on it! I think this is a great side to dry-rubbed smoked brisket, Texas style. I actually made this in the morning, because that's what my schedule permitted, and for some reason it looked like it needed fried eggs. Two in the pan with some melted butter, over easy for runny yolks, slide 'em on top of the bean dish. Yum. Yum, yum, yum. Thought about adding a warm tortilla or two, but either way, this is a nice, filling breakfast and one that's not even that bad for you. I also made a second batch and served it alongside a steak I'd done a spicy dry rub on and grilled, pairing it with an also-spicy Zinfandel for a super flavorful dinner. Nice variety from just this one side dish, all the way around.

BACONATED GRILLED HASSELBACK POTATOES

I love a hasselback potato. Crispy on the outside, soft and mellow on the inside, they also make a nice presentation on the plate. Lots of things can be stuffed in those accordion slits, the most common being some simple herbs and butter or a little parmesan cheese. I, of course, went with bacon. Here's what you'll need for each potato:

1 large Russet baking potato
1½ bacon slices, uncooked
ground pepper to season
¼ cup of your favorite shredded cheese

1. I actually hadn't made hasselbacks before, though I've eaten them. With a burger going on the grill, I stared at the lone remaining Russet in my larder and decided to give it a go. I Googled a half-dozen recipes or so; some said to parboil the potato a bit, others not. I opted for the parboil, figuring it would cut my time on the grill down and make the potato easier to work with. It did both.

2. Taking a potato that's as uniform in cylindrical shape as possible, take a sharp knife and make slits across the width of it, spaced uniformly apart somewhere between an eighth of an inch and a quarter-inch. Do not slice all the way through. You want to make the potato fan a bit, but you don't want to force it into that arrangement. You may try a potato or three before you get the hang of it. Also, it's important to keep the almost-slices uniform in width, of course for cooking purposes, but also because 1) if you get them too thick and not enough of them, the potato will tend to break upon stuffing, or 2) if you get them too thin, you'll end up overstuffing the dish, cooking will get all wonky, and you're also more likely to break the potato.

3. While you're busy semi-slicing the potato, bring a saucepan of appropriate size to boil. When it's there, put in your spud (or spuds). Four to eight minutes, depending on the size of your tater (I went eight on a fairly large Russet). You don't want to cook this all the way through, you just want to get it a *leeeetle* bit softened up, so that there's some flexibility in the potato leaves. That will allow them to spread apart and take whatever stuffing you want to put in them without the leaves snapping near where they're still a part of the still-intact potato base.

4. Once I hit the eight-minute mark (a knife tip would insert into one of the ends, but there was still a lot of resistance), I took a pair of tongs, lifted the tater out of the boiling water

and let it drip-dry a second before I set it on a waiting piece of aluminum foil. When it was cool enough to handle but still hot, I stuffed mine with about a slice and half of bacon that I'd cut into even one-inch squares, letting some of the bacon lay on top of the hasselbacked tater. I cracked a little pepper over the top, pulled the sides of the foil up around the sides, but not over the top of the potato, and set it on the rack of my hot grill, lid closed.

5 About fifteen minutes in, I began the burger for the Margherita bacon cheeseburger, so all told, the potato roasted on the medium hot grill for about forty minutes, give or take.

During the last few minutes, I sprinkled over a little fresh shredded parmesan, working it down into the crevices against the bacon, then let it settle down on the cooling grill after I'd removed the burger for its setting time and turned off the grill's flames.

6 I love this potato grilled better than I ever have in the oven. The outside was crispier, the inside was softer, and the parmesan had taken on a nutty, lovely flavor. And the bacon? It was everything I'd hoped it to be, cooked to perfection, with its salty, meaty, smoky goodness permeating the potato's overall goodness. Then again, what would you expect? Has it ever done a potato wrong? Has it ever done *anything* wrong?

BACONATED KUGEL

Just as fall was shedding its final leaves and the first snowflakes were teasing the air, I ran across something in some magazine or online, or maybe it was on a TV show, I don't remember, but the word of the day ended up being "kugel." Now, according to Wikipedia, Kugel is "a baked Ashkenazi Jewish pudding or casserole, similar to a pie, most commonly made from egg noodles." A pie? Made of *noodles?* Oh, I could baconate that! Here's what you'll need:

1 pound of thick and heavy egg noodles, preferably Amish made

2 cups of sour cream

2 cups of whole milk ricotta

2 8-ounce bars of cream cheese

4 eggs

3 medium-large sweet onions

1½ cups light brown sugar

1 cup chopped toasted walnuts

1 cup chopped raw walnuts

2 cups cooked bacon, rough chopped

8 tablespoons of butter

2 teaspoons of salt

1 tablespoon of cinnamon, plus extra for sprinkling on top

1 teaspoon of allspice, plus extra for sprinkling on top

1 Cook your bacon first, though not to crispy doneness, and set it aside to cool; you'll likely need about a pound and a half uncooked to get to the two-cup cooked measure. Once it's cool, go ahead and give it a rough chop, either by hand or in a food processor, and put it in a large mixing bowl.

2 Once your bacon is done, give one cup of the walnuts a quick roast. Simply dump them on a cookie sheet and give them ten to fifteen minutes at 365°F. The minute they smell nutty, get them out of the oven, for they'll go from tasty to burnt in a flash. Alternately, you can toss them in a sauté pan, flipping the pan from time to time to keep the nuts moving around and preventing burning. Same rule applies there; once they smell fabulous, get'em off the heat. Once the walnuts are toasted, give them a rough chop and add them to the bowl with the bacon. Many of the recipes I ran across simply used walnuts for the kugel topping and didn't require pre-toasting, but since this recipe has the walnuts incorporated into the pie structure itself, the roasting is a sound step to preventing that bitterness walnuts often have in the raw.

3 Next up are the noodles. I used the thickest, densest egg noodles I could fine. The large grocer I frequent in the next town over has an amazing noodle aisle, with multiple Amish brands to choose from. These tend to be much thicker pasta than other types of egg noodles, and I wanted a really good "tooth" to this pie. I ended up choosing a brand called Harrington's Amish Style Hand Made Noodles, and lest you think you can't find these, a little Googling showed that both Walmart and Amazon have these available.

4 If all you've ever cooked before is spaghetti, know that you'll need to give these quite a bit longer in the boiling water to get the noodles to al dente. The package said something like 11 to 12 minutes—I went twenty, until I could push a fork through a noodle without fighting it. Also, know that unless you leave this in a boiling pot for a *loooooong* time, you're not going to get these noodles butter-soft, and they're not meant to be. They're meant to be substantial in texture.

5 While the noodles are cooking, caramelize the onions. Take your sweet onions, halve and slice them, and add them to a large saucepan in which you've melted several tablespoons of butter. Add in a quarter cup of brown sugar and cook until the onions are translucent, reduced, and silky smooth. Add them to the bacon and walnuts.

6 Once your noodles are cooked, drain them and add them to the bacon and walnuts, tossing to combine and keeping the noodles from clumping and sticking together. Now, moving quickly so that the noodles don't cool too much, put the sour cream, ricotta, and cream cheese into a stand mixer and combine until smooth. Add the eggs one at a time, making sure you've mixed each in well before you add the next. Finally, add the spices, salt, and the melted butter, combining until you have a smooth mix. Pour over the noodle and bacon mix and, taking a large, rubber spatula, gently combine until the noodles are evenly coated.

7. Butter a 9x13 or other deep-sided casserole in this size range—I used an oversized deep-dish ceramic pie plate from Emille Henry), and pour in the kugel mixture. Now, take a little of the leftover brown sugar, maybe a quarter-cup, and put it in a gallon ziplock bag. Add in a bit more of the cinnamon and allspice, maybe a teaspoon of the first and a half-teaspoon of the second, and massage it into the brown sugar. Now take four tablespoons of cold butter, cut into teaspoon patties, plus the cup of chopped, unroasted walnuts, and add them to the bag of sugar and spices, massaging until you've got everything kind of evenly distributed. Then, using your hand, dollop teaspoons of the mix across the top of the kugel. Into a 350°F oven for forty-five minutes to an hour, depending on how deep/tall your kugel is; I went the full hour in that deep-dish pie pan. The top should be lightly browned and the edges and sides of the kugel should be pulling away slightly from the baking dish when done.

8. What a wonderful treat! Not only does it work well as a side to all sorts of deep-flavored roasts—chicken, beef, pork, lamb, it works for all—it also worked well as a dessert. I even had it a couple evenings reheated, with a scoop of good vanilla ice cream on the side—and I wasn't sorry one little bit.

BACONATED REFRIED BEANS

I once went on a deer hunt in Mexico, in country far, far away from anything but a few copper mines we could see lit in the distance, like viewing a tiny city from a mountain miles and miles away. The property where we stayed was vast, four 20,000-acre parcels owned by a brother and his three sisters. Our group stayed in an old but charming *hacienda,* the small home away from the home the brother used when he needed to stay over on ranch business, and it came complete with a woman of diminutive size who looked like she'd morphed into life from a gargoyle on a Mayan temple. She spoke no English, bowed slightly, and smiled at our heartfelt *"Gracias,"* when she set down her platters of food before us. I never saw her not cooking in the week I was there, her tiny, gnarled hands making fresh tortillas at every turn, cast iron skillets smoking before on an old gas stove I think she could barely reach over to stir and turn.

There was nothing that woman cooked that wasn't memorable—and I know I'll never eat Mexican cuisine as authentic as that was, no matter the name-brand chef or the number of Michelin stars hanging outside their kitchens. This was the real deal. I traveled home with a buck Coues deer very nice for a draught year, but perhaps more importantly, at least to who I am today, I left for the long ride back to the border with an obsession for authentic Mexican cooking.

I bought a cache of books when I got home, a couple from Rick Bayless and another just on tamales, and I cooked a good many recipes out of them in the months after that trip. But the one thing I made every week, by hand, from scratch, in an effort to replicate that Mayan woman's dish, were refried beans.

I love refried beans when they're done right. Done wrong, they're a flavorless, unattractive paste. Done right, they have a creamy texture and an earthiness mellowed by a hint of melted butter— that last part's due to the lard many recipes call for. Now, I've made refried beans several different ways, and I thought the best I'd come up with, and the recipe that most closely matched what I'd enjoyed in Mexico, was when I'd done an overnight soak on the beans, then a long slow cook on the stove (maybe with some herbs, a little fat, but mostly just water), followed by a hand-mashing in the pan with a potato masher, adding the pot liquid to the pan with each new bean addition, allowing the liquid to evaporate as you mash and, thus, truly becoming refried beans.

As it happens so often, the other weekend I had a craving, this time for refried beans. I found the required pinto beans in my pantry, but in gathering up the few other things I needed, I couldn't find my potato masher. I dunno, I've moved four times in the last ten years, crisscrossing half the country in the process, and lots of stuff has disappeared. So I did what I do best and improvised— and, of course, I baconized. Here's what you'll need:

1 pound pinto or black beans or a half-and-half combination of both

5 cups of chicken stock

1 pound of cooked bacon, rough chopped

1 teaspoon of Mexican oregano

1 tablespoon of onion powder

1 tablespoon of crushed garlic

1 16-ounce can of whole peeled tomatoes (drained)

1 whole dried *guajillo* pepper

Water

Salt and cayenne to flavor

1. Confession here. I find I never get to an overnight soak of my beans. But that's okay, because I have a slow cooker that does what I need it to do beautifully (I used a Breville combo slow cooker/rice cooker that has both a low and a high setting on the slow-cooker controls). I dumped my dried beans into the pot (and I've done this recipe with a variety of beans, the only ones I didn't like being kidney beans, so mix it up if you like), added the rest of the ingredients down to the whole guajillo pepper (no, whole tomatoes aren't usually a component of refried beans, but like mashed potatoes, once you get the basics down, you can add a variety of elements to

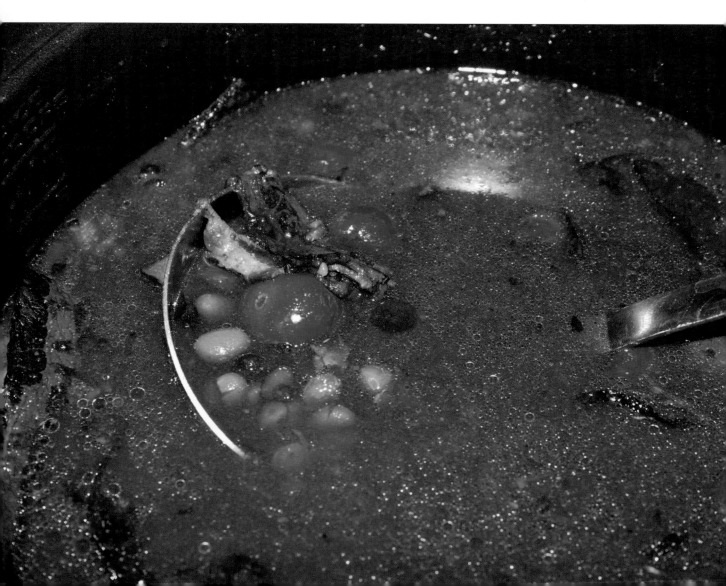

give the foundation dish some variety), then added water so that there was a good four inches of liquid above the beans. It was about 11 in the morning when I started this, and I set the slow cooker to low and ignored it for the rest of the day.

2 In fact, I ignored it right up until bedtime, when I went into the kitchen to make sure everything else was turned off and saw the "keep warm" light glowing on the slow cooker panel. I cursed a little at not having remembered to actually finish the beans, but figured I really hadn't done any harm, so I unplugged the appliance and went to bed.

3 The next morning, I looked in the pot, added another cup or two of water, and set the cooker back on low. I let it go all day again, but this time I remembered to do something with it at dinner. The first thing I did was remove the guajillo pepper from the pot and take its stem off, then put the pepper back in the pot. Taking my blender, I set the pot next to it and, with a ladle, filled the blender about halfway up with both beans and liquid. I started the blender on low remember to cock the little plastic thingamajig in the top of the blender lid, otherwise the contained heat and steam will blow off your blender top and you'll be

cleaning beans from your walls and ceiling instead of eating them off a plate. Once I had a good start on low, I accelerated the blender to its high setting and let it run until the mixture was one smooth homogenous mamajama.

④ Meanwhile, I had a large All-Clad saucier heating on the stove at about medium heat, with a tablespoon of lard melting in it (you can use butter, even solid Crisco, if you like). I poured the first batch of puréed beans into this heated saucier, mixing to make sure the lard became one with the beans. I puréed the next batch of beans, added them to the pot on the stove, and then repeated one last time with the rest of the beans, letting each addition to the saucier cook down and thicken, bubbling lowly, before I added the next.

⑤ I cooked the entire pot down on heat somewhere between medium-low and medium (the beans will scorch and become the new bottom to your pan on any higher heat) for probably another thirty or forty minutes or so, frequently stirring with a wide rubber spatula both the side and bottom of the saucier and keeping a lid half-cocked on top of the pot in between, because even at a very low rumble, when a surface bubble of beans pops, you get bean splatter everywhere. When the pot was starting to really thicken, I took a little taste-test, stirred in a little salt and a pinch of cayenne, then took the pot off the heat and left the lid on it. Thirty minutes later I had thick, hot, refried—and *totally* baconated!—beans ready for my dinner plate. And they were the *bomb*! The bacon absolutely and without a doubt added a definite richness to these silky beans. In fact, the next time I made these, I left the lard out and instead used just a bit of bacon fat to get the refried end of things going. Either way, I might actually have made that little Mayan woman proud.

BLANKETED ASPARAGUS AND BACON

As much trouble as my brain has coming up with something creative for green beans, there's almost nothing in which I won't use asparagus. I especially love the tried and true side where asparagus stalks are wrapped in prosciutto and grilled. But everyone knows how to do that. Then I ran across something on the Internet, whereby someone had wrapped asparagus spears in puff pastry. Cool, but I could do better. Here's what you'll need:

6 strips of cooked bacon
1½ cups of asparagus tips
1 cup of Italian dressing

1 sheet of puff pastry
8 tablespoons of whipped cream cheese

① Take your average bunch of grocery store asparagus and cut off the stalks at the halfway point. You really want the most tender part of the vegetable for this dish, plus the short length is easier to work with. You can certainly cut off only the really hard ends of the stalks and steam the remaining bottom halves for a salad or to toss with pasta, so as not to waste them, but it's the tips we're after for this dish.

❷ I'll be honest. I bought a bunch of organic asparagus from my local health food store. Pretty, small-headed, and vibrantly green, I put them in the refrigerator after shopping that day and promptly forgot them for more than a week. When I rediscovered them, they were still good, but starting to wilt just a wee bit. I decided a marinade might be in order, you know, just something to perk them up a bit, and found a bottle of Olive Garden Italian dressing in my refrigerator door. I put the cut spear tips in a plastic container and poured in about a cup of the dressing. Marinate a least a couple hours, though a couple days won't hurt anything.

❸ On the day you assemble these, cook your bacon like you normally would, and let your puff pastry (in this case Pepperidge Farm) set out on the counter to warm up to room temperature at the same time. When the bacon's finished, let it drain, and while it does, roll out the puff pastry on a floured cutting board. Take a sharp knife and divide the pastry into four squares.

❹ In the middle of each square, spread two tablespoons of the whipped cream cheese. I used Philadelphia brand, and please, use the whipped version, not the dense cheese bricks you'd use in a cheesecake. This needs to be spreadable, and while I'm sure I could hauled out my Kitchen Aid stand mixer and whipped a brick of Philly cream cheese into submission, the whipped Philly is just too easy to work with to pass up.

⑤ I quickly steamed the asparagus, then plunged them in an ice water bath. A note here: I used my new Breville Risotto Plus, which has a steam basket and accompanying function, and I gotta tell you, this thing steams *fast*. I came back after ten minutes and found my asparagus past their pretty green stage. Wasn't the worst thing that ever happened to an asparagus spear, but still, for the full visual effect, you certainly want to steam this veggie, like most other greens, until it is brightly colored, then cold-bath them to preserve that color and stop the cooking. Anyway, I missed by a few minutes. At least I got to it long before they turned grey-green with overcooking.

⑥ I took my ice water-bathed (slightly overcooked) asparagus spears and drained them, then divided them into four length-wise bundles and laid each on top of the cream cheese on the four pastry quadrants. I laid a strip and a half of bacon on top of each asparagus bunch, then rolled the works up, twisting the ends to seal. I basted each with the still-warm bacon grease left on the tray from the bacon I'd just cooked, then slid the tray of four pastries into the 375°F oven. I checked it at fifteen minutes, then another fifteen minutes, and pulled them out ten minutes after that.

⑦ Holy cows and pigs, these are good. The tangy cream cheese was *perfect* with the zest the Italian dressing marinade had provided the asparagus. The asparagus, *soooo* tender it almost melted on my tongue (and yet wasn't mushy!), had all the unique flavor you'd expect from this vegetable, but with the bacon and puff pastry—oh, *oh my*.

⑧ I don't care what you serve this with. Roast chicken, grouper, steak, prime rib, zebra, ptero-dactyl. This one goes with everything. Roll-your-eyes good, this one right here is.

BROCCOLI AND BACON RICOTTA CASSOUFFLÉ

Just before Labor Day, I traveled home for my parents' fiftieth wedding anniversary. Mom and Dad were having a vow renewal and a small catered party afterwards, and in the days leading up to and after the anniversary date, there were a good number of relatives and dear friends staying at their house for the week. My dad, busy with last-minute yard work before the party, asked me to step in and take over cooking for the masses in an effort to keep Mom out of the kitchen and de-stressed. Since I have developed a habit over my years away from home of taking over my mom's kitchen when I do visit, I was only too happy to oblige.

The first night in, I planned on roasting two chickens with lemon and rosemary under the skin, enough to serve six and have some chicken left over for lunches the next day. Mom and I had done a massive grocery run earlier in the day, in which we both promptly forgot to buy chickens. I dashed back to the Walmart in Tappahannock, snagged two pterodactyl-sized Perdue roasters and a bag of lemons, and headed for the checkout. That's when I reviewed the slide show in my head of what we *had* already bought (and with two full carts, that was a lot), and realized we really didn't have something for the side. Now, Virginia at the end of August is generally a hot and humid affair, and this long weekend was no exception. Now, most people would have gone for some sort

of salad. I like salad well enough, but, truthfully, I find most of them boring. I wanted something warm and green, but not heavy. I hit the Epicurious app on my iPhone and searched under "broccoli" for something that inspired me. Bingo: Dutches County Broccoli and Cheese Casserole—but done up the Bacon Maven's way. Here's what you'll need:

4 large broccoli heads and stalks
6 eggs
3 cups of ricotta cheese
2 cups of shredded cheddar cheese
¼ cup of all-purpose flour
1½ cups of whole milk
½ stick of butter
1 large onion
2 cups of cooked bacon, chopped
Salt and paper to taste

1. Get your bacon cooked first. Standard oven method, about a pound and a half should yield the two cups of chopped bacon you'll want, though more certainly can't hurt. Set it aside to cool and drain.
2. Next up is the broccoli. Separate the heads and stalks, trimming off the leaves and disposing of the toughest, lower halves of the stalks. As with most anything, you want uniformity so

that cooking occurs evenly in the dish, so slice up the heads so that the florets are generally of the same size. Quarter or halve the upper parts of the stalks, making roughly one-inch slices to match the size of the florets as best you can.

3 Though the Epicurious recipe didn't call for it, I decided to blanch the broccoli. I've found that doing this with many vegetables to be used in casseroles, but especially broccoli, ensures that you don't end up with several problems: undercooked broccoli that's tough to the bite; overcooked broccoli that's lost its color and flavor and has turned to mush; that kind of nasty odor and flavor overcooked broccoli ends up with in leftovers. Blanching, while an extra step, gives you tender, bright green, and true-to-flavor broccoli that doesn't change or go flat in either the initial bake or in reheated leftovers.

4 Blanching is simple, but in case you haven't done this before, you'll need a large bowl of ice water and a slotted spoon. Steam your broccoli on the stovetop as you normally would, and just as the color gets to its most vibrant hue, take your slotted spoon and ladle the hot steamed broccoli into the ice bath. This stops the cooking process at its moment of perfection, leaving the broccoli tender and firm and the prettiest green you ever saw.

⑤ Chop the onion while you're waiting for the broccoli to chill (with four large heads of broccoli, you'll likely steam and blanch in batches, adding more ice to the ice bath as needed), then run your cooled bacon through the food processor to reduce it to a small, uniform dice. Drain the broccoli through a colander and put it in a large, wide-mouthed mixing bowl. Add in the onion and bacon and either toss lightly with a flat wooden spoon, a large rubber spatula, or your hands—note I said "lightly." You just want the three ingredients to be evenly distributed with each other, but you don't want to mash all that perfectly cooked broccoli in the process.

⑥ Up next is the ricotta and cheese sauce. Using a KitchenAid stand mixer with the standard mixing blade, combine the ricotta and the eggs, adding the eggs one at a time and making sure each is incorporated before adding the next. Melt the butter and add that and the cheddar cheese to the ricotta and eggs and combine. In a separate measuring cup or small bowl, whisk the flour into the milk until thick and there are no lumps. Add that to the cheese and egg mix and combine again. Give it a taste, add salt and pepper as needed, and pour the works over the bacon, onion, and broccoli mix, again, gently combining just to coat. Pour into a deep, buttered, 9x13 casserole pan, and into a 350°F oven for forty-five minutes to an hour, or until the dish has firmed up and pulled just slightly away from the edges. A little brown on top adds some nice toasty color to this pretty dish.

⑦ This was a hit with the anniversary crowd and a great side to the roasted lemon rosemary chicken (I think everyone that night had seconds of both this dish and the chicken). Light and fluffy—thus my invention of the hybrid "cassoufflé"—no one flavor trumped another. Broccoli, bacon, ricotta, and cheddar all played nicely together … much like children giggling and playing tag on the last warm summer evenings before school starts. I think it was a perfect way to start a golden weekend celebrating a golden anniversary.

Note: A big thanks goes out to Karleen and Lanny White, two of my parents' dearest friends. They were our neighbors back when I was in grade school in New Jersey. I don't think I'd seen them in early high school, sometime back in the early '80s. Anyway, Karleen got the flour whisked into the milk when we couldn't find cornstarch and while I was juggling working lemon slices and rosemary under the chickens' skins and blanching what seemed to be an endless stream of broccoli. She is also a one-woman dishwashing machine—I couldn't set a bowl or fork near the sink without it getting sudsed. Lanny, fascinated that baking bacon in the oven precluded the mess of frying on the stove, not only got my rhythm of rotating trays of bacon in and out of the oven and getting a lot of it chopped for various dishes over that weekend (I nicknamed him "José my sous chef"), he helped with photo props and set-ups. My thanks and love go out to both of them.

CANDIED BACON BRUSSELS SPROUTS

Brussels sprouts. There's no middle ground with this tiny cabbage; rarely does anyone say, "Eh, I could take 'em or leave 'em." No, this little veggie usually elicits an "Oh, I *hate* those stinky things," as if that person had once survived a bitter tasting poisoning by them, or, on the other end, "Oh, *oh*, Brussels sprouts, I l-o-v-e *love* those sweet little cabbages." They don't even seem to grow on those who hate them like, say, spinach often does. Nope, once a hater, always a hater. Me, I'm a Brussels sprouts lover.

It's a surprisingly versatile vegetable, one that takes on well a range of herbs and other flavorings, from lemon and garlic to apples and raisins, sherry and cream, parmesan and seasoned breadcrumbs, and you can cook them up nearly any way you can imagine—roasted, shredded, sautéed, fried, pickled, and steamed. About the only thing I've never heard people do with them is eat them raw or put them in a juicer (but I'm not really one of those wheat-grass smoothie folks, so I might be naïve here). Anyway, bacon ranks high among the list of common Brussels sprout additives, but I wanted to try something I didn't find in an Internet search or among my various cookbooks. Here's what you'll need for a two-person serving.

12 good-sized Brussels sprouts	½ teaspoon of ground black pepper
2 tablespoons of butter	6 slices raw bacon
1½ tablespoons of turbinado sugar	Balsamic vinegar (optional)*

❶ Chop the bases off the sprouts and put them in a gallon-sized ziplock bag. Melt the butter and pour it in the bag, then add in the turbinado (or light brown sugar, if that's all you have access to) and ground black pepper. Give the bag a couple shakes to make sure all the Brussels sprouts are evenly covered.

❷ Take your bacon slices and cut them in half. Roll each in one of the halved slices—there shouldn't be much overlap. You're really looking for just one complete wrap-around. Place the wrapped sprouts in a small, shallow casserole or gratin dish so that they are close together.

❸ I was working on using a new Staub grill pan for a T-bone steak, and making that steak successfully requires a quick sear in the hot grill pan on the stovetop, then about ten to fifteen minutes in a very hot oven (375° at the very low end, on up to 500°F in restaurant ovens—most home ovens won't go that high). I wanted, of course, to time it so the sprouts were done at the same time the steak finished, so here's what I did.

❹ I put the little china casserole dish I had, without a cover, in the oven at 350° and set the timer for forty minutes. At the bell, I stuck the tip of a sharp knife in one, and found it nearly done, but the bacon was still a little pale. I set the timer for another fifteen minutes and started the Staub pan, stovetop, on its way to sear status. With five minutes left on the timer, the bacon was closer to where I wanted it, so I lidded the dish, placed it on the bottom rack of the oven, and boosted the oven temp to 395°F.

5. My grill pan not sear-hot, I hit the T-bone for a minute on each side and then quickly slid the pan onto the top rack of the oven to finish. Ten minutes later, I brought the steak out to rest, and set the Brussels sprouts dish on a slightly raised trivet.

6. I could not have imagined how unbelievable the Brussels sprouts would be. I dished out six, took the steak off the still-hot grill pan and onto the plate to rest a bit more, and took a fork and knife to the first sprout. Wow. *Wow.* The little steak knife slid through the bacon and halved the sprout like it was cutting through room-temperature butter. Yet the sprout wasn't mushy, and it hadn't lost its color! But the best treat of all was the underside. There, sitting on the rack above the glowing element for its last 20 minutes, the sugar between the bacon and the sprout, on the bottom side of each bacon-wrapped sprout, had melded into this glossy, slightly sticky candy. *Candy!*

7. How good was the Bacon Maven's rendition of Brussels sprouts? I ate the remaining six the next morning—cold—with Big Maybelle belting out *Candy* playing in my head.

Note: I made these to go with a meal I made for parents one night. My dad is not at all a fan of Brussels sprouts, but I drizzled this batch with some really high-quality Balsamic vinegar—something he does like—before I roasted them, and it totally converted him.

CUMIN-SPICED TWICE-MADE POTATOES WITH BACON AND CORN

I made up this dish to go with the smoked prime rib steak I made with the Roasted Poblano and Bacon Relish. Just a few ingredients—and bacon, of course—take everyone's favorite spud to new, flavorful heights. Here's what you'll need for roughly a four-person dish:

6 to 8 medium Gold potatoes (yellow, thin-skinned)

1½ cups of cooked bacon, lightly cooked and rough chopped

1½ cups of fresh or frozen yellow corn

1 tablespoon of cumin

1 teaspoon of cayenne

2 tablespoons of butter

2 tablespoons of bacon fat

Salt and ground black pepper to taste

Diced spring green onions to garnish

① Cook or bake your bacon as normal, keeping it on the flexible side, rather than crisp, and set aside to cool. You'll need about a pound and a half of bacon, maybe a little les, to get 1½ cups of cooked bacon. If you want more bacon in this dish, you certainly have my blessing. Once you have the bacon cooled, give it a rough chop with a knife.

② Peel your potatoes and cut them into one-inch cubes. You'll want approximately a cup to a cup and a half for each person; the reason I listed six to eight medium Gold potatoes is that, increasingly, the yellow potatoes I've been seeing in the supermarket are just so damned small in size, a third of a decently sized baking Russet. Anyway, use your best judgment according to the number of people you plan on feeding. The worst that can happen is you underestimated, while the best is that you'll have some yummy leftovers.

③ Boil a stockpot of unsalted water and add your potatoes. Cook on a low boil until almost done. You want to be able to push a fork or knife tip in them, rather than have such a utensil slide in effortlessly, almost but not quite done. When you get them to this stage, start another large pot on the stove to medium heat and add the bacon fat to get it melting. Drain your potatoes, give them a quick rinse in cool water, and add them to the melted bacon fat. Now add in your corn and spices. I use frozen corn most of the time. Obviously summer sweet corn is a seasonal thing and, so, not available outside those summer sweet months, but frozen corn, like frozen peas, also tends to hold up better in many dishes. I find that frozen corn and peas retain that bit of pleasant "snap" to them, when their fresh counterparts turn to mush.

④ Give the spices, potatoes, and corn a good stir now and then, until the potatoes start to brown. If you find them starting to stick a bit, go ahead and toss the butter in, and you can also lower the temp under the pot and keep a lid on it, though tilted enough to let out a little steam. Once the spuds start to brown, add in the bacon and give it all several vigorous stirs over the next five minutes or until the potatoes are fork-tender. Serve up as a side to roasted, grilled, or smoked anything, especially and particularly those meats spiced with cumin, cayenne, etc., and these spuds are certainly just as at home aside dishes spiced along Indian curry lines, the bacon providing its lovely savory profile, a somewhat unexpected delight with these heavier spices, and certainly one that counters those heavy-handed with the cayenne. Garnish with a few chopped raw spring onions, both whites and green, for a nice extra little peppery bite.

DOUBLE CABBAGE, RICE, AND BACON ENDS PIE

I know I've covered Brussels sprouts a time or two before, but of all the vegetables out there that can pair with bacon, this is the one that really stands up to such an element of strong flavor. Yes, I love all manner of vegetables, from the mild zucchini to the mouth-warming nuttiness of a baked potato to the earthiness of broccoli and cauliflower. But, to my taste buds at least, there's not another vegetable that complements bacon so completely (insert "You complete me" line from *Jerry Maguire*) as does the Brussels sprout.

And then there's the Brussels sprout's big brother, cabbage. From the slightly tarter red cabbage perfect for pickling to the average head of green coleslaw destined for an Irish colcannon, from the silkier Napa cabbage wonderfully light in Asian inspired soups and spring rolls to the toothsome, almost bitter bite of bok choy, and to curly, I love them all.

Running around a nearby town with my parents during the Thanksgiving holiday week, thankful for a couple 40°F days, we were on the search for a quilt shop. My mother is an extremely talented quilter, and she very proudly showed me an app on her iPhone that showed the location of any and all quilt and quilt supply shops via the phone's GPS system (yes, that means there really is an app for everything). We pinpointed one and headed for it, a little surprised to find it in a five-store strip mall on the outskirts of one of my region's larger towns. Now, I wouldn't quilt if you paid me, nor sew anything more than was necessary to reattach a button, so I'd brought a book along with me to while away the hour it would take her to sort through and buy material. But two doors down from the quilt shop was a sign that had the words "organic" and "food" in it. Fifteen minutes later, I had two jars of locally sourced mustards and a giant stalk of organic Brussels sprouts. My wheels turning, I hit the grocery store on the way home to secure the rest of the ingredients blending in my head. Here's what you'll need to make a 9x13 casserole dish, serving approximately eight good-size helpings:

1 large stalk of Brussels sprouts, approximately 35-45 sprouts

1 medium head of green cabbage

3 cups of cooked basmati rice

3 cups of cooked bacon ends, rough chopped to bite-sized pieces

1 cup of shredded Asiago cheese

4 tablespoons of butter

2 tablespoons of light olive oil

Salt and Pepper to taste

14 sheets of filo dough

reserved warm bacon fat

1 Get your bacon ends cooked and chopped first, then set them aside. Next get your rice cooked, preferably in a rice cooker, and keep it on warm while you get the cabbages ready.

2 Take your Brussels sprouts off the stem as close to the base of the sprout head as possible, then trim off whatever tough stalk part might remain. If you're using individual sprouts, trim the tough bases and discard any old loose and discolored leaves that fall away. Either way, take each whole sprout and cut it in half.

3 Up next is the cabbage, and there's not much to getting this prepped. Simply core it and chop/slice it down to thin, two-inch-long strips.

4 In a large sauce pan or sauté pan, take half the butter and half the olive oil and heat on slightly hotter than the medium setting. Add a teaspoon of salt to these and a couple good twists of black pepper as it heats, releasing the oils from the pepper and allowing the salt to break down a bit. When the butter and oil start to bubble a bit, add your Brussels sprouts to the pan, stirring to coat. I then let them cook for a bit, maybe another ten minutes or so, stirring from time to time so as not to brown them, and then I stuck the lid on the pot and reduced the heat a bit, letting the sprouts steam in their own heat for about another five minutes. When they reached a point where a sharp knife could penetrate with just a decisive push down—somewhere between the forceful cut necessary to cut the raw sprout and the fork-tender consistency of a fully cooked vegetable—I added in the chopped cabbage and the other half of the butter and olive oil, giving it all a vigorous stir to combine. Another seven or eight minutes with a couple stirs here and there, and the cabbage was just coming off its brightest coloring. Once again I put the lid on the saucier I was using, letting it go another five minutes, until the cabbage was fork-tender and the Brussels sprouts were nearly done.

5 Moving my warm rice to a waiting wide-mouthed bowl (I kept it warm so it wouldn't clump and have to be broken apart at this stage), I added in my chopped bacon bits and mixed, then poured the cabbage and sprout mixture over the top, spreading it out to cool a little as I got the first filo dough layer ready.

6 I prepped a fairly deep 9x13 casserole dish by swiping some warm bacon fat over the bottoms and sides. I laid the first sheet of filo dough in the bottom, then dipped a soft pastry brush in the warm, melted bacon fat and swiped the sheet top to bottom and side to side. Now before you get all carried away, know that you're just painting the sheet of filo, you're not saturating it. Your pastry brush should not be dripping fat as you move it from the bowl to the pastry. Repeat with five more sheets of filo, swiping each one with the pastry brush, for a total of six sheets to form the bottom crust of the pie.

7 Back to the filling. Add your grated Asiago cheese to the top of the cooling cabbage mix—I waited to add the cheese in until just this moment, so that I wouldn't end up with clumps of melted cheese just here and there in the dish—and immediately toss with the warm rice and bacon ends underneath. Salt and pepper to taste, then, when all the ingredients are evenly combined, spoon the mixture on top of the bottom filo sheets. Add eight more sheets of filo, repeating the layering on top as you did on the bottom. If you want a very crispy top, you can scramble an egg and very lightly do an egg wash over the final sheet of filo dough, but it's not necessary.

8 I slid my dish into a preheated 365°F oven, checked it at thirty minutes, gave it fifteen minutes more, which was just enough time to sear a steak for my dinner, and dished up a fragrant square. And I loved it. The moist rice, super-tender sprouts, and succulent cabbage were wonderful, especially when a nice chunk of smoky bacon end was on the fork. The little bit of crisp filo top and bottom kept it all together. Altogether a really nice side dish for a prime rib steak with a nice crust or a caramelized roasted loin of pork, and a great way to combine two vegetables in the same family.

MAPLE PECAN BACON DATE WHEAT LOAF

I have long been a bread baker, my time with the loaf pan extending back to my youthful days in 4-H. Then, the quest was for the perfect, blue-ribbon loaf of sandwich white, where the middle was required to be a bastion of hole-less uniformity and the bottom seam had to be straight as the seam on a pair of fishnet stockings.

Over the years, I've come a long ways away from that kind of regimented bread baking. These days, when the yearning strikes, it's free-form artisan loaves or focaccia that fills my kitchen with lovely warm tones for my nose. Too, I've found such unstructured loaves are a great place for bacon, case in point, this hearty number. Here's what you'll need.

1½ cups of warm water, 90-100°F
2 tablespoons of active dry yeast
4 tablespoons of pure maple syrup
2 tablespoons of pure honey
2 cups of stone-ground whole wheat flour
1¾ cups of bread flour
½ cup of quick-cook Quaker oats
2 teaspoons of salt
1½ cups of pecans, rough chopped
1½ cups of cooked bacon, finely chopped
1 cup of chopped dates

1. In a small bowl, dump in your yeast and then add in your hot water and both the maple syrup and the honey. Stir to combine, then set aside for about five minutes to rest.

2. Now take a large mixing bowl and combine the oats and both flours, then add the salt and whisk or fork it around to make sure the salt's distributed. Pour in your yeast mixture and combine until the dough starts to come together.

3. A little confession is necessary at this point. I started out with my KitchenAid stand mixer, but, for me, this became a really dense dough, and I just wasn't getting anywhere with the dough hook, so I made this a second time and, once the dough started to come together, I added in my bacon, dates, and nuts, gave it a couple spins so that the dough hook started to pull those heavier ingredients into the mix, then I dumped the works on a floured wood cutting board to knead and combine by hand. In fact, having made this twice to get it right, it wouldn't be a bad idea with this loaf to add in a little vital wheat gluten. I didn't, because

I found nothing but an empty box of wheat gluten in my pantry when I went to look for it, but a tablespoon and a half or two can certainly help add back a little elasticity to a heavy dough like this.

4 Your dough should be smooth when you've kneaded it enough. Not smooth like white bread dough, because the stone-ground wheat isn't going to lose its grainy texture, but in general you should come away with a nice, neat, smooth ball of dough. It should not be sticky, and it should not resist holding together in a ball. If you've arrived at a too-dry stage, sprinkle on a little warm water (same temperature you used to activate the yeast), and even

a little light olive oil, working either or both into the dough gently but thoroughly until you come away with the desired results.

5 Take another large mixing bowl and wipe the inside with a little light olive oil. Place the dough ball inside, cover with plastic wrap and a towel, and set in a warm place to rise until doubled in size. I started this loaf during very cold weather, which is totally counterproductive to getting bread to rise, so I preheated my oven to its lowest temp, 225°F, shut the oven off, and left the door open for five minutes, then put in my bowl of dough, shut the door, and put the oven light on. It worked well enough, though had I made this in summer, it would have been better. You work with what you have. I went about three and a half hours

before I felt it had risen enough. Check yours at the ninety-minute mark and then every thirty minutes from there until you see the size has doubled.

6 Once the first rise is done, gently lift the dough out of the bowl, give it a quick knead, and reform into a smaller, tighter bowl, then repeat the rising process again, including the plastic wrap and towel. This rise shouldn't take as long as the first before you see the dough double again—I went about two hours, again, mostly because of the cold.

7 Through with the second rising, I carefully lifted out my dough ball and set it in a cloche baker, basically a stone focaccia baking dish with a large domed lid. You can use just the straight focaccia pan or a pizza stone, even regular old loaf pans if you like. Either way, I sprinkled on a few more rolled oats, pressing them slightly into the dough to stick. You can also take a knife and tic-tac-toe the top for extra effect.

8 If using the cloche, preheat the oven to 450°F and include a baking or pizza stone inside, set the cloche baker on the stone, and bake for about twenty-five minutes before turning the oven down to 400 and going another twenty-five minutes. Then and only then should you peek inside the dome to see what's going on. If it's toasty brown and crusty, stick a long bamboo skewer in the center to make sure there's no raw dough; if it's just not quite there, give it another five to ten minutes.

9 If you're using anything other than the cloche, lower your starting temperature to 400°F and spray the oven with water (a small bottle used for ironing and filled with bottled water will work) three times when you first set the bread in, then again at the ten-minute mark. Reduce your second temperature setting to 375°F at the twenty-five-minute mark and keep an eye on the doneness when twenty more minutes have passed, again judging the crust and using the skewer through the middle to test for doneness.

10 Whether you bake bread once a year or every week, you'd be a complete liar if you said you didn't want to rip a hunk off a loaf fresh out of the oven the minute your fingers could stand it. This one's no exception, but the kicker is you *should* eat this one warm. I tried it at room temperature and wasn't excited. But warm, oh, *oh,* the bacon comes out to play, and the maple, honey, and roasty-toasty pecans are as in harmony as their aroma would indicate. Slice a hot wedge of this bread and halve it to slide in some sweet honey ham, or tear it off in hunks and slather tabs of butter over it, or dip it in more warm syrup. Add in a hot cup of chocolate and a lazy Saturday afternoon, and the only thing you'll want after this treat is a nap.

PORK LOVIN' PORTOBELLO CAPS

I had some herbed, cornbread-based stuffing leftover from a chicken I'd roasted a couple nights ago. After a couple days of eating leftover chicken, I was wanting something different. Steak was the easy answer—I often pick up a prime rib for one weekend dinner, if my week hasn't gone too badly and I have enough funds—but I still had quite a bit of stuffing left to deal with. I wandered down the produce aisle of the grocery store, snagged a package of giant Portobello caps, a fresh group of thin-stalked asparagus, and then a package of prosciutto over at the deli, and with those three in hand and the leftovers at home in the fridge, I had a plan. Here's what you'll need:

4 large Portobello mushroom caps

Tips and middle sections from 10 asparagus stalks

10 prosciutto slices

2 cups of pre-cooked herb stuffing

1 cup of cooked ground regular or sage breakfast sausage

¾ cup of cooked bacon, chopped fine

4 teaspoons of butter

1. Start with the asparagus. Trim off the tough ends, then take the remaining stalk and cut in half. Your tip and middle stalk sections shouldn't be any longer than your Portobello caps are wide. Either steam the pieces until bright green or sauté in a little butter until bright, but either way, have an ice water bath ready to shock them when they reach that just-tender stage. Since the asparagus is going to get reheated in the mushroom caps, you don't want to put them in there warm and have them turn to mush. Once your asparagus pieces are cooled in the ice water bath, drain them, pat them dry with a paper towel, and set them aside.

2. Take your leftover stuffing, break it apart with a fork (mine was a very moist stuffing, so chilled in the refrigerator, it was quite homogenous), and add in your finely chopped bacon and cooked sausage (I used Jimmy Dean sage breakfast sausage, to pair with the herb profile in my stuffing). I chopped my bacon in a small food processor, as I usually do, which allows me to control the size of the chop and the uniformity without working so hard or endangering my fingers with a knife handle slicked with bacon grease. If you don't have leftover stuffing on hand, no worries. You can either make a small, fresh batch of stuffing from something like Pepperidge Farm's prepackaged and seasoned herbed or corn stuffing mix, or you can toast some other appropriate bread and then reconstitute it in a pot of just a little boiling water or stock and some herbs and butter, just as you would follow the directions on the Pepperidge Farm stuffing bag. Really, it's so simple, even I wonder why I don't make stuffing more often.

3. Take your Portobello caps and either brush them with a mushroom brush to remove any dirt, or very gently run them under some warm water and pat dry with a paper towel. Spread a

little olive oil in a low-sided gratin dish, then set in each of the mushroom caps, top-side down. Reserving eight asparagus tips, wrap the remaining asparagus sections with small strips of prosciutto (you may have to slice the ones you've purchased down their length, if they're wide pieces), and evenly distribute in each of the four caps. Slice a size-appropriate piece or two of prosciutto and lay on top of these asparagus sections. Take a heaping serving spoon of stuffing and mound it over the asparagus, spreading it to the inside edges of the mushroom caps, but being careful not to press down or outwards too hard, so as not to crush or tear the mushroom. Place a teaspoon pat of butter on top of each stuffing mound.

4 Divide your last eight asparagus tips into four pairs. Take a slice of prosciutto and wrap each pair of asparagus tips, placing each wrapped pair on top of each stuffing mound. Into a 365°F preheated oven, about twenty to twenty-five minutes. The prosciutto should look a little sizzly, the stuffing should be browning at the edges, and you should be able to smell the mushrooms as roasted. If you're unsure about the doneness of the mushroom, take a sharp knife and, inserting it into the stuffing under the top asparagus tips, press gently down and through with the tip of the knife and see if the mushroom yields easily. Portobellos, being as thick and meaty as they are, naturally take longer to cook than the everyday button mushroom, and while there's no harm in eating one a little undercooked, the texture and flavor are much better when cooked all the way. If you find yours a little undercooked but your top is done, loosely tent the dish with foil to keep the tops from drying out and check every five minutes until the mushrooms are done.

5 This was an excellent side to a thick steak, especially if you like your steak on the rare side and you have a plate full of beef juices. Everything in this nifty little side pairs well with those juices, so you won't have any need to mop up with a separate piece of bread, and the deep, earthy flavors of the Portobello and the asparagus are, of course, a natural pairing to something as dense as a grilled prime rib. The real bonus ended up being the baconated stuffing, which actually seemed to lighten up the entire meal, proving once again that bacon truly is the most versatile food in your kitchen.

ROASTED POBLANO AND BACON GRILL RELISH

Over this past summer, a friend recommended I try smoking one of my weekend steaks, instead of grilling it. I thought that was an interesting twist, and so I did a dry rub on a well-marbled slab of prime rib and slid it into the smoker. Close to done, it smelled heavenly when I opened the smoker door to check on it, and all smoky aromatic goodness had me craving something other than the usual mushroom and onion topping. I initially was thinking this would be genius use for bacon jam, but the steak was almost done and there wasn't time for that. Here's what I came up with:

2 roasted poblanos, chopped fine

2 cups of cooked bacon, chopped very fine

2 tablespoons of ground dried cayenne pepper

2 tablespoons of minced garlic

1 tablespoon of bacon fat

½ teaspoon of salt

½ cup of leftover brewed coffee

½ of a medium onion, diced very fine

2 tablespoons of light brown sugar

1. I already had the roasted poblanos on hand, but these don't take long to do and you can certainly get this done before you start your grill or smoker. I simply took two peppers, deheaded them, then sliced them in half lengthwise and removed the seeds. I placed them flesh-side down in a small gratin dish, drizzled with a little olive oil, sprinkled with a little sea salt, and slid them into a 365°F oven for about forty-five minutes. The peppers should be buttery soft when done, including the skins, so there's no need to remove the skins. If you roast yours over an open gas or grill flame and want to remove the charred skins, by all means, have at it.

2. My poblanos roasted, I ran them quickly through a mini food processor, getting them down to a fine dice, but not pulverizing them. I swapped out the peppers for my cooked bacon, again, reducing it to a very fine chop.

3. On the stove, in a small saucepan set to medium-low, I melted my bacon fat and added the garlic, cooking the garlic until it started to brown and had become nuttily fragrant. I added in the diced onion and upped the heat to medium, and once the onions became translucent, in went the bacon and poblanos, stirring to combine. Once it was bubbling away, I added in the rest of the ingredients. I brought the mix to a boil without a lid on the pot, let it roil

for roughly five minutes, stirring occasionally, then lowered the heat to medium-ish. What I wanted to do was reduce the liquid and let this mix thicken. It took a bit of time and some stirring, probably thirty minutes total, maybe forty. You'll have to play with the temperature—too low and it will take an eon to reduce, too high and it just doesn't seem to come together as well, plus you run the risk of burning. No harm in going up and down, and no harm in going lower and slower. What you want in the end is a thick, dark, chunky relish, the closer to room-temp-molasses thick you can get without burning, the better.

4 Personally, I thought this was *genius* on top of my smoke-infused prime rib, a rich, almost decadent topping with just a hint of sweetness playing off the complex smoke flavors in the meat. Indeed, this would pair well over any smoked meat or grilled fare that you've prepped with a cayenne-based dry rub or other deep-spice type of treatment. If you like strong toppings on your meats, this should definitely be a go-to relish to add to your repertoire.

SPAGHETTI SQUASH AND BACON STUFFING (WITH SMOKE-ROASTED CHICKEN)

In addition to keeping up with www.TheBaconAffairs.com (well, trying, at least), I'm starting work on a second cookbook and I've agreed to do some writing for the revamped Bradley Smoker website, www.BradleySmoker.com. I promised the marketing gal at Bradley that I'd have something ready for her by mid-December, but, frankly, as I type this, it's a whopping 5°F and snowing here in central Wisconsin. It's been single-digits for several days now, and even though I keep my smoker covered, I almost didn't get its door open, and the racks and drip pan stuck to my fingertips (which leads some credence to denying the challenge issued to Flick in *A Christmas Story* to stick his tongue on the schoolyard flagpole). Alas, though I looked like some weird smoker version of Edward Scissorhands when I made my way back into the kitchen to wash said racks, I decided to go ahead and brave the 5°F smoking experiment. The focus of this book, of course, is about bacon, and, as such, there's a generous helping of that heavenly bit of pig in the side dish, but that side dish turned out to be such a perfect companion to the main course, I've included both recipes. Here's what you'll need:

For the Chicken
1 6-pound or larger roaster (no fryers)
1 teaspoon of ground black pepper
1 teaspoon of fine sea salt
1 teaspoon of crushed sage
1 teaspoon of crushed rosemary
½ of a lemon squeezed for juice
2 tablespoons of light brown sugar

Get your chicken prepped first, as this is going to take some time in the smoker before you get to anything else in the recipe. Bring your roaster to room temperature. This is going to be especially important if you're smoking in super-cold outside temps, where your smoker—any smoker—is going to struggle to maintain a decent temperature. While this recipe won't smoke the chicken until it's cooked all the way through, you do want it to get at least partially done, so that the smoky taste is present when you're finished.

Once your cluck is at room temperature, mix up the rest of the ingredients in a small bowl and pour it over the chicken (breast-side up), rubbing it all over the bird and inside the cavity (remove the bag of gizzards and liver). Try to slide some under the skin, as well, but don't let the skin tear so that the meat is exposed—the white meat will dry out too much if you tear the skin back. If you're using your smoker in super-cold weather like I was, up your temp a little; I went to 235, instead of my usual 225, and you could probably go a little higher than that, especially if, after the first hour, your smoker just isn't keeping the temperature where you want it. As for the wood, I used mesquite for this recipe, to balance out the sweetness of the brown sugar and citrus from the lemon juice. I went three hours, adding smoke after the first hour for two full doses of smoke. I also kept the vent closed to its maximum, due to the outside temperature.

Once you've got the chicken started in the smoker, you can move on to working on the stuffing. Here's what you'll need:

For the Stuffing
Two cups cooked of bacon or bacon ends, rough chopped

1 cooked spaghetti squash

½ a loaf of soft French bread

1 stick of butter

3 tablespoons of brown sugar

½ teaspoon of dried ground sage

½ teaspoon of dried rosemary

1 teaspoon of cracked black pepper

¾ teaspoon of salt

1. Roast the squash. I Googled a bunch of ways to do this, and the simplest is to simply set the whole squash, uncut, into a shallow baking dish (I put a little olive oil on the bottom of mine and wiped the squash with a bit of oil, too—oh, and remember to pull off the produce sticker) and put it in a 375°F oven for about an hour and a half. Sure, you can cut it in half and roast it cut-side down, and there are plenty of different recipes that do it that way. However, unless you have a cleaver, spaghetti squash, like most large gourds of this type, are difficult to get a knife through at all, let alone with any kind of ease to allow a neat halving. Add to the problem the gourd's roundness, and you're just as likely to slice some part of you as you are the squash. Take my word for it, when you can, roast this one whole.

2. When the first hour has passed on the roasted squash, get your bread toasted. I used about a half-loaf, maybe a little more, of a really long loaf of semi-soft French bread (not one of the super-crusty baguettes). I tore it by hand into one-inch or so pieces and distributed it evenly across a large cookie sheet, then popped the tray into the oven in the rack under the

roasting squash. Another thirty minutes and the squash was done and I had toasted bread-crumbs you can pull the bread out earlier if it starts to get too brown. (By the way, I know lots of stuffing recipes call for stale, day-old bread, but I think toasting fresh bread provides more flavor, plus you can include some drizzled olive oil, butter, or bacon fat and some herbs to really add more *oomph*.) Pour the toasted chunks into a large mixing bowl and set aside.

3 With the squash finished roasting, remove it from the oven and let it rest and at least cool down enough on the outside so that you can touch it without pulling away. When you can get to that point, take a sharp knife and split the squash open and in half along its length. Roll the halves on their backs and let the seeded, fleshy side be exposed to the air to cool; you don't have to let it get all the way to room temperature, but you do need to be able to work with the flesh without taking the prints off your fingers.

4 Okay, the squash cool enough to handle, take a fork and start to tease the seeds out. There are plenty of them, but it's not an overwhelming job. As you remove the seeds that are closest to the flesh, you'll notice the flesh strands pull free, almost by magic, as the tines of your fork stroke it, hence the squash's name. It's the only squash I know of that behaves in this manner and, frankly, it's a delightful treat both in vision and texture, compared to the baby-food soft-ness of most other squashes of the fall and winter seasons.

5 Once you have all the seeds removed, get a sauté pan started on medium-high heat and melt half the stick of butter. Once the butter's liquefied and starting to bubble, add in the brown sugar and herbs. While the sugar is melting and mingling with the herbs and butter, take your fork and shred the squash all the way down to the skin. When the herbs become aromatic, lift the squash strands by big forkfuls and add them to the pan. Keep your fork handy, lifting and turning the squash so that it's coated in the sugar, butter, and herb mix-ture, while also permitting its excess moisture to evaporate. You don't want to try to brown the squash, but you do want the pan to eventually end up close to dry when you're finished. When you think you're getting close, add in the chopped bacon, toss with the fork to com-bine, give it another five minutes to meld and let the bacon loosen up and become flexible again, then add it to your toasted bread hunks in the mixing bowl.

6 Melt the other half of the stick of butter and pour over the top. Now take a large spatula and turn to combine everything. Take some time with this; the spaghetti squash can clump a bit, but going slowly and using the tip of the spatula to separate strands that are in too big a knot is better than smashing the squash into the bread. When you've got this mixed to your liking, either set it aside until three hours have passed on the smoker, or pull your chicken off the smoker if you're at the three-hour mark. Either way, set the bird in a roasting pan and stuff

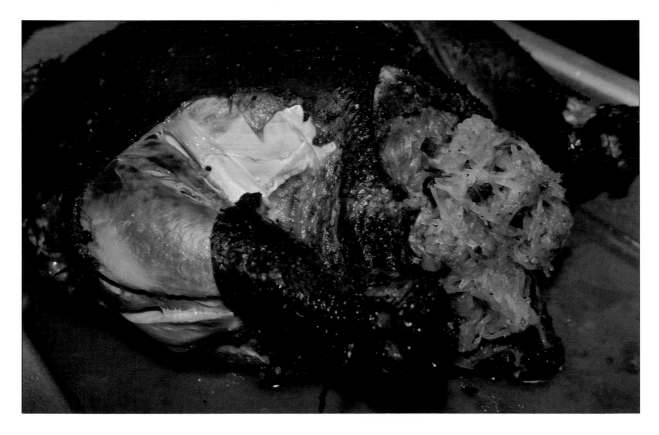

it with the squash mixture, then put the remaining squash stuffing in a baking dish. Into a 350°F oven with both, the bird on the bottom rack, the squash stuffing on the top. I went about forty-five minutes and the bird was finished. Obviously you'll have to vary your time depending on how long you smoked the chicken and how cooked it got during that process. You'll know it's done A) if you pull the leg away from the body and the juices run clear, or B) your bird has a pop-up timer that gives the visual. If you want to go the technical route and use mercury, stick an appropriate food-safe thermometer in the deepest part of the breast and make sure it reaches 160°F before you take the chicken out of the oven. All in all, and depending on how long you had the bird in the smoker, check at thirty minutes, then every fifteen minutes until you're satisfied the bird is done. Meanwhile, check the squash stuffing at the thirty-minute mark, too. If it starts to get brown before your chicken's done, cover it with foil.

7 Remove the chicken from the oven, tent it with foil, and let it rest for fifteen to twenty minutes before carving; I took the foil off the squash and bacon stuffing and let it sit in the oven, the oven turned off and with the door partially opened while the chicken rested. In truth, I don't know how much actual knife work you'll need to do. My bird nearly fell apart when I threatened it with a fork and knife, it was so tender. I ended up slicing the breast, but the leg and thigh pulled off with barely a gentle tug. And it was *divine*. I tried it by itself, then the stuffing by itself, smacked my lips and danced a little jig. Then I ate a forkful of chicken and stuffing together, and felt the need to dance in front of a full-length mirror—and I was too in love with this dish to care that I was a lousy ballerina.

THE BETTER BACON CHEESEBURGER

- The Mushroom Bacon Swiss Burger
- Margherita's Italian Job
- The Better Cheddar
- The Bacon Nacho Cheeseburger
- The California Bacon Cheeseburger, Dude

THE MUSHROOM BACON SWISS BURGER

This won't be news to anyone with a passing interest in this blog, but I am a meat eater. Love the stuff. Ridiculously thick cowboy steaks like I used to get in Texas, standing rib roasts and lamb chops pink on the inside like the blush of a virgin on her wedding night, succulent pulled pork Carolina-style that came after our annual opening day dove hunts, turkey injected with a butter marinade and deep fried, and beer can chickens so moist you almost can't believe they're actually cooked. And burgers, oh, for the love of burgers. Stack 'em high with the best beef you can find and load 'em with toppings, wear two napkins and elbows up in the air to keep the goodness from running down your forearms and dripping off your elbows. Those things, those burgers, are the things that make me salivate like a hard-worked hound dog with dinner hitting his stainless feed pan.

Since this is a bacon blog, you, dear reader, are almost without doubt thinking I am headed for a dissertation on bacon cheeseburgers. Okay, the headline gave that away—a girl's gotta maximize her SEO on this kind of thing. But why? I mean, come on, how hard is it to lay out a bun, layer on your favorite toppings, slap on a patty, a couple slices of bacon, a slice of melty American cheese, and call it a day?

It's not hard. It's also often not good. Think about all the bacon cheeseburgers you've had. At most, you get two slices of bacon, and god forbid the line cook puts them in that dreaded criss-cross arrangement, which leaves you with far too few bites that include the bacon with the beef. Too, the bacon is almost cooked beforehand, which is fine, but if you don't properly reheat it you A) take a bite of your burger and the whole strip of bacon comes out of the burger assembly, or B) they do reheat it and now it's overcooked, so see A) again, but with a worse mouthfeel and taste. Blech, either way. The Bacon Maven can do better, and, so, in her newest of her two in-blog series, she's gonna do a bacon cheeseburger as many ways as she can, making sure you never experience either A or B. For the first burger, here's what you'll need.

½ pound of premium ground beef
¼ cup of seasoned bread crumbs
¼ pound of raw bacon, diced
4 strips of cooked bacon, slightly underdone
1 cup of button mushrooms
½ cup of sliced onions
4 to 6 substantial slices of Swiss cheese
Oversized hamburger bun
Toppings of your choice (the Bacon Maven likes mayonnaise and yellow mustard for this
    particular burger)

1. Bring your hamburger to room temperature and mix in the breadcrumbs as if you were making meatloaf, but without all the extra ingredients. I used seasoned breadcrumbs, but it's certainly fine enough to use plain and then add in salt and pepper and a dash of Worcestershire, whatever you normally use. If you're asking why breadcrumbs, well, I saw a chef at a burger joint on *Diner's Drive-Ins, and Dives* who said he thought the breadcrumbs better kept the juices and fat inside the burger. I thought this was a pretty good idea and went for it, and if you're using a higher fat content in your burger than 80/20, then it's probably a very good idea—why would you want all that finger-lickin' flavor to leak out? Added benefits: If you're on your stovetop, using breadcrumbs tends to reduce the spatter factor; if you're on the grill, your chance of a flare-up and charring your burger into a charcoal hockey puck are greatly reduced.

2. I used a burger press set to make my patty pretty damn thick, then set the burger aside to rest for a bit under a towel while I heated up the grill (i.e., don't put the thing back in the refrigerator). Anticipating this was going to be a messy burger (which it was), and because

I needed to sauté the onions, mushrooms, and bacon, I put my Lodge cast iron grill plate on my gas grill, flat-side up, and painted it with a little bacon grease to keep it in business. While it all heated up, I sliced the onions and mushrooms and chopped the bacon (see note at the end). Once the grill plate was heated, I piled on that mix and let it do its thing, stirring periodically to make sure the bacon was getting cooked.

3 Just as the onions got translucent and the mushrooms were starting to lose some of their moisture, I added the burger to the other side of the plate, then closed the grill top. Five minutes, and I flipped the burger over and laid four strips of bacon on top of it, shutting the lid again. After two minutes, perhaps three, I laid cheese to mostly cover both the mushroom-bacon-onion mix cooking on the side and a few thinner slices on top of the bacon on the burger. Lid down, give the cheese a chance to melt without turning into a molten puddle. Check this—depending on your grill, it can go fast, and you want the cheese to be as much a part of this as everything else, not melted into a memory of what it used to be.

4 Just as the cheese on top of the burger is becoming one with the bacon and the burger, take a nice, wide, solid spatula, scoop up a pile of the mushroom mix, and load it onto the burger.

Shut the lid and turn your burners off, let it sit there a couple minutes. Now pull it off the heat altogether and set it on a plate to rest—ideally, you can put it in an oven that had been heated, turned off, and was close to cool. This allows the burger juices to gather back inside the meat, but the meat itself to stop cooking. Two to three minutes should be all you need, otherwise the burger's going to go cold on the outside. Time up, slide it onto your toasted bun (done with the last of the heat of the grill, and you do want to do this, otherwise you end up with a soggy roll that won't keep this kind and amount of works together). Top as you like.

5 Worried about getting your mouth around a tall boy like this? Don't. Once the burger has set up off the heat for a couple minutes and is setting on its bottom roll half, top it with the other bun half and press down to compress a bit. From there, stack up the napkins next to you, then follow the Guy Fierri *Triple D* method—unhinge your jaw, lean over your plate, and stick your elbows up in the air like a chicken trying to fly. This burger is so good that I promise, no one will care what you look like—and neither will you.

MARGHERITA'S ITALIAN JOB

One of the simple pleasures in life is a Margherita pizza. A good crust, mellow mozzarella, fresh basil leaves, and an earthy tomato sauce combine to make a simple but flavorful pie, one perfect when you're just not feeling that "I'll take an extra-large pie with everything, and throw in the kitchen sink" kind of feelings. Too, basil is one of my favorite herbs to use fresh; I love how it fills the back of your mouth and your nasal cavity with its perfume.

The other night, I was kind of craving a Margherita pizza, but it was too late to make dough and I was too broke to order one. What I did have on hand, though, were the makings of Better Bacon Cheeseburger No. 2. Here's what you'll need (per burger):

½ pound of premium ground beef, either 80/20 or even 90/20 if using ground sirloin or organic grass-fed beef

1 teaspoon of garlic

½ teaspoon of pepper

½ teaspoon of ground dried basil

4 fresh basil leaves (not ground dried basil)

3 slices of prosciutto or cooked bacon, finely chopped

1 large slab of beefsteak tomato

4 generous slices of fresh mozzarella (use a whole piece of mozzarella, not shredded)

½ cup of marinara sauce

❶ For each burger, you'll want to divide the half-pound in half. You may season with salt and pepper if you wish, but remember that a Margherita pizza has just three ingredients besides the crust. In that spirit, I kept my ground beef, which was ridiculously expensive but worth it organic grass fed beef, seasoned with just a little bit of crushed garlic, a little dried ground basil, and ground pepper. Make a ball of the quarter-pound by hand and place it on a piece of waxed paper. Cover with another piece of wax paper and gently press down on the ball with your hand to start to flatten it. Then, take a rolling pin and gently, *gently*, roll the patty out until it's a good half-inch beyond the borders of a bun if you were to set it on one. The rolling pin allows you to get the meat to an even thickness all the way around, while at the same time stretching the patty to the desired diameter. Repeat with the next patty.

❷ Remove one of the patties from the waxed paper and set it on a non-stick cutting board (or simply uncover it and leave it on the waxed paper). Place the prosciutto (which should be thin) or your crumbled bacon on the patty, then place on the basil leaves and one of the mozzarella slices. Arrange these ingredients so that there's room at the edge of the burger patty, maybe a quarter-inch or so. Now, take your other patty and cover the one with the stuffing ingredients, pinching the edges of the two rounds together to seal the "middlings" inside.

❸ I chose to do mine on the grill, but knowing that this burger was going to be messy, I also used my Lodge cast iron griddle with the flat-side up. After the burger was done on one side and turned, I slapped the tomato slice on the hot iron, as well as the bun to toast up a bit. Toasting the bun is going to be essential. This is a fairly "wet" burger, so toasting helps the bun to not become a soggy, disintegrating mess. It's one thing to have to use a knife and fork (which you might, with this one), it's another thing to have the bun reduced to flavorless mush.

❹ When the burger was just about done, I pulled the bun off and set it on a plate. Next I slid the hot grilled tomato on top of the burger, finally topping that with the three thick rounds of mozzarella I'd set aside. I closed the grill lid, turned off the flame, and gave the cheese a chance to melt a bit. Back in the kitchen, I'd started a small saucepan of marinara sauce on the stove, and once it was bubbling, I took it outside. Placing the finished burger on the bottom toasted bun, I then ladled about a half-cup of the marinara over the top, which further helped to melt the gooey cheese, then set the other side of the bun on top.

5 I let this set up for a little bit, a minute or two, just like you'd let a steak hot off the grill set for a bit and let the juices come back up through the meat. It also gives that piping-hot marinara and cheese a chance to cool down, so you don't take that first layer of skin off the top of your mouth. When I was ready, I cut it in half, expecting to fork-and-knife this one, but, in fact, the toasted bun, a thick soft Kaiser roll, had held up very well and I was able to eat this like a normal burger. And oh, it was worth it to eat it this way, with a bite that had all the layers in it all at one time. What a total, wonderful, stupendous mouthful of Margherita pizza flavors—and I'd do it again in a heartbeat.

THE BETTER CHEDDAR

Burgers have taken on a kind of cult status these days, with restaurants and pubs everywhere refining this humble American fare and producing burgers that are loaded with all sorts of decadent (and sometimes bizarre) toppings. I love them all, love the ability to experiment and discover that there's so much more you can do with this handheld meal than we ever used to think. Still, sometimes your mouth just wants the basics—bacon, lettuce, tomato, a little mayo, and some really good cheese—but that doesn't mean that you can't improve on basic. Here's what you'll need for the classic cheddar bacon cheeseburger (this recipe makes one thick burger), done better the Bacon Maven's way:

½ pound of organic beef

1½ cups of excellent quality aged sharp cheddar, half sliced, half shredded

6 slices of thick-cut hickory smoked bacon or pepper bacon, cooked and cut in half

⅓ cup of cooked bacon (about 3 slices), finely diced

1 loose cup of spring mix lettuces

2 slices of beefsteak tomato

2 tablespoons of mayonnaise

One thick and wide (oversized) hamburger bun

Salt and pepper to season

❶ Take your three slices of bacon, lightly cooked, not crispy, and pulse in a food processor until finely diced. Add this to the half-pound of organic ground beef (either 80/20 or 90/10 will work fine) and combine by hand, working the bacon into the ground meat until there's an even distribution.

❷ By the way, I emphasized organic, grass-fed beef for a couple reasons. One, I prefer the taste, even if I don't prefer the price, but since I only cook a burger or two at a time, even the price isn't a huge issue. More than the taste, though, what I get is a burger that holds together better both in forming while raw (especially when mixing in other ingredients, such as the bacon here), and certainly better on the grill or in the skillet. That, it turn, means it also holds together between the bun, and that's important when you're looking for that burger bite that has a little bit of all the ingredients in it, rather than a clump of cheese and a crumb of burger or a torn piece of bun with nothing but lettuce and bacon. Also, the organic 80/20 actually seems to be leaner than non-organic 80/20. I just don't get the grease puddle in the pan or the greasy trail running down my arm, rather I get more beefy juice. Then there's the whole GMO thing and slaughterhouse treatment, etc., that's more than this book is meant to tackle, but on those points, regular, corn-fed commercial-grade ground cow leaves cold these days.

❸ The organic isn't for everybody, either because the price point precludes it or because it's simply not available. Not problem. When making a thicker burger like this, work with the burger cold from the refrigerator as you work the bacon in and form your patty. You can certainly let it sit and come to room temperature after forming and before you cook it up.

❹ I sprinkled both sides of the patty with a little salt and pepper—again, this is a really basic burger and, as such, I wanted to keep the seasoning simple—set it in a hot stove-top grill pan (I use a heavy, ridged, coated iron pan from Le Creuset). Just as the first side was starting to look close to done, I lowered the temp on that side and started to warm a small, non-stick sauté pan on the burner next to it. Just as I flipped the burger (hint, if it doesn't come away easily from the pan, it's either not done on that side or you've cooked it way past done—flip when a spatula pries the burger away without leaving half of it behind), I lowered the heat under that pan and then laid half of my half-strips of bacon in the warmed non-stick pan. Within a minute or so, the bacon was flexible again, just starting to snap, and as soon as I saw that, I dumped a handful of shredded cheddar over it. I let it sit there for about thirty seconds, then took a measuring cup of water, poured just a dash into the pan, and slapped the lid over it quick, letting the steam from the water hitting the hot pan melt the cheddar and bacon together (this also helps to keep the bacon flexible while it's re-cooking). When I heard the hiss of the steam start to die down, I slid the pan, still covered, off the burner.

❺ Back to the burger. Almost done now on the second side, I laid several slices of cheddar on the top, followed by the other half-strips of bacon and three or four more slices of cheese to cover that. I took a large domed lid from one of my stock pots, poured a little water on the hot iron grill pan, and quickly slapped the lid over the burger, giving the cheese a chance to melt on top (of course, the seal between the lid and the ridged grill pan isn't as tight as it is on a flat-surfaced sauté pan, but it still works pretty well). When the sizzle died down this time, I removed the burger from the pan altogether, setting it on a small plate away from the stovetop to rest a minute.

❻ While the burger rested, I prepped the bun. For burgers of this size and depth, I'm gonna tell ya right now, don't even think about using one of the cheap grocery store hamburger buns that not only increasingly look like they'll only hold a burger of slider-size these days, but are of so little substance that, regardless their width, will be rendered a sodden mess at the first dollop of ketchup. Find a bigger grocery store that has either a well-stocked bread aisle or has its own in-store bakery and buy a better roll. If that fails, at least use a large, soft Kaiser roll.

7 In keeping with my very simple theme, I used only mayonnaise on the bun. Certainly this is personal preference, so add ketchup and mustard or Heinz 57 as you like. I covered the inside surface of each bun half with my mayo, then, on the bottom half, stacked some really good organic spring mix greens I'd chopped a bit—I *hate* it when I bite into a burger and pull out an entire lettuce leaf! I laid the two beefsteak tomato slices on top of that, then I grabbed the nonstick pan and spatulaed the mound of now perfectly blended bacon and melted cheese and slid it on top of the tomatoes. Then came the burger, and then the top bun. I pressed down lightly, squarely on the top, then let it sit a minute or two, you know, to kind of become one, as it were.

8 As for how it turned out, all I can say is, if you don't want to take the time to make it this way after looking at that picture, well, you probably ought to consider going vegan.

THE BACON NACHO CHEESEBURGER

The Super Bowl week in the past, spring far too many weeks in the future, and the endless strings of sub-zero temps of 2014's Polar Vortex had me deep in the grips of cabin fever. For the past couple winters, I've stopped in at one of the local pubs from time to time, had a brew, some piping hot fried mushrooms, and a juicy burger or a pizza. But this year, sheesh, it's just been too damned cold to think about leaving the house more than I had to. That left me with a decided craving for bar food—and thank god bacon was there to save the day. Here's what you'll need for two bar-food-esque, loaded half-pound burgers:

1 pound of 80/20 ground beef (organic preferably)
24 Dorito chips, original nacho flavor
1 cup of refried beans
8 slices of cooked bacon
3 cups of shredded sharp cheddar cheese, plus several
½ cup of guacamole
½ cup of sour cream
Thinly sliced and diced red onion
2 large hamburger buns, halved and toasted

1. Divide your ground burger in two and make two patties. As I nearly always do, I suggest using organic beef, not only because I think it tends to taste better, but because even in the same 80/20 mix of regular ground beef, it doesn't seem to be as greasy. Set your patties aside on a cutting board or plate, cover, and allow to come to room temperature.

2. Get your nachos started. I used a small, oval gratin dish for mine (it was only me needing one burger), and I kept the nachos simple. Not that I don't like a plate of loaded nachos, but I really wanted the bacon to shine in these. I simply laid down a layer of Doritos (because why *wouldn't* I use Doritos instead of regular old tortilla chips?), dolloped on some refried beans, laid in four strips of bacon, and topped with a layer of shredded cheese. I repeated with a second layer of everything. Into a 365°F preheated oven.

3. While the nachos were getting cooked, I heated a sauté pan to medium-high, set in my patty, and immediately reduced the heat. Nachos don't take that long to cook, but I wanted them to end up done to medium rare the same time as the burgers, and I didn't want to put a lid on the meat except to melt the cheese. The low-temp, slower cooking matched up perfectly to the roughly twenty minutes the nachos were in the oven (that twenty minutes including about five minutes to heat up the sauté pan). Naturally I turned the burgers over halfway through, and when the second side was almost done, I piled on a big handful of shredded cheddar cheese, stuck a lid over the works, and turned off the burner, though I

didn't remove the pan from that burner. The last thing I did was take a really thick, bakery made hamburger roll and stick it, halved, in the oven for the last five minutes the nachos were cooking.

4 The burger done and the cheese melted, I removed the lid from the pan and set the pan on a trivet to let the burger set up away from any heat and let the juices come back to the surface. Needing just a couple minutes for this, I took the bun out of the oven, setting the broiler on high to the nachos to get them really hot, and prepped the bread. I spread a generous dollop of guacamole on the bottom half of the bun, laid on some shredded red onion, and set the burger on top. The top half of the bun got dressed with an equally good dollop of sour cream. I pulled the nachos from the oven, estimated a burger-sized helping of it, and cut into it, lifting it out with a large serving spoon and setting it on the waiting burger. Finally, I laid on the top bun with its sour cream, pressed down to seal the deal together, and, lacking the jaws of an anaconda, cut the works in half.

5 I admit, I stopped at just one half. This is a really filling burger. It's also barfoodarific—I liked it so much I ended up snatching a bit out of the cooling second half every time I walked through the kitchen over the next hour until it, too, was gone. A second burger for dinner used up the rest of the nachos, and, paired with an ice cold beer, I'd almost forgotten it was winter outside.

THE CALIFORNIA BACON CHEESEBURGER, DUDE

I've been on a bit of a burger kick, lately, something I've actually found a bit difficult to keep under control. I hit the grocery store with three themes running through my head, and $200 later, I've got fixings for twenty different bacon cheeseburgers. Sheesh.

Anyway, I got home from such a trip the other day, sorted through my groceries, and tried to match them up to all the ideas I'd had two hours earlier. I was staring out into space, imagining a hearty burger with all sorts of peppers coming together, and when I brought my focus back to earth, I found myself staring at my lonely, snow-covered grill. Thoughts of warm sunshine, beaches, and a salt-rimmed margarita crowded my head—and I instantly had my next bacon burger. Here's what you'll need for three third-pound burgers:

1 pound good quality 80/20 ground beef, preferably organic

3 large flour tortillas

2 avaocados, sliced

1½ cups of fresh bean sprouts

15 slices of bacon, six cooked, nine raw

8 ounces of soft, mild chevre

salt and pepper

1 tablespoon of bacon fat

1 Preheat your oven to 375°F.

2 Take your ground beef and divide it into thirds. Take each third and, rather than make your traditional round patty, make one that's rectangular, though not very wide. Sprinkle each side with salt and pepper, set on a plate or cutting board, cover, and bring to room temperature.

3 Heat a large sauté pan to medium-high and melt your bacon fat. If you don't have any bacon fat on hand, shame on you, but go ahead and use a little butter instead. Once your fat source is sizzling, lay your hamburger rectangles in and sear quickly on both sides, but don't really cook them. Once both sides are brown, remove from the heat to a plate to drain while you prepare the wraps.

4 Take each tortilla and warm them for thirty seconds in the microwave so that they're flexible. Next, lay a third of the bean sprouts in the center of each tortilla. Lay your still-hot burger on top of the sprouts, dollop an equal amount of chévre on each, and then lay on two slices of cooked bacon slices. Top with slices from half an avocado (you'll have half an avocado leftover for a salad or as a garnish to the finished dish) and pull up the sides of the torrtilla to wrap around the filling, meeting at the top like a giant soft taco. Wrap three slices of raw bacon around each wrap to hold the works together.

⑤ I set my three Cali burgers in an oval gratin dish, but any shallow casserole will do. I went just about twenty minutes in the oven, which was enough to cook the bacon on the outside of the wraps and heat the insides through.

⑥ This truly was a California-style burger, with all the flavors and textures you imagine in foods from the Sunshine State! Crunchy sprouts, creamy avocado, and a bit of funky chevre, all in a neat, bacon-wrapped, hand-held package. The burger was so tender the juices ran down my arms, yet it wasn't greasy in the slightest, and the bacon added the right amount of saltiness to, well, all of it. All it left me wanting was a seat under a palm tree and a drink with an umbrella in it.

Note: Eat these right away. Not that you wouldn't, but living by myself, I cooked enough for the pictures and, so, I had leftovers. I wrapped one of the burgers in foil the next day and reheated in the oven. While most of it was just fine, the bean sprouts did not take kindly to being cooked, refrigerated, and reheated. I didn't even bother reheating the last one.

Chapter 7

BACON DESSERTS

- Apple, Pear, Cranberry, and Bacon Cobbler
- Bacon-Pecan Crusted Four-Layer Dream Pie
- Baconated Apple Spice Cake
- Liquored Up and Nowhere to Go Bacon Bread Pudding
- Peanut Butter Bacon Coffee Cake

APPLE, PEAR, CRANBERRY, AND BACON COBBLER

Fall is, without a doubt, my favorite season. This is the one I'd make last the longest, were I to have such powers. Cozy sweaters, rosy cheeks, frisky puppies, a favorite coat, wood fires burning, hot toddies, crunchy leaves, everyone scurrying around battening down the hatches before winter sets in. Oh, and apples.

I like apples alright, enjoy the occasional apple pie, a crisp slice with a bit of cheese, the juices running down my chin. But not often. I'm not a huge fruit eater, or a sweets eater, for that matter. Still, I like apples alright.

Apples put me in a rut; I always seem to get stuck at pie. Oh, I did a strudel, to rave reviews I might add, when I first moved here to Wisconsin, but really, such a thing isn't a far cry from a pie. I'm not a fan of fruit with meat, so, again, I'm back at pie. The worst of it is, I am besieged by apples. The grocery stores devote bin after bin after bin to the seemingly endless varieties and, around here, you can't drive a country mile without seeing a "Pick Your Own!" sign pointing to one orchard or another. Every cooking magazine oozes apple this and apple that. It is apple overload, and I feel, um, obligated—I sucked it up and bought eight round, shiny, overpriced Honeycrisps this past weekend, went home, and scrolled through my Pinterest board. Here's what you'll need:

For the Filling

6 small Honeycrisp apples

4 medium apple pears or 5 Bosc pears

16 ounces of sweetened dried cranberries

1 tablespoon of cinnamon

¼ teaspoon of nutmeg

2 tablespoons of white table sugar

½ cup of orange juice

2 tablespoons of butter

1 cup of cooked bacon, finely chopped

For the Pastry

1½ sticks of butter

2 cups of white table sugar

4 eggs

1 teaspoon of vanilla extract

1 teaspoon of salt

3 cups of self-rising flour

1½ cups of honey Greek yogurt*

❶ I confess, I had the apple pears on hand and needed to use them (then again, that's how half my recipes come into being). Apple pears are, well, pears that look like apples, kind of like the Golden Delicious variety. They are thin-skinned and soft-fleshed, which is why I said to use Bosc pears for a substitution. The taste, at least to me, is similar. The apple pears showed up in my grocery store not that long ago in this neat little four-pack, each fruit cradled in a soft, woven net of sorts. I figured that was the reason for the high price, thought they must be something special, and into my cart they went.

2 Prep the filling first. Peel and core the apples and apple pears and slice them into uniform widths, about a quarter-inch. You want them to stand up to cooking and not turn into mush. As you're slicing the last couple pieces of fruit, set a large sauté pan to just over medium and melt the butter. Once the butter starts bubbling, add in the apples, tossing to coat. Next add in the sugar, cinnamon, and cranberries, again, tossing to coat. Stir occasionally for about four minutes or so, then add in the orange juice. Stir again until the cranberries have plumped up and the excess liquid has evaporated. Remove the pan from the burner, add in the finely diced cooked bacon, toss to combine, and set aside.

3 Up next is the pastry. Cream your butter and sugar in a stand mixer until combined. Add in the vanilla, then the eggs, combining thoroughly before each next egg is added. You should have a smooth, thick, cream-colored start to your batter at this point. Add in your yogurt and flour, alternating a cup of flour with a third of the yogurt until both are consumed. Your end product should look like white cake batter, but thicker.

4 Take a 9x13 baking pan and grease and flour it (I used a non-stick Cuisinart baking pan, but sprayed it down with Pam just in case). Spread about three-quarters of the batter evenly across the bottom of the pan. On top of that, evenly distribute the apple filling, but gently. There's no need to press the filling into the bottom of the batter and, in fact, you'll risk burning fruit that touches the bottom if you do. Now take the rest of the batter and dollop it over the top—you want some space, some fruit showing through, so that the dish vents its steam as it cooks, thereby preventing the bottom layer of batter from becoming a nasty sponge. Into a 350°F oven for forty-five to sixty minutes. I waited for mine to become light golden brown at the top and stuck a long toothpick through to the bottom just to be sure.

5 I declare that this dish is the way to break out of the apple pie rut. The orange juice and cranberries, along with minimal added sugar, served to keep the filling bright, instead of the goopy sweetness apple pies can often be. The pears, too, served to mix the flavor profile up, something my tongue was more than happy about. The batter poofed nicely, with a moist, cake-like texture and, when served warm over some pan-hot excess filling, the bacon added just this hint of, oh, you know by know, that *thing* that bacon brings to everything: depth, richness, a bit of the savory cutting though an otherwise sweet dessert. Skip the bacon and I promise, you'll regret it.

BACON-PECAN CRUSTED FOUR-LAYER DREAM PIE

Pies are a staple of America's cafés and classic diner counters. My favorite has always been the tall, pudding-based types with mounds of whipped cream on top, rather than fruit. There's just something about them, maybe just that it's in a pie wedge and not a bowl, that lets you enjoy a moment of your childhood without actually acting like a five-year-old—I mean, c'mon, who *doesn't* like *pudding*?

Recently I've run across several recipes for these kinds of pies, including a couple that layered different pudding flavors and layers of whipped cream. Me, being the Bacon Maven that I am, thought I could improve on this and, well, "adultify" it, if you will. Here's what you'll need:

1 cup of crushed graham crackers	1 package of vanilla, butterscotch, or cheese-cake Jell-O pudding mix
2 cups of chopped pecans	
¾ cup of sugar	3 cups of heavy whipping cream
1 cup of finely chopped bacon	1 8-ounce package of cream cheese
¾ stick of melted butter	1½ cups of powdered (confectioner's) sugar
¾ cup of cake flour	
4 cups of whole milk	Fresh raspberries and your favorite choco-late pieces for garnish
1 package of Jell-O chocolate pudding mix	

❶ Start by making the crust. Combine the graham cracker crumbs, sugar, cake flour, and chopped pecans in a bowl. Take your cooked bacon and whirl it in a small food processor until it's finely and uniformly chopped—you don't want big chunks for this. Melt the butter and add that and the chopped bacon to the graham cracker mixture, thoroughly combining so that all the components are moistened.

❷ Press the mixture along the bottom and sides of a 9x13 pan that you've prepped with a little non-stick spray. Make sure there are no holes in the bottom or corners. Pop it in a preheated 350°F oven for twenty minutes. The crust should be lightly browned and smell *amazing* when done. Set it aside to cool completely.

❸ Note: I used my KitchenAid stand mixer with the whisk attachment for each of the following steps. One appliance and one extra bowl kept clutter and mess to a minimum.

❹ For the first layer, begin by taking one cup of the heavy whipping cream and whip until you have, well, whipped cream, of course. Spoon that into a separate bowl and set aside for a

moment. Back at the stand mixer, combine the cream cheese and one cup of the powdered sugar until thoroughly combined and silky—make sure to scrape down the sides of the bowl and the bottom a couple times. Now, take a rubber spatula and fold in the whipped cream you made earlier until just combined. Don't overmix and turn it into soup. Gently spread this layer along the bottom of the cooled bacon-pecan-graham crust.

5. Make the chocolate pudding per the instructions on the box, with two cups of whole milk and continuing to use the whisk attachment on your stand mixer. Spread the pudding before it really begins to set across the top of the cream cheese layer. Go slowly and carefully, as you don't want to mix the chocolate into the layer beneath. Repeat the next layer with your next flavored layer of pudding.

6. While the second layer of pudding is setting up, whip the last two cups of cream in the stand mixer. Add in the last half-cup of powdered sugar as the whipped cream comes together, then gently spread the finished whipped cream layer across the top of the last pudding layer. Refrigerate at least four hours before serving.

7. I loved this. Creamy and dreamy every bit like I'd imagined it would be, the fresh whipped cream gave a truer, richer flavor than Cool Whip could ever dream of. Cool Whip, by the way, is what most recipes of this type call for—I promise, it's worth the rather minimal effort to whip your own from fresh heavy whipping cream). Freshly whipped cream, even with a little powdered sugar, is far less sweet and much less cloying on the tongue than commercial whipped toppings, and since this is already a sweet dessert, toning this component down gives a better taste balance. That there's bacon in the crust—and the crust is what so many people leave behind on their plates with a dessert like this—completes the overall bite, that little bit of savory and salt playing in a most excellent manner against the sugary elements. I loved it all, and then I added in a handful of fresh tart raspberries—do that, add that little bit of sophistication and another flavor to play with the others, and no one will ever question your "kid's" love of pudding.

BACONATED APPLE SPICE CAKE

I like a good spice cake, but usually only my own. Too many of them are dry and lifeless, while the other end of the spectrum seems to deliver nothing but a harsh mouthful of cinnamon. And as for those who glop something like German chocolate or some envelope-sealing sticky caramel icing on it and muck it up, well, to you I say, *pfft!* I like mine deep and rich, the spices working in harmony, but the cake itself light and airy, moist, and *sans* icing.

This fall, the annual crop of apples, in all their varietal splendor, called my name as I walked through the sliding glass of the grocer's one fine Saturday morning. I dismissed the Fujis, the Granny Smiths, the red delicious, and bagged up a half-dozen medium-sized Honeycrisps. Snagging a pound of bacon, I sped through the twenty-items-or-less aisle while the idea for an upgraded spice cake was making the rounds of my brain matter. By the time I got home, ten minutes later, I had it worked out. Here's what you'll need:

2½ cups of cake flour	1 teaspoon of cinnamon
5 eggs	1 teaspoon of allspice
¼ cup of melted butter	½ teaspoon of nutmeg
1½ cups of light brown sugar	½ teaspoon of ground cloves
1 cup of whole milk	1 teaspoon of ground ginger
1 teaspoon of vanilla extract	½ teaspoon of ground cardamom
1 teaspoon of salt	3 cups of ½-inch diced fresh apples
½ teaspoon of baking soda	1¾ cups of finely chopped cooked bacon
½ teaspoon of baking powder	2 tablespoons of light brown sugar

❶ In a stand mixer (or in a large mixing bowl, if you're going to mix by hand), combine the flour, salt, baking powder, and baking soda. Add in the sugar and spices and combine again. Add in the eggs (preferably at room temperature) one at a time, combining thoroughly before adding the next. Add the milk, vanilla, and melted butter, combining on a low to medium speed until you have a smooth and medium-thick batter. Add more milk if needed—you don't want this batter to be stiff, but you don't want this to be a cake-batter kind of consistency, either.

❷ Once you get the batter where you want it, add in the chopped apples* and all but a quarter-cup of your chopped bacon. I ran my bacon through the food processor to get that

very fine dice, so that it would distribute very evenly through the batter. Run your stand mixer just until these last two ingredients are distributed throughout the batter, no more.

3 I took a square springform** pan, greased it with a little butter, and floured it, just in case. I poured in the batter, then took my last apple and cut it into thin, uniform slices, laying them in a pretty pattern around the edges of the cake, repeating and working in toward the center until the surface was covered. Last, I took the remaining quarter-cup of chopped bacon, tossed it in a ziplock bag with a couple teaspoons of light brown sugar, and sprinkled that over the top of the cake. Into the oven, 360°F, about forty-five to fifty minutes for a large springform like this, maybe a bit longer. Put a toothpick in the middle until it comes out clean, the house smells irresistible, standard cake-testing stuff, you get it.

4 I let the cake cool, removed the outer part of the springform pan later that night, and had a piece. Eh, meh, so what. Seriously, meh?

5 The next night I cut a slice and stuck in the microwave for thirty seconds. Eh, meh, and so what? Not a *chance!* With just a little warming up, this cake had *everything.* Warm soft apples, succulent bacon, and rich spices, all of it coming together in harmony.*** Bliss, I tell you, pure autumnal bliss.

*Note: As you chop the apples in preparation, keep a bowl of cool water with a teaspoon or so of lemon juice mixed in beside you. As you get the apples chopped, scoop them up and put them in the water-citrus bath. This will keep them from becoming brown before you're ready to mix them into the cake batter.

**Note: I used a springform pan mostly because I couldn't find one of my regular cake pans (don't ask). However, because this is such a thick batter, it worked out grandly. I'd suggest you stick with the springform. If you elect to use regular cake pans, fine, but keep an eye on your time. I'd look in at two normal nine-inch rounds after about twenty-five minutes, keeping an eye on it every five minutes or so until the toothpick comes out clean.

***I did get carried away one night and added both some Häagen Daz pure vanilla ice cream and a drizzle of caramel syrup. Nothing but my waistline regretted this alteration.

LIQUORED UP AND NOWHERE TO GO BACON BREAD PUDDING

I love bread pudding, and I usually stick to a bourbon-infused recipe I have in a book of low country cooking. Looking through Terry Thompson-Anderson's *Texas on the Plate* for a dinner dish I could redo with bacon, I ran across a dessert called "White Chocolate Bread Pudding with Frangelico Sauce and Raspberry Chantilly Cream." I almost didn't make it past the words "white chocolate." I don't indulge in candy very often, but, when I do, I'll almost always reach for white chocolate before the choco-chocolate variety. Anyway, the idea of combining white chocolate, Frangelico, and bacon seemed a good one.

The *Texas on the Plate* recipe was kind of intense. And long. In fact, there were three distinct parts to it. There was the making of the bread pudding, the cooking of the Frangelico sauce, and the whipping up of the raspberry Chantilly cream. I lost interest at the end of the Frangelico sauce section, especially since it involved a double boiler, a kitchen tool I fairly despise. I figured I'd never get to the Chantilly cream portion, so I redid nearly the entire recipe. Here's the recipe for the bread pudding portion as I devised it.

1 long, rather thin French baguette, plus ¾ of a loaf of plain Italian bread

1 cup of fresh blackberries

1 cup of golden raisins

3 tablespoons of Frangelico liqueur

2 tablespoons of sugar

2 teaspoons of vanilla extract

3 cups chopped bacon

For the White Chocolate Sauce Bath

12 ounces of Ghiradelli white chocolate

3 cups of half-and-half

1½ sticks of butter

For the Binder

5 eggs

1¼ cups of sugar

2 teaspoons of vanilla extract

¾ cup of coconut flakes

❶ Macerate the blackberries and golden raisins with the Frangelico, 2 tablespoons of suger, and the vanilla extract. I actually did this on a whim. I didn't want to the berries to go bad, but I'd had to postpone the bread pudding making for a number of reasons. I figured the liqueur would save their lives and give them some extra kick all at the same time. Given how well this dessert turned out, I'd stick with this. Go at least eight hours, holding the dressed fruit in the fridge. I actually went five days, meaning either I had blackberries with some unbelievable shelf life to them, or the maceration plan revealed a bit of personal genius. I'm going with the latter.

2 I had chopped up the bread into one-inch chunks and let them go stale, air-drying them in a large stainless bowl for a couple days. I also accidently sort of toasted them in the oven. I'd needed to run into town for a quick errand and had put the bowl in the oven to keep the puppies from grabbing it while I was gone. (And, yes, that's how I ended up with three-quarters of a loaf of Italian bread—Lucy had grabbed what had been a dual loaf bag off the counter while I was putting laundry away earlier in the week, managing to eat one loaf with her brother Hayden. The other loaf was still in the bag, and while one end had been stepped on, it had escaped the dog saliva, so I salvaged the unmolested remains of that loaf.) Later that night, I turned on the oven to preheat it for something, forgetting the bowl of bread cubes was in there. I remembered just as the oven beeped that my preheat was done, so the cubes were definitely drier than I'd had them before. No harm, no foul—the bread cubes weren't even brown—and the extra little warm in the oven might have even done them some good, but there's no need to actually toast the bread if you don't want to.

3 To the dried bread cubes I added in the chopped bacon and macerated fruit, but did not yet combine them. On the stove I slowly heated the butter, half-and-half, and white chocolate (I'd broken this last ingredient into chunks to aid the melting). I stirred it occasionally over a medium-low heat setting until all was smooth, then poured it over the bread and fruit. Taking a large-paddled rubber spatula, I then combined, folding gently and making sure all the bread soaked up some of the white chocolate bath.

4 The next part of the recipe in the *Texas* book called for combining the eggs and sugar (though the original recipe had different quantities than mine) in a mixer on medium speed for about seven minutes. I did just that, then added in the vanilla and coconut. That, too, got poured over the bread mixture, and I folded once again to combine and distribute the coconut evenly.

5 Into a preheated 325°F oven it went. The *Texas* book said forty-five to fifty-five minutes. I checked it at forty-five, went another ten minutes, then another and final ten minutes. My quantity of bread pudding was about half again more than the recipe in the book, so this made sense. When the heavenly aroma of Frangelico and sweet warm white chocolate and cream reached my nose at the 1:05 mark, out it came, bubbly, aromatic, sweet, toasty brown on top, and begging for a spoon.

PEANUT BUTTER BACON COFFEE CAKE

Skimming through my Pinterest page the other day, something I've opted to fill, lately, with more posts on desserts to balance out my days spent in the kitchen with so many main courses, I ran across something called a Polish coffee cake. Wasn't much to it. There was a pretty standard, heavier crumb bottom cake layer that got a cheesecake type layer and then a pretty usual crumb topping. As "standard" and "usual" ran through my head, I thought, *Hmmm, I can fix that.* Here's what you'll need for this terrific peanut butter and bacon twist on the morning's sweet tooth fix:

For the Cake Layer

1½ cups of sugar

½ cup of butter, softened to room temperature

1 cup of sour cream

1½ cups of creamy peanut butter

2 cups of cooked bacon, chopped medium-small

1 teaspoon of baking soda

1 teaspoon of baking powder

2 eggs

3 cups of all purpose-flour

For the Cheesecake Layer

2 8-ounce bricks of cream cheese, room temperature

1 cup of creamy peanut butter

1 cup of sugar

1 egg

For the Crumb Topping

2 cups of roasted, salted peanuts

¾ stick of butter, melted

1 cup of light brown sugar

1½ cups of quick-cook oats

1. Prep your baking pan first. I used a 9x13 sheet cake pan, which I greased and floured, then set aside and set the oven to preheat at 350°F.

2. Make your cake layer. Combine the sugar, butter, peanut butter, and sour cream in a stand mixer until smooth. Add in the baking powder and one cup of the flour and combine, then

add in the baking soda and the other two cups of powder, combining until incorporated. This is going to be a pretty stiff batter, but if you find your stand mixer struggling, add in a bit more sour cream and/or peanut butter. Last, add in your chopped bacon; bacon should be in quarter-inch to half-inch pieces for this recipe, as you really want the bacon to be a true bite, rather than an ingredient that serves just as a flavor booster.

3 Take a big rubber spatula and dollop your cake base evenly across your prepared pan, but don't spread it with the spatula and undo the grease and flour job you've done. Instead, spread out the dough gently with your fingertips until the bottom of the pan has an even covering.

4 Wash out your mixing bowl and move on to your cheesecake layer. No rocket science here, merely combine everything until very smooth. When you've got it there, pour it across your cake batter layer, spreading it around with a rubber spatula for easy distributiton.

5 Finally, time for the crumb topping. I took a couple cups of dry-roasted, salted peanuts my mom sent me from Virginia and pulsed them briefly in a small food processor. Virginia is renowned for its peanut farmers nearly as much as Georgia is, and the peanuts my mom sends me are super crisp. They have a decided "snap" to them, really excellent crunch, and great flavor. You can, of course, use Planters or your grocery store's in-house brand, not a problem there. The only thing I would caution is not to buy a super-salty brand. In fact, a low-salt label would be excellent, but don't go with unsalted. You want the salt to play with the brown sugar in the topping.

6 Anyway, I pulsed the peanuts in a small Cuisinart food processor until I had a mix that ranged from the size you'd find in chunky peanut butter to full halves. This gives a nice range of texture and crunch to the topping. I added the peanuts to the brown sugar and oats, then poured the melted butter on top and combined, before spreading all of it across the cake.

7 I set my first timer for forty-five minutes, but a toothpick stuck in several places returned questionable results, plus I noticed the top really jiggled when I slid the pan back in the oven. I went another fifteen minutes, then another five, before I was satisfied the cheesecake portion had set. You'll likely have to do this same kind of trial and error, but I'd say the moment you see no more shimmy in the top, you're done. I will say I think I overcooked my first go at this just a smidge. I'm not a big edge person when it comes to things like sheet cakes, bar cookies, and brownies; I always go for the soft middle pieces. I ended up running a knife around about a half-inch to the inside of the crust and all the way around the pan, then cutting the larger center portion into squares—yes, more or less like cutting the crust off a sandwich for a picky four-year-old. The edges were just too solid for me (though the

cheesecake portion was just perfect at the edges, so go figure). If you're a person who likes the edges, you'd have been perfectly happy.

8 I let this cake cool to room temperature before I stuck a fork in it, and I was pleased to fully taste the bacon, the cheesecake, and the sugared/salted peanuts. It was quite a mouthful, one anybody fond of peanut butter and peanuts will love. The cake truly did have the mouthfeel of a coffee cake—in fact, a fresh pot of coffee really was the thing to go with here—and what could have been a really sweet cake was something more subtle, thanks, I think, to the sour cream and the salted peanuts. Oh, I should tell you, I did get carried away and poured some melted peanut butter over the top one afternoon—with a cold glass of milk in hand, I don't regret that move one bit.

ABOUT THE AUTHOR

Jennifer L.S. Pearsall is a well-known writer and editor of outdoor journalism. She has long been an avid cook, one who never leaves her guests wanting. Pearsall resides in central Wisconsin, along with her two Great Pyrenees dogs, Lucy and Hayden, cooking and eating bacon nearly every day. This is her first book with Skyhorse Publishing.

METRIC AND IMPERIAL CONVERSIONS

(These conversions are rounded for convenience)

Ingredient	Cups/Tablespoons/ Teaspoons	Ounces	Grams/Milliliters
Butter	1 cup=16 tablespoons= 2 sticks	8 ounces	230 grams
Cream cheese	1 tablespoon	0.5 ounce	14.5 grams
Cheese, shredded	1 cup	4 ounces	110 grams
Cornstarch	1 tablespoon	0.3 ounce	8 grams
Flour, all-purpose	1 cup/1 tablespoon	4.5 ounces/0.3 ounce	125 grams/8 grams
Flour, whole wheat	1 cup	4 ounces	120 grams
Fruit, dried	1 cup	4 ounces	120 grams
Fruits or veggies, chopped	1 cup	5 to 7 ounces	145 to 200 grams
Fruits or veggies, puréed	1 cup	8.5 ounces	245 grams
Honey, maple syrup, or corn syrup	1 tablespoon	.75 ounce	20 grams
Liquids: cream, milk, water, or juice	1 cup	8 fluid ounces	240 milliliters
Oats	1 cup	5.5 ounces	150 grams
Salt	1 teaspoon	0.2 ounces	6 grams
Spices: cinnamon, cloves, ginger, or nutmeg (ground)	1 teaspoon	0.2 ounce	5 milliliters
Sugar, brown, firmly packed	1 cup	7 ounces	200 grams
Sugar, white	1 cup/1 tablespoon	7 ounces/0.5 ounce	200 grams/12.5 grams
Vanilla extract	1 teaspoon	0.2 ounce	4 grams

OVEN TEMPERATURES

Fahrenheit	Celcius	Gas Mark
225°	110°	¼
250°	120°	½
275°	140°	1
300°	150°	2
325°	160°	3
350°	180°	4
375°	190°	5
400°	200°	6
425°	220°	7
450°	230°	8

INDEX